THE
TELECOMMUTER'S
HANDBOOK

THE TELECOMMUTER'S HANDBOOK

How to Work for a Salary— Without Ever Leaving the House

BRAD SCHEPP

PHAROS BOOKS
A SCRIPPS HOWARD COMPANY
NEW YORK

First published in 1990.

Library of Congress Cataloging-in-Publication Data:

Schepp, Brad.
    The telecommuter's handbook : how to work for a salary—without ever leaving the house / Brad Schepp.
        p. cm.
    Includes bibliographical references.
    ISBN 0-88687-571-4 : $9.95
        1. Telecommuting—United States—Handbooks, manuals, etc.
I. Title.
HD2336.U5S34 1990
658'.041—dc20   89-39995
                                                                       CIP

Printed in the United States of America

Pharos Books
A Scripps Howard Company
200 Park Avenue
New York, N.Y. 10166
10 9 8 7 6 5 4 3 2 1

To Deb, Stephanie, and Ethan

CONTENTS

Acknowledgments   ix

1. Telecommuting Today   1
   A Nation of Jacks (and Jills) **1**   Enter the Telecommuter **1**
   What's So Great About Telecommuting? **5**   Nothing's Perfect
   6   Becoming a Telecommuter **7**

2. Telecommuting's Advantages: The Upside   10
   The Biggest Advantages **10**   Other Advantages **14**   Families
   and Telecommuting **17**   A New Lifestyle **20**

3. Telecommuting's Disadvantages: The Downside   23
   Psychosocial Problems **23**   The Drawbacks of Working from a
   House **28**   Looking Ahead **37**

4. How to Become a Telecommuter   38
   Telecommuting: What Enters Into It **40**   Working as a Telecommuter: Suggestions for Job-Hunters **48**   Working as a Telecommuter: Convincing Your Current Employer **52**   Start
   Slow **63**

5. 75 Jobs for Telecommuters   65
   Why Telecommuting Fits So Many Jobs **65**   What the Profiles
   Show **66**

6. 100 Companies with Telecommuters   112
   How the Companies Were Located **112**   Two Types of Companies **112**   How to Use the Profiles **113**   What the Profiles
   Show **115**   Alphabetical Listing of the 100 Profiled Companies **115**

7. Your Hi-Tech Home Office   172
   The Basics **172**   The Telecommuter's Wish List **186**
   Buying Equipment **191**   Give It Time **194**

8. Telecommuting and the Disabled   196
   Some Striking Demographics **196**   When Telecommuting
   Makes Sense **198**   Recommended Resources **198**

9. Working with Consultants   203
   Consultants—Two Types **203**   What Consultants Do **204**
   Getting Ready for the Consultant **205**   Four Steps to Tele-
   commuting **205**   What Consultants Charge **208**

10. Resources for Telecommuters   210
    Books **210**   Free Software **215**   Magazines **216**   Mail
    Order Sources **217**   Newsletters **219**   On-line Services **220**
    Organizations **224**   Miscellaneous Resources **227**

Appendix. Getting Telecommuting Under Way:
Sample Memo   229

Index   234

Acknowledgments

Most telecommuting advocates share a common interest in using technology to make people's lives easier and more rewarding. Equally important, they see telecommuting as a way to help preserve the earth's dwindling resources. It was my pleasure to speak with many of them in researching this book.

Thanks to the following telecommuting consultants and authorities: Joanne Pratt, Gil Gordon, Pat Mokhtarian, and Jack Nilles. Also Susan Herman of the City of Los Angeles and Carol D'Agostino of Link Resources.

Special thanks to Dr. Grace Boynton of Digital Equipment Corporation, whose groundbreaking theories on how best to position telecommuting for today's managers shaped my thinking on this. Thanks also to Debra Schepp, and Sheryl Ricci and Ann Kelly for their editorial assistance.

Many telecommuters who use the CompuServe Information Service gave freely of their on-line time to contribute to this book. I especially want to thank Dianne Breen, Diane Yeager-McIntosh, Paul Danaher, Tom Johnson, Sarah Stambler, Fred Wilf, Jesse Levine, and Dale Lewallen. Also, thanks to Dan Swan of GEnie.

Many other telecommuters shared their experiences for the purpose of helping others telecommute. They include Paul Andrews of the Seattle *Times,* Joan Orke of Honeywell, Jim Jacobus of the Merrill Corporation, Carol Nolan of Pacific Bell, Charlotte Purvis of MultiLink, Cheryl Mahaffey of Psychological Services, Inc., and Alex Malcolm, Reynolds Lee, and Barry Trask of John Hancock.

Thanks also to the many public relations, marketing, and human resources managers who took my phone calls and answered my surveys.

Thanks to good friend and mentor Alfred Glossbrenner for always being there. Also, thanks to Shari Jee of Pharos Books, who so early on shared my vision for what telecommuting could mean to people. Her editing skills also made this a better book.

Finally, to my family—Deb, Stephanie, and Ethan—who most gracefully tolerated my absence and preoccupation for the sake of the words between these covers.

B.S.

THE
TELECOMMUTER'S
HANDBOOK

1
Telecommuting Today

It's 7:00 P.M. and Jack Rogers, manager, husband, and father, is arriving home from another ten-hour day at Acme Publishing. Struggling to swim through the crowded waters of middle management, Jack works late most days—only to bring home a briefcase at night and on weekends to work still more. His neighbors all do the same. Once inside, Jack faces a succession of chores: meals to prepare; kids to feed, bathe, and tuck away for the night; a house to clean, straighten, repair, and improve. Then there's that briefcase.

A Nation of Jacks (and Jills)

In 1989, according to a Boston University study, only about 10 percent of all U.S. families fit the *Father Knows Best* mold of a happy homemaker who cleaned house, cooked meals, and raised children all day while Daddy, the breadwinner, trotted off to work. Father knows best is no more. Instead, in most cases, both men and women spend ten to twelve hours away from home each working day. If they are in day care, their preschool-age children do the same. In the evening all converge on the home to regroup and recover, but not often to relax. There's too much to do. The bleak cliché "No Rest for the Weary" was never more apt than it is today.

Enter the Telecommuter

These may be the worst of times for some people, but for others they are among the best of times. These people have gained more control over their work lives and their lives in general. They do the same job, but in a different place, one presumably much more to their liking. They have become telecommuters, employees who work for their companies from home.

Thanks to cheap but powerful computers and social trends switching the emphasis away from corporations and back to their workers, millions of people have regained lost freedom and time by taking their jobs out of the rat race and putting them back into the home, where people used to work. Telecommuting won't bring back the 1950s, but it can make things easier. "Telecommuting removes most of the pressure associated with having two parents working," says Dianne Breen, who has worked at home as an editor for more than a year. By working from home instead of an office building, Dianne sees her children more, works more productively, and feels more in control of her life.

How Many Are There?

The number of telecommuters is increasing by 20 to 30 percent per year, a pace maintained since the mid-1980s. One to two million people now work this way, according to Professor Jack Nilles of the University of Southern California, who coined the term *telecommuting* in 1973 and remains its leading authority today. Most people telecommute just one or two days a week, reporting to the office the rest of the time. A sizable number, however, work from their homes full time. Some telecommuters go weeks, even months, without setting foot in their employers' offices.

Why You Will Telecommute

These days, managers can no longer afford the luxury of clinging to their conservativeness. Many companies feel they have no choice but to look into work options such as telecommuting. Here's why:

Business is more competitive. Foreign competition has forced companies to strip down to the bones: to get lean and mean. Most companies now consider anything that cuts costs. Since telecommuting reduces the need for office space and worker amenities such as restrooms and parking areas, it saves the company money.

The unemployment rate is way down. In February 1989 the nation's unemployment rate fell to 5.1 percent—the lowest rate in fifteen years. This means that fewer people apply for each available job. This trend will only continue. Since the peak of the baby boom in 1957, the birth rate has dropped 40 percent, from 25.3 live births per thousand to 15. The rate has stayed at about this level for the past sixteen years.

The days when employers had the pick of the crop are gone. A study of *Fortune* 500 executives found that "six out of ten companies are already feeling the employee pinch or expect to be scrounging for workers within the next five years."

People want more balance between work and family. In the 1990s, baby boomers must either commit to careers at full throttle in order to reach the top or rethink where they're headed. Many will opt for a change, in favor of a lifestyle that is more balanced between work and family (such as telecommuting).

It's already happening. In 1989, the Yankelovich Monitor survey, which has tracked trends for nearly two decades, found a shift in thinking about prosperity and what's important to people. It found many two-career couples tiring of the grind. *The Washington Post,* for example, reported that some couples in Washington, D.C., the U.S. city with the most two-career families, are changing their lifestyles—switching to part-time work or giving up one income entirely—to spend more time with their families.

The buzzword for the 1990s in personnel circles is *flexible,* as in flexible working arrangements (for example, telecommuting). Already, the giant telephone company U.S. West has a flexible work arrangements manager. Such jobs were unheard of ten or even five years ago.

Commuting just gets worse. Commuting, bad already, is getting worse despite car phones, microcassette recorders, and the other gadgets that can make it more productive. The average Southern California freeway trip that took fifteen minutes in 1984 will take forty-seven minutes by 2010. Commuters stuck in this traffic cost businesses $6 billion per year considering the value of their time, the fuel they waste, and the wear and tear on their cars.

It's this way not only in Southern California, where bumper-to-bumper commutes even spark gunplay, but in Boston, Seattle, and other cities as well. Our highway system, spectacular twenty years ago, is clogged as hell and can't take it any more.

Technology has made workers portable. Despite all these other trends, telecommuting would remain a fanciful pipe dream were it not for the technology now available. Personal computers, fax machines, copiers, and the other trappings of modern office life are moving into our homes. Setting up a hi-tech home is now well within the reach of the middle class.

The new technology is everywhere. It's no longer just for the hi-tech literate, the hackers: Average people are getting comfortable with it, using it for themselves. Along with towels and maid service, each Holiday Inn now has fax machines. It's no wonder: These handy gadgets can zap a facsimile of any document to anyone, anywhere, who's also got one. Originally something only businesses could afford, fax-machine prices fell from about $10,000 in 1981 to about $2,000 now, with some as cheap as $600.

With laptop computers and built-in modems you can create, send, and receive work from anywhere. Journalists like Dick Thompson of *Time* use them on planes, in cars, in hotel rooms, anywhere they can. Cellular phone technology means you can have a phone with you always.

Who Telecommutes?

Many telecommuters are knowledge workers—they create or manipulate information. In this Information Age, knowledge workers comprise more than half the total work force. Much of what they do can be done anywhere as long as there's a telephone, desk, chair, and, if needed, a computer handy. Most knowledge workers spend much of their time working independently anyway. Hundreds of white collar jobs can be done from home at least part-time. They include:

Accountant	Lawyer
CEO	Order entry clerk
Claims examiner	Professor
Clerk typist	Programmer
Company president	Reporter
Consultant	Secretary
Copy editor	Stockbroker
Data entry clerk	Technical writer
Editor	Telemarketer
Educational courseware writer	Translator
Engineer	Travel agent
Graphic designer	Typesetter
Indexer	Urban planner
Information broker	Word processor

Chapter 5 describes these and other jobs best suited to telecommuting, along with names of companies whose people do these jobs from home.

Companies with Telecommuters

A handful of companies, among them JCPenney, Blue Cross/Blue Shield of South Carolina, and The Travelers Companies, have formal telecommuting programs. These programs were often set up by consultants, are condoned by top management, and have been written about many times. Unfortunately, they involve very few workers; they are rarely open to outsiders and long lists of in-house people are waiting to enter the programs. If telecommuting were limited to these formal programs very few people would be working this way.

It turns out that more than 90 percent of the millions of people who telecommute do so informally, as guerrilla or "closet" telecommuters. They made private arrangements with their immediate supervisors to work from home, and few others at their companies even know about it. Their supervisors prefer it that way so that they don't have to go through the red tape of establishing formal corporate policies. These guerrilla telecommuters work for many of the nation's top companies: AT&T, Apple Computer, DuPont, IBM, Weyerhauser, John Hancock, Sears. How they arranged to telecommute and how you can do the same is largely the focus of this book.

Although a large number of telecommuters work for companies based in the western United States, home of Silicon Valley, the nation's hi-tech center, as well as the horrendous traffic and smog that have fueled telecommuting, there are telecommuters in every other part of the country. Chapter 6 gives complete contact information and other details on 100 companies that use telecommuters.

What's So Great About Telecommuting?

Telecommuters love their work style. Dale Lewallen's opinion is typical: "I sure like doing this job," says this telecommuter for *PC Week* magazine. "If I do move on, I'll either press to work at home or be miserable." Like Dale, workers find many reasons for telecommuting's appeal:

More control. Telecommuters can work when they are at their best, run errands when it's convenient, schedule things to meet their needs. In short, they are more in control of their lives. How much you feel in control of your life, psychologists say, greatly affects your state of mind.

Money savings. Telecommuters save money on gas, tolls, clothes (no more dress-for-success routine), and restaurant lunches.

Less stress. Telecommuters eliminate many sources of stress, including the stress that comes from commuting and working closely with people you might otherwise have little to do with. Symptoms of such stress include trouble concentrating, a productivity drop, and health problems such as headaches, even heart disease.

Little or no commuting time. Commuting is a poor way to start your day. Battling other drivers gets your blood flowing hot and tires you out even before your work day has started. And, if your commute is especially bad, the thought of having to do it again at night nags at you during the day. Some commuters travel a round-trip commute of four hours a day. Think of all the extra time they'd have if commuting meant traveling from one room to another!

Greater productivity. On the average, telecommuters are 20 percent more productive than their office-based counterparts.

Nothing's Perfect

Telecommuting has its drawbacks as well. For example:

A feeling of being cut off. Telecommuters can be cut off from office intrigue and gossip, some of which they need to know to get ahead or at least protect themselves.

Isolation. Telecommuting can be lonely. Most neighborhoods are deserted these days from 8:00 A.M. to 6:00 P.M. Someone who works from home may not see anyone else the entire day except maybe the letter carrier or another delivery person.

Little respect. Fellow workers may not really believe telecommuters actually work when they're at home. And until they lay the law down, they become the neighborhood dropoff for UPS or the emergency baby-sitter.

Constant temptation. For some, the constant presence of the refrigerator or liquor cabinet are too much to bear.

Need for self-discipline. Because there are no supervisors or coworkers nearby (which may also be a plus), telecommuters must push themselves to keep at it.

Being bumped off the fast track. If you want to zip up the corporate ladder, you'll have to work hard to ensure that telecommuting does not hold you back. You need to be noticed by those who can help you move up.

For some, perhaps 20 percent of telecommuters, these problems soon send them back to the office. But, given the choice, most telecommuters would never go back. (Chapter 3 covers these drawbacks in more detail and explains how to deal with them.)

Becoming a Telecommuter

How do you become a telecommuter? Do you have to get a new job and arrange to work that way from the start? Or can you arrange to take your current job home? What are its drawbacks and rewards? Who hires telecommuters?

The Telecommuter's Handbook answers these questions and more, taking the mystery out of telecommuting. It's designed to help you take advantage of this work style now—to reap its rewards today, not tomorrow. It may not help you find a new job, but it will explain how you can become happier and more productive in the one you have.

The Telecommuter's Handbook explains how you can join such telecommuters as technical writer Tom Badgett. Tom's office is in the hills of Tennessee, but the publication he works for, *Digital News,* is based in Boston. Tom gets full company benefits and even has three part-time telecommuters working for him. Another telecommuter, Reynolds Lee, a consultant for John Hancock, is so enamored with telecommuting he says he never wants to work in an office again. "Once you've tasted honey you don't want to go back," says Lee.

Entrepreneur or Telecommuter?

Why do it partway? Why not just opt out entirely and go into business for yourself? Isn't that the route most freedom-seekers now take?

Entrepreneurs are the new heroes of the American scene. Millions aspire to match the success of such homegrown businesses as Domino's Pizza, Amway, Apple Computer, Baskin-Robbins Ice Cream, Nike Shoes, and Mrs. Fields Cookies.

The Reality. While four out of five new businesses no longer fail within the first five years, the odds remain stacked against entrepreneurs. A recent study co-sponsored by the Small Business Administration and an entrepreneurship professor at Babson College found 40 percent of new businesses survive at least six years. That still means six out of ten fail!

Even for those who make it, it's rough. Entrepreneurs take three times as long as they thought it would to reach their salary goals, says Jeffrey Davidson, author of *Avoiding the Pitfalls of Starting Your Own Business.* Their first-year expenses are usually double what they had expected.

Then there are the other headaches. Entrepreneurs must market their own wares and deal with tax questions and legal issues. Sure, they can get help, but accountants and lawyers are not cheap, and most people have little experience in dealing with them.

In short, "Not everyone wants the responsibility of having their own business," says cottage industry expert Joanne Pratt. Telecommuting offers many of the advantages of working for yourself but few of the risks.

The Story of One Who's Made It

Jim Jacobus is a project manager for Merrill Corporation, a printing and publishing services company based in St. Paul, Minnesota. He works for Merrill from his home in northern Illinois. Jim explains how he began telecommuting:

> I sort of fell into telecommuting when I changed jobs in May 1986. I'd been working as a network specialist for the research and development group of a large pharmaceutical manufacturer for three years. It was a very good job, and I learned a great deal there. However, I'd gotten tired of working for a large firm, because their upward career path wasn't to my liking. During this time, I had also worked as a consultant to a financial printing firm with whom I'd had a longstanding working relationship.
>
> I was making some pretty good bucks part time, so I decided to quit, find another job or do independent consulting full time. I spent the next month doing full-time job hunting. I had about four good offers. One of the offers was with the financial printing firm I'd been working with. They wanted me to be an internal consultant type working on large projects as a project manager. This would be a nice position in a company of about 350. The only problem was that their main production facility was in St. Paul, Minnesota, and I live in northern Illinois. I did not want to relocate because most of my professional contacts are in Illinois and my wife has a horse-training business here that she has been building for the past ten years.
>
> I proposed to them that since I was going to be more of a consultant, and that my job would take me around the country quite a bit (not to mention they wanted and needed me on their staff), I'd set up shop at home. I could dial into a dedicated telephone line in their Chicago office from my house, so the telephone charges to their computers would only be from my house to Chicago (they pay for the second telephone line in my house/office). They needed no office space for me; and, if it didn't work out, neither side would have risked much in dollars, time, and energy.

Well, that was three years ago, and it has worked out well for both sides. I hold a relatively high position in the company and travel around the country working on various projects. When I'm not traveling, I'm "home." When there, I spend a lot of time on the telephone dealing with clients, vendors, support people, computer operations, and programming. There are a lot of good and bad points about telecommuting, and it's not for everyone. However, I've been encountering more and more employers who are interested in how I work, how it works for the company, and how it works for me.

2
Telecommuting's Advantages: The Upside

*B*rzzzzzzz! It's 6:20 A.M., wake-up time for editor Jack Rogers, who obediently begins to rouse himself from his night's sleep. He never finds this easy, but now that it's winter and his bed is even more snug than usual, it's even tougher. But there's no avoiding it: The alarm signals the start of another work day. For Jack that means shaving, dressing, eating, then rushing to catch the commuter train, only to sit in a cubicle typing on a keyboard. He slings one leg over the bed, then the other, then stops suddenly. "Hey, wait a minute, I don't have to get up," he reminds himself. "This is my first day as a telecommuter!" He gets the same feeling he gets when his body's time clock wakes him at 6:20 on a Saturday, and he realizes it's the weekend and he can stay in bed.

So Jack dozes off for another half hour or so. Then, feeling rested, he gets up, slips on his bathrobe and slippers, and walks the twenty steps from his bedroom to his home office. He checks his "to do" list, sees the note about that memo that's due, and decides to get it out of the way before breakfast. He's at work and it's only 7:00 A.M. But somehow he doesn't mind.

Jack Rogers' experience hits on several of telecommuting's obvious boons: greater flexibility, an end to commuting, and less stress. Any one of these advantages may justify giving telecommuting a try, but they are only the beginning. There are other, less obvious advantages as well that will help you in many aspects of your life—not just how you earn a paycheck.

The Biggest Advantages

1. Greater Productivity

Surveys from Pacific Bell, a company with more than 1500 tele-commuters, have found that telecommuting's chief benefit is in-creased productivity. Telecommuters are an ambitious lot. They don't choose this lifestyle because they want to escape the watchful eyes of their managers and work less. Actually, they are interested in producing more. They like their jobs and want to do the best work possible.

Working from home allows them to do just that. While estimates vary, on the average telecommuters produce 20 percent more than their office counterparts, according to telecommuting consultant Jack Nilles. Newsletter editor Dianne Breen says she actually works only twenty to thirty hours a week. However, "My thirty hours at home are equal to about forty or fifty office hours," says Dianne. "When I'm working at home, I'm working *hard* because I know I only have certain hours available without distractions. I don't have meetings to go to, phones ringing every few minutes, or fellow work-ers to distract me." Being more productive makes telecommuters feel good about their work and themselves. Remember, these are people who enjoy their work and who want to do a good job.

2. Greater Flexibility

The next most frequently cited advantage is increased flexibility. Because telecommuters choose their working hours (and are their own bosses in a sense) they can better balance the demands of work and family. For Dianne Breen, who has two children at home, the chance for a more flexible schedule is what led her to try telecom-muting in the first place.

Having more choice over their working hours also allows telecom-muters to work according to their internal time clocks, not the nine-to-five hours of the working world. You can work according to your body's own rhythms, when you are at your best. In other words, you can work when your engine is revved up and all systems are go. This is a great advantage.

Picture a "rise and shine" morning person who gets the most done between 6:00 and 10:00 A.M. After playing subway sardine for forty-five minutes, he gets to work around nine o'clock. He'll then need some time to unwind, to recover. He'll be lucky if he starts work by nine-thirty. He's just wasted his most productive hours.

Contrast this to the early riser who telecommutes. He can get up at six and be at his desk, working, by six-fifteen if he chooses. By nine-thirty, when his office-bound counterpart is just getting started, he's already put in a solid three hours' work. He's ready to take a break, secure in the knowledge that he's made the most of his morning.

The benefits are similar for the night owl who works best after dark. If that person holds a regular office job, she's forced to be at her desk at times when she's feeling low, the early morning. She could choose to take work home, of course, and work nights on her own time. The problem is that since she spent the whole day in the office, by the time evening rolls around she's too tired to get much work done.

"It's a real benefit to work when your body wants to," says John Hancock's Barry Trask. Barry, who's neither night owl nor morning bird, sometimes finds himself waking up at two or three, bright and alert, ready to get something done. He can get up, be at his home office and get right to work, then work until ten or eleven at night.

By working in synch with your body's energy, you are working smart. You are producing better work in less time. Here's how one telecommuter, an editor who works as an independent contractor for a technical publisher, sums up this advantage: "Because I work from home, I set the rhythm of my own day. My schedule responds to the changes in my life. I can work productively on a Sunday night, because Monday morning doesn't mean the same thing to me as it does to people who work away from home. If I worked in an office, my rhythms would have to conform to those of the people I worked with, within the constraints of a time clock. Now when I work, it represents an appropriate portion of the life I lead. I live, I take care of my children, I work all the more reasonably, because I have established my own patterns. Within these patterns, I get more accomplished, and I feel happier with my work than ever before."

Working this way also benefits the company you work for. If you are working when you are at your best you are able to produce your best work—regularly. It not only means you can work when you want; you can also stop when you want. When psychologist Cheryl Mahaffey's production falls off, she stops for a while. As she puts it, "I get to work at a pace and intensity I like without having to fill in time."

3. Greater Satisfaction with Their Lives

While greater productivity and flexibility are easily understood, the one advantage that's not so concrete may actually be the most important one. Jack Nilles, who has worked with companies to set up telecommuting programs for more than fifteen years, says telecommuting's main advantage is actually an emotional one. In brief, telecommuters feel more in control because they can shape their work around the rest of what's going on in their lives. Telecommuters say that they are more satisfied. "I'm not harried, I'm not rushed, and it makes me a happier worker," reports Dale Lewallen, a telecommuter for *PC Week* magazine.

Telecommuting's other advantages contribute to this emotional plus. Greater productivity, more time with family, a sense of control (masters of their own destiny) add up to a greater feeling of emotional well-being. Just knowing that you can take care of that errand, let the repairman in without a problem, or pick up your child from school leads to a peace of mind that translates into greater productivity and contentment on the job.

Consider the following scenario from the office worker's vantage point. Your car registration must be renewed immediately or state troopers everywhere will hound you. But you work all day and the motor vehicle office is open only during regular working hours. That means you must drive there during your lunch break (which, of course, is when everyone else is also taking care of chores) and disrupt your whole day. You've picked the worst time to run your errand because you have no choice.

The telecommuter, on the other hand, can schedule his errand when the roads are less crowded and the motor vehicle office isn't busy. Or he can arrange to do it when there are other chores to take care of anyway. Perhaps it's a time when his productivity is normally ebbing (early morning for an evening person, late in the day for a morning person). The point is that he can do it when he wants. He has control. This control, in turn, alleviates stress.

Perhaps Carol Nolan, a Pacific Bell manager and former telecommuter herself, captured this emotional plus best when she said telecommuting was, in a word, "wonderful." Carol telecommuted for a year before she had to give it up after a promotion into a new job that called for more face-to-face interaction. "Being back in the office full time was a real culture shock," she says. "For the first five months I was back, I hated my job. I walked around with a frown on my face all the time."

4. The One-Minute Commute

For some people, ending that twice-daily rendezvous with the car, bus, or subway is more important than anything else. "Telecommuting cuts my commute time down to zero," says Jim Jacobus, a project manager who works from his northern Illinois home. "If I had to commute into Chicago each day, that would take me more than an hour each way, so telecommuting saves me two hours and twenty minutes every day."

Anyone who can eliminate commuting time—no matter how long—is going to have some additional time in their day. Telecommuting gives systems analyst Barry Trask an extra four hours per day, since his commute to John Hancock is two hours each way. When he must commute, he says he "can't get enough hours in the day." When he doesn't commute, "I can sleep an extra hour and still get started two to three hours earlier than office workers," Barry says. His work days may actually be shorter because the commute is eliminated, but he gets more done. Plus there are other things you can do besides work during the time you save by not commuting.

Other Advantages
Goodbye GQ, Hello Jeans

Telecommuters can dress as they choose—dressing for success gets replaced by dressing for comfort. Women can dispense with makeup, men can skip shaving. "I don't have to wear a suit (or anything, for that matter)," says Jesse Levine, a programmer who works in upstate New York. Few people would mind putting these early-morning rituals off for a while. "Shaving," says Barry Trask, "is the worst way to start a day." Eliminating dressing for the office also means saving even more time. You can get up, make a cup of coffee, and be at your work area in ten minutes. Ending the primping also forces people to judge you more on what you produce than on how you look.

Peace and Quiet

While working at home brings its own distractions (such as interruptions from family members and neighbors), these are more controllable than the interruptions most office workers must contend with. Telecommuters sometimes find that when they work at home co-workers are less likely to interrupt them than they would be if they worked in the office. Because of the distance they create between themselves and other employees (which admittedly has its disadvantages as well) they only get interrupted when it's really important. So for the most part, quiet reigns. "There are no silly meetings, no distractions; I just sit and work," says programmer Jesse Levine. A phone machine takes care of his calls, and express mail and UPS delivery people know to leave packages at the door.

For people who create, being able to work uninterrrupted is crucial. A simple thing like being able to complete a thought is no longer a problem. Unwelcome interruptions are more than annoyances—they are setbacks that impinge on productivity.

Boosting Your Bottom Line

Increased productivity, flexibility, and control are fine, but for some the fact that telecommuting saves them money is as important an advantage as any. Consider the commute itself. If you normally travel by car, telecommuting saves you gas expenses, tolls, parking fees, and maintenance costs. Not only that, you'd pay less insurance since the number of miles you drive per week helps determine your insurance premium. You may even save the expense of the car itself. Honeywell's Joan Orke was able to put off buying a new car entirely when she got her telecommuting job. Of course, if you would normally take public transportation, telecommuting would spell the end of tokens or bus fares.

Other expenses, such as your at-home wardrobe, for example, would be much different and much less expensive. All those incidental expenses that are part of the working world (which, when you add these up turn out to be not incidental at all) are reduced. The birthday cakes. The Girl Scout cookies or peanut brittle your boss or co-worker is selling for his or her kids. The good-bye luncheons. The welcome-to-our-group lunches. Even just lunch in general, if you eat out every day.

Your Office, Your Home

Another advantage (which plays into productivity) is that at home your work space is what you've made it. As more of us face working in office environments that are actually counterproductive this advantage grows in importance.

Many businesses now divide work areas into cubicles. While this design saves money for the company, it forces workers to put up with increased noise, clutter, and lack of privacy. It's not surprising that Steelcase, an office furnishings leader, found in a 1988 survey that 65 percent of all respondents wanted more private work space. Despite their efforts to personalize them, workers still find cubicles artificial and small.

Being able to arrange your own working space means you can create an environment that's productive for you. "I can completely control my working environment," says Jesse Levine. You select the type of chair you find comfortable, the computer and software you need. You decide whether a Gershwin rhapsody or rock music fills the room. Even down to what you choose for your walls, you can personalize your home office more than you could the office you'd have at work.

Full-time telecommuters, particularly, have much more freedom in where they choose to live. This may explain why *Business Week* reported that in attractive areas such as upstate New York, rural Maine, and the Sierra Nevada (areas once viewed as too removed from work centers to be practical living areas) home prices are skyrocketing.

Better Communication

Although this is a case where an advantage can be a disadvantage for the most part, communication can actually improve. For example, if you communicate with your boss by electronic mail, you'll find that no matter how busy she is your message is seen. And when telecommuters do show up at the office, communication is more to the point and more productive. Think back to the last time you were away from the office for a few days. When you returned, after your boss gave you the lowdown on what happened regarding your work responsibilities, you probably picked a co-worker to fill you in on the grapevine. In just a few minutes, someone distilled days' worth of gossip for you. While some of the color and texture may have been missing, you still got all the salient details.

Good-bye gossip. For psychologist Cheryl Mahaffey, one of the big advantages of telecommuting is that it removes her from office politics. While Cheryl concedes that some people may not like this, she does.

Hi-tech Prowess

Another less obvious advantage to telecommuting is the familiarity you gain with microcomputers, modems, fax machines, and other useful tools. You may already use these machines in the office, but having them at home is different. John Hancock's Reynolds Lee found his PC skills improved tremendously once he started working at home. Honed skills boost productivity both at home and at the office.

One reason your skills sharpen is that you use the tools more when they are close by. "If you put the machine in the person's house, he will get caught up in doing work with it," says systems analyst Barry Trask. "He will probably play some games, but the employee will also turn to it on a rainy Sunday afternoon when the Celtics have been losing and he doesn't feel like reading the paper. It's an insidious, seductive technology."

Also, you may be exposed to technology you would not have used otherwise, such as a modem (which, combined with a computer, allows you to send and receive information over telephone lines). A modem is a very handy thing to get on comfortable terms with. By allowing you to communicate with other computers, it makes researching easy. Modems also enable you to send electronic messages, which eliminates phone tag since they always reach their destination. With these tools in your home, you'll gain new skills and gain them faster than you would have otherwise.

Families and Telecommuting
Telecommuters and Childcare

It's becoming the norm for both parents to work. The options for two-career couples with children are few in the United States. Daycare is not a satisfying option for many parents. Faced with a dearth of childcare choices some school districts "help" working parents by extending the schoolday, but that seems sad more than anything.

Telecommuting gives family members more time to spend with one another. And while it doesn't solve childcare concerns, it can still make a parent's job easier. Although you cannot be available to your children while you are working, there is still a peace of mind that comes with knowing that in an emergency you are only a few steps away instead of across town. "I can be there if he's upset; can go out for a hug, greet him after a nap, soothe him if he's been hurt," says Joan Orke, a telecommuter for Honeywell who has a 10-month-old baby at home.

An at-home parent can easily arrange to fit medical checkups and dental visits into her schedule. She can also arrange to participate in special programs, from the nursery school years onward. You no longer need to take a vacation day in order to be at your child's nursery school Mother's Day luncheon. Even simple things, like rework-ing your schedule to take your kids to see that matinee of the Disney classic you loved so much when you were six, are easier for the tele-commuter. These are the benefits of working from home that your child will remember.

For the telecommuting parent the serious concerns, the ones that would nag at you if you worked in an office, are no longer an issue. These concerns include who stays home when a child is sick or wor-ries about the child getting hurt, or even just missing you. "I'm near my family more," says editor Dianne Breen. "Even if I am busy and distracted at times, at least I'm there, and can be available if they need me." Again, this translates into peace of mind.

Once your children are in school, the fact that you are there when they arrive home also benefits them. You may still be working, but your kids don't have to come home to an empty house and pass sever-al hours unsupervised. Maybe you can arrange your day so that a break occurs when the kids get home. A snack with some time to visit and talk about the day may be followed by a return to work for every-one: you get back to your task and they do homework. At any rate, your lifestyle shows them that you are a family that's committed to home and to each other. This is bound to be an advantage to any kid who is growing up in our times of disintegrating family structures and value systems.

When they're older, being home with your children gives you the chance to show them things they may not have been exposed to other-wise. "People who have children older than the age of eight can in-corporate them into their workdays," says Chicago psychologist Gi-sela Booth, an expert on working at home. "Get them to help you collate, help with a mailing. This is a terribly positive thing to do. For one thing, it exposes them to the world of work. Most kids have no inkling of this."

This way the telecommuter's children not only feel they are help-ing out, they get a feel for what you do for a living. Also, by seeing how hard you work, how seriously you take your job and how you go about doing it, they may develop habits and insights that will benefit them when they go out into the working world (or bring it home, as you've done).

When baby makes three. But don't fool yourself. While your chil-dren are young, you'll need a babysitter. A cartoon accompanying a 1985 article on telecommuting in a major computer magazine shows a woman telecommuter busily typing away at her home computer keyboard. She's dressed in office clothes, but playing at her feet is her crawling baby. Just beyond her desk is her washer and dryer, with a freshly folded load of laundry sitting atop the machines. The cartoon implies that telecommuters can easily fit work in between laundry and childcare. While an old cartoon, the myth persists.

People who try to solve their childcare problems by telecommuting may find the resulting tension so great that they wind up leaving the organization, according to Mary Van Glinow, a University of Southern California professor of management science who has researched this issue. The reality is that people who work at home and have children in their care can rarely balance work and parenting without help.

In her survey of 14,000 *Family Circle* readers who work at home, Kathleen Christensen found that about half of the professional and clerical women used babysitters so they could get their work done. Those who didn't have help often worked late into the night after their children were asleep. (Telecommuters with school-age children were in a different category.) The telecommuters she surveyed were just not able to get as much done during the day as they thought they could.

This is why consultant Jack Nilles makes it clear to his clients from the beginning that telecommuting and full-time child care don't mix. Trying it may add stress not only to the telecommuter's life but to her boss' life as well. "You don't need a sitter with an advanced degree; you just need someone to supervise them, someone who is responsible, and who knows to call the parent in an emergency," says Nilles.

You only need a babysitter, of course, when the children are pre-school-age, when you have to worry that "they will drop jelly into your keyboard," as Jack Nilles puts it. But after that, when the kids are in school, your sitter worries diminish considerably.

Another approach to the childcare issue. While most experts feel telecommuters with small children should hire babysitters, some telecommuters do blend childcare and work successfully. Jan Fletcher, who edits the newsletter *Home Business Adviser* from her home, is one. Jan has two children (two-and-a-half and five) and was expecting her third when interviewed for this book. Her office is in the middle of her house, where her kids can easily see her, although many experts counsel that a home office should be more secluded.

The location of her office isn't the only thing that makes Jan's approach different. She also works with her kids nearby, sometimes in the same room. "I taught myself how to concentrate with kids in the same room," says Jan. "This meant learning to deal with interruptions: how to stop work and then go back to it."

She also has her house set up to minimize the chance of her kids getting bored. Gyms are set up both inside and outside. To reduce interruptions due to snack requests (which were a problem at first), Jan arranged to have healthy snacks readily available so her kids could help themselves. Finally, Jan taught her kids the importance of independent play. She also worked hard to eliminate sibling rivalry, so her kids would play together peaceably. Of course, Jan still needs to stop to change diapers, and so forth, but for the most part she's able to get her work done without babysitters.

Admittedly, not everyone could work this way. Many people would prefer not to even try. Yet, if nothing else, Jan's story shows that it is possible if the commitment to do so is strong enough.

Eldercare

While telecommuting and childcare does not always work out, eldercare is another matter. This is something that will challenge more of us now that people are living longer. In 1950, according to Census Bureau reports, there were 12.3 million Americans over age sixty-five. By the year 2000, over 35 million Americans will be over sixty-five. Since we all have parents, eldercare is something even childless couples may be concerned about.

Taking care of an elderly relative usually does not involve the same kind of constant care that caring for a child would. More often it entails running errands and other things that can be worked manageably into your working day.

The need to offer eldercare is what motivated Rosalin Dano, owner of Direct Data (a company profiled in Chapter 6) to work at home. Rosalin's ninety-year-old father-in-law lives with her and, although he is in good heath, she needed a job that would give her flexibility so she could balance her career with her family responsibilities.

A New Lifestyle

Telecommuting can be an entree into a working style that is more flexible generally. For example, you may actually only telecommute one or two days a week. Other days, though, you may come in later to bypass the rush-hour traffic. This is how John Hancock's Reynolds Lee works. He'll work two or three days a week at home. The other days he'll come in at ten-thirty or so to cut down on his commuting time. "The issue is not time spent working in the office, it's time spent working," says Lee. This kind of flexibility benefits the entire Lee family since Reynolds' wife is in medical school.

Telecommuting means going against the grain. It gets you thinking about options that can open you up to possibilities that go beyond how you earn a living to how you live your life. "What this is all about is integration," says Nathan Edelson, a designer of home office furniture who also covers management issues for the *Wall Street Journal*. "Integrating working, living, and having fun."

3

Telecommuting's Disadvantages: The Downside

The headline from an early *Wall Street Journal* article on telecommuting asked WORKING FROM HOME: IS IT A LIFE OF FREEDOM OR A LIFE OF FLABBY LONELINESS? Telecommuting always brings freedom, but a life of flabby loneliness? Unfortunately, that can be part of it too.

In some ways, Pacific Bell's Carol Nolan was a lot like many other telecommuters in that she loved the lifestyle. In other ways she was unique: "I'm very well-organized and self-motivated, so it was nothing for me to adjust to telecommuting," says Carol. Most telecommuters find that telecommuting takes some getting used to, so there might be something to that *Wall Street Journal* headline.

Telecommuting's drawbacks are serious enough to send an average of one in five telecommuters packing for the office. A national survey of people who work at home done by New York market research firm Link Resources found 20 percent of homeworkers were unsure enough about telecommuting to want to go back to work or at least reduce the time they worked from home.

Psychosocial Problems

Isolation: The Biggest Drawback

Former *Fortune* magazine writer Peter Schuyten now works as editorial director for a *Fortune* 500 publisher. A company on the cutting edge of electronic information delivery and technology, it would seem an ideal place for telecommuting. Yet it's unlikely that Schuyten's staff will work from home any time too soon because his experience at *Fortune* soured him on the idea. "Most of our stories were 5000 words long back then," says Schuyten. "We'd do our research, then spend two weeks at home writing up the story. I hated working at home. I even hated the room I worked in. You need an office. You need the contact."

Schuyten is not alone in finding working from home lonely. Almost all telecommuters feel this to some degree. This, more than anything, can end telecommuting for some people. MultiLink, one of the companies profiled in Chapter 6, had two employees who didn't work out as telecommuters. In both cases they were people who thrived on a lot of daily contact with others. If you need minute-by-minute input, telecommuting is not for you.

Part of the problem is that some telecommuters feel disconnected from their offices once they start working from home. People who telecommute full time are especially prone to feeling they are no longer part of the team. Psychologists call this company-connectedness feeling *organizational identification,* and it is important because how much you identify with your company affects how high you'll climb the corporate ladder.

How to avoid it. Perhaps the first step toward dealing with the potential problem of isolation is understanding when being alone is beneficial and when it's not. Dr. Gisela Booth, a Chicago-based clinical psychologist specializing in relationships and working women, says that being alone does not have to make you feel bad. You can feel alone even if you are in a room full of people. It's when you feel isolated or cut off that problems arise. This is a much more negative feeling, and one that telecommuters need to guard against.

Isolation can mean either loneliness or solitude. Solitude is OK; that's the peace part that goes along with peace and quiet. However, "loneliness," says Dr. Booth, "is when you feel that no one knows that you exist. It's the 'Christmas feeling' we can have when we feel cut off."

To keep from feeling lonely, you have to make sure that when you are in your home office you don't feel adrift or cut off. One thing that helps Dianne Breen is making use of the CompuServe on-line information service. CompuServe's electronic mail features let her network with other people who also work from home. Not only that, it improves communication between her and her boss. Dianne's boss logs on at least once a day, so she handles most of her business correspondance with him by electronic mail. That way she's sure she'll have his total attention at least once a day.

Effective use of your telephone can also help. Make it a point to call your boss or a peer at your office at least once a day. By arranging to do this at the same time every day you can prepare for these telephone chats. Also, knowing that you'll have at least that much contact ahead may help ward off feelings of loneliness.

Some companies with established telecommuting programs have formal strategies worked out for helping telecommuters stay connected to the office. U.S. West, for example, brings its telecommuters into meetings by speakerphone. The company's motto is that their telecommuters are "Not really out of touch, just out of the office."

Michael Trigoboff, a software engineer who has worked from home for about a year, both on his own software and under contract to software companies, has his own solution to the loneliness problem: "I listen a lot more to talk radio shows since I started working at home," he says. Trigoboff even bought a short-wave radio so he'd have even more to listen to (and, presumably, a ready way to connect with a lot of people).

But for most people, electronic communication—the kind a telephone, short-wave radio, or on-line service provides—cannot replace people contact. When you talk with someone on the phone, you don't see the body language that can reveal a person's true feelings. Freelance writer Tom Johnson is one telecommuter who believes that "while telecommuting is efficient, economical, and fun, it should not replace face-to-face contact." Tom, a heavy user of modems and computers, works for many different companies and finds keeping in touch important. He takes occasional trips to meet with his various editors, just to talk things over face-to-face.

To stave off loneliness, reporter Paul Andrews sometimes takes printouts of newspaper articles he is working on to a local café for copy editing. Other telecommuters set up regular coffee breaks or even more formal meetings with other people who work from home. Exchanging shoptalk is part of the reason for these get-togethers, but the main reason for them is the people contact.

This "schmooze or lose" phenomenon strikes telecommuters of all types. AT&T repair crews who received assignments for the next day by computer terminal in their homes found they missed rubbing shoulders with each other. Soon they started gathering each morning at a local restaurant for coffee. Unfortunately, AT&T executives then branded telecommuting a failure. Actually, it just showed that employees can miss being with one another, something that should be planned for.

Dr. Booth counsels people who work at home to structure their work days so that they don't feel isolated. She recommends that telecommuters make lunch dates, make phone calls, and get out and contact people who also work home. She suggests that telecommuters schedule appointments and other activities during the day rather than outside their regular working hours. "Go to exercise class or go to the dentist during the day, don't go in the evening. Develop some other contacts aside from your office, such as people in your neighborhood who also work at home—they'd welcome the contact," says Dr. Booth.

Other effects of isolation. Another drawback of working away from co-workers is that you miss out on their input unless you make a conscious effort to solicit it. The sense of team spirit that helps pull workers through tough projects is missing when you work from home. The Federal Reserve Bank of Atlanta ended its telecommuting program because it found that most of the people eligible needed to be on the premises. Its researchers, in particular, had to be on site for the "intellectual ferment."

When the UK's FI Group—the first and still among the largest users of telecommuters in the world—found that several of its workers felt isolated, it created local work centers where they could work together. In the United States, however, such satellite offices are rare.

Some telecommuters also complain that once they started working from home they no longer got regular feedback from supervisors. The pat on the back is a little hard to manage long distance (literally and figuratively). Be aggressive about seeking feedback and otherwise remaining a part of the office. Make sure your co-workers know they should call you at home (during your working hours) as freely as they'd call you if you worked in the office. This needs to be stated because some co-workers may hesitate to call you at home for fear of bothering you.

Some telecommuters don't mind at all the isolation that goes with the territory. "I like to work alone," says software writer Diane Yeager-McIntosh, sounding a lot like Henry David Thoreau. "My early experiences with offices involved co-workers who were addicted to Mary Tyler Moore (boring) and hated me because they were always dieting and I was always snacking (without gaining weight), and because I like to work when I work."

In the end, how much you miss working with other people will depend on how much you had relied on the office for socializing. Those who purposely separate work and social life or more introverted types make better telecommuters.

Workaholic Tendencies

The television newsmagazine *20/20* recently had a segment on flexible work options, including telecommuting. To show some of telecommuting's drawbacks, it featured a Salomon Brothers currency trader who often works from home. Set up in his bedroom was a Telerate terminal, complete with its constantly pulsing numbers. To stay linked with traders worldwide, the trader took phone calls at the rate of one every forty-five minutes, day and night. This meant that he never slept for long; he cat-napped through every night. Obviously, this is one very extreme example of what working from home can be like.

It's easy for those who work at home to slip into workaholic ways, at least in the beginning. The likelihood should concern every prospective telecommuter. With your office right there in your house and reminders of unfinished work constantly before you, the office is always with you. You never get away from it. Carol D'Agostino, a telecommuter for Link Resources, says that during her workaholic period she often worked on Saturdays and Sundays.

Pity especially the poor workaholic telecommuter whose office is in his bedroom (not an uncommon location), like systems analyst Barry Trask. When a thought or idea strikes him, it's just too tempting to plug it in anytime, night or day. Barry admits that if he worked in an outside office "I may just wait until the morning and roll over."

Equipment often has a great deal to do with turning telecommuters into workaholics. Link Resources' survey of homeworkers found 66 percent of those who use computers and modems (against only 26 percent of all homeworkers) said it was "hard to separate personal and work life." Many telecommuters would agree with Barry Trask when he says there are moments his family gets irritated at the amount of time he spends on his computer. He not only gets obsessive about his own use of the computer, he also gets obsessive about other family members' use of it. He believes they should use it for everything but frying omelets. "In an odd way, it impinges on my time at home," says Barry. "I must work very hard at maintaining a balance."

One way to push aside these tendencies is to set goals for yourself.

Meet them, certainly—but when they've been met, knock off for a while. You can always get back to it later. One Beverly Hills writer begins his day by taking a walk, then going for a swim. If, at day's end, he finds he has not written enough pages, he works until he completes his quota.

In short, telecommuters are not under the same constraints they were at the office. While they should set realistic goals for themselves, it's up to them how those goals are met. Working in a telecommuter's favor is greater productivity. Keep this in mind when setting goals. "Because you are more productive you don't need to keep at it all day," says Gisela Booth. "Take a walk: you can't work for more than three hours in one sitting anyway."

Slipping into Bad Habits

With no boss to keep them in check, some telecommuters slip into bad habits, indulging their weaknesses. It's understandable how this can happen, even to the most strong-willed among us. Who would know if you catch a nap in the middle of the afternoon, have your early evening cocktail at 3:00 P.M., or end the day early to play a set or two of tennis?

We all have our weaknesses, all of which are easily indulged at home. For some people it's overeating, for others it's smoking too much (no need to make a trip to the smoking room like you'd have to do at the office). For still others, it's drug or alcohol abuse.

Overeating seems to be the number-one indulgence of telecommuters. In fact, for one Chicago lawyer overeating is the main disadvantage of working at home. He says he's definitely gained weight since he started working at home—"not so much that my mother's upset, but it's noticeable." Some telecommuters go back to their offices for this very reason; at home they just put on too many pounds. Once back in the office for a while they lose the weight.

Like overeating, working from home makes it easy to get an early start on the after-work cocktail. Just how widespread alcohol/drug abuse is among telecommuters is not known; it's not the kind of thing people readily admit to researchers.

It may not be fair to blame bad habits on telecommuting; weight gain, for example, can also happen at the office. There are many reasons for overeating besides accessibility to the refrigerator.

Slovenliness

The freedom to dress as you want is one of those disadvantages of telecommuting that can turn against you if you let it. Since they no longer have to dress for success, but only for themselves, it's easy for telecommuters to fall into sloppy ways. Writing in *New York* magazine, writer and homeworker William Geist was unusually candid about his "lapses in personal hygiene." He advised prospective and fellow homeworkers that "occasionally laundering that plaid flannel shirt can be essential to maintaining a modicum of self-esteem, basic to mental health." Productivity, not hygiene, is the issue. Wearing comfortable clothes is fine, but people work better when they feel good about themselves.

The Drawbacks of Working from a House

Dealing with Distractions

With no taskmaster nearby, the telecommuter can easily be distracted. That unmade bed, the floor that needs polishing, the ready-for- emptying dishwasher—they can all beckon. Obviously, these are not distractions you would face in an office, which is set up for work. In an office, if you don't feel like getting down to work, you can more easily do other work-related things, such as open mail, discuss new assignments with a co-worker or supervisor, even check job postings on the bulletin board.

There are several things you can do to help keep your mind on the task at hand. Some can be pure self-deception. *The Wall Street Journal,* for instance, described a telecommuting stockbroker who donned a three-piece suit every day and played tape recordings of sounds from his old office.

Your neighborhood is another distraction that would not normally affect you at the office. It's amazing how many times telecommuters find themselves wheeling their chairs over to the window when they hear cars go by. When they were at the office, their neighbors, of course, got by just fine without them. But now that they are home, they feel the neighborhood needs them to stand guard.

If you are easily distracted by the goings-on outside your house, close your curtains. If the noise gets to you, use a white-noise machine to mask it out. These are available at electronics stores, although an ordinary household fan can work just as well.

Some people find the TV tempting. For them it takes real willpower to overcome the temptation to catch their favorite sitcom or the noontime headlines. One way to put TV out of mind is to put a VCR to work and record those shows. That way you don't have to feel you are missing anything by working.

A whole other set of distractions comes from other people. Door-to door salespeople and telephone solicitors, for example, can rob you of productive work time. Once interrupted, it may take you a half-hour or even hours to get back to work. Because you are home, people think you are "available." Friends and neighbors are more likely to stop by, and at home there are no secretaries, receptionists, or co-workers to shield you.

Software writer Diane Yeager-McIntosh still has friends who call, expecting to make midweek lunch dates. "Part of the problem," says Diane, "is that we have friends who do not really think I work," even though she has worked at home exclusively for more than four years. To deal with such time-stealers, Diane has learned to accept losing a few "friends." She's also "learned to live with the telephone machine all the time and the associated unpleasantness when people think you are screening your calls (because you are)."

You may have to train your friends and acquaintances not to call you during your working hours. To ensure your privacy, get a separate business line, which is something you may want to consider anyway for modem or fax use. Otherwise, you'll have to let a phone machine get your calls—personal and business.

Getting People to Take You Seriously

Women telecommuters may have more trouble convincing people that they are at home to get a job done than male telecommuters do. Many women who responded to researcher Kathleen Christensen's survey of 14,000 *Family Circle* readers who work from home said they were not taken as seriously as people who work outside of the home. Christensen feels this problem is especially acute for women because of their traditional roles as wives and mothers. This may be why some telecommuters have as much trouble getting family members to take their work seriously as they have with neighbors and friends. Editor Diane Breen says that sometimes family members forget you have work to get done: "My son will interrupt seven times in ten minutes or my husband will actually expect things to get done around the house just because I'm home."

To make working from home a success, you will have to learn how to cope with your family during the daytime if they are there. During your working hours, you must make it clear that you are home in the role of company employee, not, for example, wife or mother. When you are in your home office, it has to be as if you are fifty miles away (except for emergencies). Getting this across may not be easy, but it has to be done for telecommuting to work. "I've had to learn to be firm about *my* time and *my* needs (not always easy for a mother)," says Dianne Breen. Remind your family that telecommuting benefits not only you, but them as well.

Fortunately, most telecommuters find problems in being taken seriously eventually fade. Many say that they used to go to great lengths to disguise the fact that they work from home. That soon passes. "Gradually I've come to see that it usually doesn't matter to the clients where I work," Dianne says, "as long as the work gets done." She's now more comfortable telling people she telecommutes. Her business cards even have both home and office phone numbers on them.

Be careful that in your bid to guarantee peace and quiet you don't get too much of a good thing. You'll welcome the solitude of your home office when you must concentrate. The chance to concentrate for long stretches may be a major reason why you chose to telecommute. But too much quiet can work against you if it promotes boredom. People with routine, data-entry type occupations sometimes shy away from telecommuting for this reason. They realize they need the companionship of other workers to get through their days and remain alert. Satellite offices, rather than home offices, make the most sense for such people.

Adding Stress to Your Household

As a telecommuter you'll be more accessible to your family, which they'll welcome. But telecommuters bring more than just equipment and files home. They can also bring the stress. "If you're working on a tight deadline in an office, then things get hectic there," says Dianne Breen. "But if I'm on a tight schedule at home, then things get hectic here, and the whole family feels the pressure—dinner doesn't get cooked, laundry doesn't get done, homework isn't supervised."

Like telecommuting's other drawbacks, there are ways to deal with this one too. Here are two ways Dianne shields her family from the pressures her job can create:

1. Arrange to meet deadlines comfortably. "I work ahead so I don't find myself under the gun."
2. Prepare for it. "This may entail stocking up on frozen dinners, teaching my older son to do his own laundry, or arranging babysitting."

It's a good idea to hire a sitter who's willing to also do some chores around the house. A sitter who will stick dinner in the oven and watch the kids may be worth the extra money.

Even so, Dianne admits that it isn't always possible to avoid having her work affect life at home. "If I was in an office and the kids were in day care, the crazy days wouldn't result in our house looking like a combat zone. But since we are all here, things tend to get a little disorganized (and that's putting it mildly) when I'm under pressure with work."

Having a telecommuter around can also disrupt family relationships. In a family where one person who perhaps was used to being home alone is suddenly joined by a spouse, one or the other may have trouble adjusting. An older man who worked for Pacific Bell, asked if he wanted to take part in that company's telecommuting program, said that if he worked at home, "My wife would leave the house at seven A.M. and not return until seven P.M. Not only that, she'd spend the whole day shopping."

For telecommuting to work, you have to be on good terms with the people you live with. You must want to spend more time at home. If things are not going well there, then consider whether you want to be home an extra eight to ten hours each weekday.

Office Services You'll Miss

Even though there are some parts of office life you can do without, others you'll miss: ready access to office machines (copiers, fax machines, typewriters, even telephones) and reference materials from the corporate library, not to mention the office support staff. John Hancock's Barry Trask finds that at times he'll need to make unlimited phone calls, but he does not want to incur the cost at home. Other times he'll need to make a lot of photocopies, but he does not have his own copier.

To avoid frequent trips into the office to handle these things, arrange your visits carefully. Allocate part of each regular visit to using facilities available there that are not available to you at home. Take care of phone calls, heavy photocopying, faxing, and the like. Plan out the reference materials you'll need ahead of time and gather them while you are there. While this means that occasionally you'll have to haul a boxful of materials between home and office, it still beats interrupting your work at home just to make a "reference run" into the office.

Zoning Laws

Zoning laws have not kept up with the times. Many municipalities still have laws against people working out of their homes. Many of these laws were enacted in an era when the typical neighborhood business was a beauty parlor or auto repair shop. Understandably, communities wanted careful regulation of such businesses; they brought noise and traffic.

Lawmakers did not have in mind the electronic cottages of the 1990s when they passed these laws. Yet Chicago, which has the toughest regulations against working at home in the country, bans the use of electricity for running a home business. So, technically, it's illegal to use a computer or word processor. Although it's illegal to work at home there (except for clergy, doctors, and lawyers), a lot of people do so anyway. Chicago's zoning department gets about twenty-five complaints a day from neighbors who object to home businesses run in their neighborhoods. But there is little follow-up.

The "outlaws" have little to fear since there's a de facto practice across the U.S. not to enforce these laws. Even when enforced, they are more a worry for entrepreneurs than for telecommuters, since it's the entrepreneur who is in business for himself.

Homeworker Exploitation

Companies have abused their work-at-home employees since the early part of this century. Many garment workers then worked at home, often working long hours for poor wages. Will telecommuting bring a new, hi-tech type of abuse, creating "electronic sweatshops" in the process?

Unfortunately, this has already happened: A few companies have taken disadvantage of their telecommuters. To cut costs, they paid them less than office workers, yet demanded more from them. In fact, some people suggest that telecommuting and similar work options will split workers into two camps: the haves and have-nots. The haves will enjoy full benefits. The have-nots will work on a piece-meal basis; despite fancy titles such as *independent contractor* or *consultant,* they'll get no benefits. This wouldn't be so bad, except that employers sometimes expect these workers to work as if they were employees in every other sense.

In 1986, eight women telecommuters sued California Western States Life Insurance, claiming the company forced them to work up to fifteen hours a day. One mother of five said she consistently worked ten hours a day to meet her quotas. Another telecommuter for the company told *The New York Times* she routinely worked from five in the morning to nine at night. All the telecommuters were claims processors, participating in a telecommuting program that at one time encompassed nearly thirty people. Each processor was considered an independent contractor. According to the newsletter *Telecommuting Report,* to participate each worker had to provide proof of a rider on her insurance policy that covered the equipment; pay a rental fee to the company for the equipment; pay to have a dedicated phone line installed; and agree to pay any phone charges incurred. (Despite these terms, the company had a waiting list of people who wanted to participate in the program.) The case was eventually settled out of court.

The independent contractor issue. Whether exploitation is part of it or not, any company benefits by adding to its payroll independent contractors rather than salaried employees. The employer pays less to the government in payroll taxes. And these workers rarely receive benefits such as health insurance and disability. Such benefits boost an employee's salary by about 30 percent. So, even though independent contractors may earn more per hour than office workers, they can wind up with less if they pay for their own coverage.

How to categorize telecommuters is something employers often wrestle with. The company profiles in Chapter 6 specify in each case whether the company classifies its telecommuters as independent contractors or salaried employees. Often small companies, who hire telecommuters as they would any other freelance or part-time employee, classify telecommuters as independent contractors. Review this information to be sure you know what you are getting into before approaching any company. If an employer wants to hire you as an independent contractor and you can get health benefits and life insurance through your spouse's employer, it does not matter. If not, think twice about working for them. Providing your own coverage is expensive and, with health costs rising much faster than the overall inflation rate, the cost will jump each year.

A few employers are not sure how to proceed, so they experiment. Dianne Breen and her employer have gone back and forth about her status. For a time her status was the same as those in the office but her employer recently switched her to independent contractor status.

Where status is negotiable, you might mention that management is already saving money by allowing you to telecommute. For example, it may save on office space and other facilities. It almost certainly saves money because of your greater productivity. So there's no need for it to skimp on benefits as well.

The IRS is cracking down on companies too quick to label workers independent contractors. The IRS' concern is that it loses tax revenues when companies misuse the independent contractor designation. Under IRS rules, if an in-house employee begins telecommuting but still does the same job, the employer cannot take him off the payroll by labeling him an "independent contractor, partner, co-adventurer, or the like."

Also coming to the telecommuter's defense are state governments. New Jersey recently introduced a bill, for example, that specifies that telecommuters and other employees who work at home cannot be asked to work more than a normal work week or normal work day. It would also protect their benefits as employees. In addition, it mandates that worker's compensation laws would cover telecommuters injured by equipment they need to do their jobs (microcomputers, for example).

As competition for workers increases, companies may decide on their own to ensure the rights of telecommuters, even those working only part time. Setting the pace for this is ICL, a British computer systems firm that has more than 300 employees working from home, mostly part time. Its employees already enjoy many company benefits, and ICL is planning to bring them into its pension program. Like other progressive companies, ICL believes its home-based workers and office-based workers are equal.

Finally, help for telecommuters may come from another direction: unions. Even though many unions are against telecommuting, others realize it's an unstoppable force in the working world. Sensing a new source of members, they want to put telecommuters under their wing. For example, some members of The California State Employees' Association participate in that state's telecommuting pilot. Union official Peggy Connerton has been quoted as saying that she doesn't oppose homework "if it is done right." Her union wants to be sure home clerical workers "maintain parity" with their office-based counterparts. Its 1988 resolution warns against "a growing marginalization of office work . . . marginalization in the sense that full-time jobs are turned into part-time jobs, wages and benefits are reduced, potential for career disadvancement is limited, and working conditions are eroded."

The salaried worker who arranges to work from home is in little danger of having his employee status changed. If you had benefits before, it's unlikely that your employer will strip you of them once you start telecommuting. Many of the large companies listed in Chapter 6, including AT&T, DEC, and Apple, treat their telecommuters exactly the same as their nontelecommuting employees.

Getting stuck on the slow track. The old adage "out of sight, out of mind" haunts telecommuters. In many companies, visibility is very important. The right people must see you doing the right things for you to get ahead. The good news is that telecommuters do get promoted. Their work may not be in full view, but their results get noticed. As managers move more toward managing by objective rather than by walking around and observing employees, this concern may die.

As a telecommuter, you can make sure your accomplishments get noticed. Send memos and otherwise make sure the right people see and hear about your accomplishments. When you do appear at the office, "talk up" what you've been doing. If you do that, you may garner more visibility than some of your co-workers.

Consider the case of Debra Sorkowitz, the "invisible editor" who worked on-site for a New Jersey-based technical publisher. Even though her work was excellent, her boss admitted that she'd forgotten about her because she never made waves. This stalled her career growth. You need to toot your own horn whether you work in the office or from your home.

You are always "on call." "Telecommuting invades your personal life," says project manager Jim Jacobus. "I get calls outside of normal working hours. They know where to reach you." Another telecommuter complains "Because of my erratic hours my boss seems to think that I should be on call." Unfortunately, complaints like these are common.

There are a couple of ways to address them. If you tend to work normal business hours, make that clear to your co-workers. Outside those normal working hours they should not call you, just as someone who works in an office generally would not be bothered at home. If your hours fluctuate, set a core period of four hours or so during which your availability is guaranteed.

You can also use technology to reduce unwanted interruptions from the office. Use a separate line for your business calls and simply let a phone machine take your messages outside your working hours.

Tell your co-workers that during your core working hours you'll return their calls within half an hour or so. But if you allow people to call you at six one morning and eleven o'clock the next night with-out setting them straight, you are tacitly giving them permission to do so.

The Severed Grapevine

Gossip shared among co-workers can clue you in on forthcoming assignments, promotions, demotions, and so on. By sniffing out such news before it's generally announced you can prepare for it; that way you don't have to react to it on a gut level. *PC Week* telecommuter Dale Lewallen admits to sometimes feeling out of the loop, since he's not a part of such social events at the office as birthday parties or even coffee klatches. "While talking on the phone helps, there's no water cooler," Dale says.

Relying on voice mail or even the telephone, especially when communicating with colleagues, is possible if you have friends at the office. Personalities enter into every interaction you have with other people. This is one reason some companies don't like to hire people off the street to telecommute. Not only do they not know them, they realize that the person does not know the organization.

When Joan Orke began telecommuting for Honeywell she was new to the company. She didn't know the company jargon, and was not included in office gossip and intrigue (or even plain information sharing). This meant she not only missed out on gossip, but that at times she did not have information she needed to do her job. Sometimes this held her up for hours. To overcome this Joan sought out people she could trust and depend on to fill her in. "I had to be real aggressive in seeking these people out," she says.

For some telecommuters, communication with co-workers improves when they start working from home. Electronic mail, for example, eliminates telephone tag, so you "always get through." Because you see your co-workers less often, there's always something to talk about, information to exchange. Presumably they'll always be glad to see you since, depending on how many days you work from home, getting together will be an event. Psychologist Cheryl Mahaffey admits that since she's started telecommuting she interacts less with her co-workers, "but what interaction there is is probably heightened."

Dealing with Jealousy

You know that telecommuting has enhanced your life; its appeal will be obvious to others as well. Expect to encounter some negative reactions from co-workers. These reactions, says consultant Gil Gordon, can be a combination of "resentment, jealousy, and resistance." One telecommuter for a large hi-tech employer in the Midwest found that some people didn't believe she was doing anything at home, that her telecommuting was "all for show." Some even suggested that she was using the company.

Co-worker jealousy is one of the thorniest problems a telecommuter can face. Obviously, gloating over your good fortune is in poor taste. A less obvious way to keep feathers unruffled, though, is to ensure that your telecommuting does not inconvenience others at the office. This may mean making sure that call forwarding is set up so that you are not regularly asking others to take phone messages for you. Expecting others to take on some of your chores just so you can enjoy the freedom of working at home is a good way to alienate co-workers. Clarifying such things is part of the communication process that should take place between telecommuters, their supervisors, and their co-workers—before telecommuting begins.

Looking Ahead

This chapter was meant to prepare you, not to scare you. Enter telecommuting with your eyes open and you'll increase your chances of making it work for you. Remember, most telecommuters would never want to return to the office full time. But they work at being successful telecommuters.

Telecommuting is a trade-off. You exchange your commute for more time with your family, your high heels for your slippers. But you also exchange those pleasant water-cooler chats for time staring at your keyboard with no one to talk to for hours.

In the end, do what's important to you. If it's important to you to be with fellow workers, you may not belong at home. If you are afraid that telecommuting will slow your career growth, then by all means head back to the office. You'll be happier there. But be sure to let your co-workers know you've returned. Many of them would probably like to take your place.

4

How to Become a Telecommuter

In mid-1989, at a televised press conference, Los Angeles County announced a telecommuting program that would soon involve thousands of it employees. The star of the press conference was the county's first telecommuter, a woman who started working from home while on an extended maternity leave. Holding her baby, she told the television audience that at home she "got done in twenty hours what it took thirty to thirty-five hours to do in the office."

Her words sparked a rush of phone calls to the county from "every young mother in town," all of whom wanted to telecommute, a program coordinator later said. The calls poured in for weeks. Unfortunately, except for the very few applicants whose special skills were in demand, most of those applications were filed, permanently.

Obviously, telecommuting appeals to many people who see it as a practical answer to the demands of a two-career family or the way around a horrendous commute. But for most of them, including those who responded to the Los Angeles announcement, telecommuting will remain out of reach. This chapter explains how you can become a telecommuter—either for your present employer or for a new one. There are a number of ways to do this.

Telecommuting doesn't usually represent a new job; rather, it's a different approach to doing the job you already have. Consider the approach taken by the people who followed up on the Los Angeles press conference. As outsiders, they contacted the county, hoping to get jobs as telecommuters. Instead, they should have first checked with their current employers about telecommuting part time. Even if they were in the market for a new job, they should have planned to work on-site first, before suggesting telecommuting.

Granted, people sometimes luck into telecommuting jobs. Their skills may be so in demand that employers will do whatever it takes to snare them. This happened to Charlotte Purvis, Director of Educational Services for MultiLink, a company that offers teleconferencing training courses. Charlotte got her job because she had unique skills (including previous experience in the still-new field of teleconferencing), appropriate voice quality, and writing skills. MultiLink, based in Massachusetts, specifically designed the job for Charlotte, who telecommutes from her home in Durham, North Carolina. Now, when the company rewrites her contract every year, the document mentions that hers is a telecommuting position.

A similar thing happened to Jim Jacobus, the project manager who telecommutes for St. Paul's Merrill Corporation. At his previous job, Jim dealt with Merrill regularly. They liked his work and were eager to hire him, and Jim was ready for a change. There was only one problem: Jim lives in Northern Illinois and didn't want to move to Minnesota. So Merrill made him its first telecommuter.

Sometimes, something in your personal life occurs that makes the timing right for bringing up telecommuting. For example, if you have surgery coming up, you can ask your boss beforehand about working from home during your recovery period. By telecommuting, you'd save the company money (something sure to get attention) since it would have to pay less in the way of disability benefits. Maternity leave can also trigger the start of a telecommuting arrangement.

In these cases, telecommuting begins on a short-term basis. But in each case, the telecommuter also has the chance to establish a work record that proves telecommuting works. Before long, she's eased into regular telecommuting.

For Charlene Weiss, of Chicago's National Opinion Research Council, her husband's military transfer to another state triggered her working at home. "When I moved to Arizona," she explains, "my boss and I collaborated and proposed that I keep my job but do it from my home. When it turned out that we decided to stay in Arizona, I was allowed to continue since I was handling the job effectively." Charlene has worked from home full time for more than five years, and feels she's more productive than she'd be in an office.

Sometimes the company's situation, rather than an individual's, prompts the start of telecommuting. For example, Psychological Services, Inc., of Glendale, California, began its work-at-home program when it moved from Los Angeles to the San Fernando Valley. Rather than commute, two of its employees set up satellite offices in their homes, complete with a separate phone line and a personal computer and modem. This worked out well for both the company and its telecommuters, and telecommuting spread to other employees at the company.

In these situations, telecommuting was the solution to a problem. If similar opportunities are available to you, seize the moment and suggest telecommuting.

Telecommuting: What Enters into It

Most of us can't wait for our employer to move, or we don't have Charlotte Purvis' unique skills. Yet we'd still like to telecommute. Or perhaps you are looking for a new job anyway, and the idea of working from home appeals to you. How do you proceed?

First, you must analyze just how feasible telecommuting would be for you. The chances are quite good that your job would lend itself to telecommuting, at least part time. More than 60 percent of all jobs are now information-based, which means—given computers, fax machines, and modems—they are no longer location-dependent. So it's unlikely that your job would stand in the way of your working as a telecommuter.

The suitability of the job is only the first hurdle. Telecommuting must make sense for you personally. In other words, are you the type of person who would make a good telecommuter? And, of course, the employer must also go along with the idea.

Let's look at these considerations—the job, the would-be telecommuter, and the employer—one at a time.

Looking at Your Job

"There are some jobs in every company where telecommuting can work out," says Merrill's Jim Jacobus. It's true. Every company has a bookkeeper, someone who handles public relations, or, for that matter, a president—all positions suitable for telecommuting.

Both clerical and professional jobs can be done from home. Clerical jobs are usually more easily measured than a professional's. This means that if the telecommuting arrangement is not working out, it will soon become evident. The "numbers" (for instance, forms processed) will be down. Consequently, it's more likely for an employer to hire you off the street for a clerical telecommuting job than for a professional one. The drawback to doing data entry or similar tasks at home is that you are more subject to abuse (the so-called electronic sweatshop). It's also likely that you'll work as an independent contractor and have to provide your own health care coverage and other benefits. This works out fine for some people, but you must plan for it.

Professionals who telecommute are usually treated the same as in-house employees and receive full salary and benefits. Almost always, however, professionals must first work in-house for the company before they can telecommute.

What to consider. Could you do your job from home? Take a close look at your job responsibilities to decide if there are days you don't have to be on- site. Begin by asking your boss to list the attributes most critical to your position. With that in hand, you're ready to see if working from home is feasible.

Joanne Pratt, a national expert on working from home and adviser to the State of California's telecommuting pilot program, recommends this approach. "Sit down with a pad and pencil and analyze the part of the job that you can do at home. Lay it all out carefully. Then, see if you can cluster those tasks better done at home so they can be done one or two days a week." Those one or two days a week will be the days you work at home. (Count on starting small until you prove yourself; you can always increase the amount later.) The kinds of tasks best suited to a home environment are the all-important, value-added parts of your job: those that call for thinking, writing, or planning.

Once you conclude that you could work from home, you'll have other issues to work out. Are there files at work that you need regular, everyday access to? If so, could you arrange to have duplicates of those files at home? (Or, if there are just a few, can you carry them back and forth?)

Who will pay for the equipment you'll need at home—you or your employer? The survey of telecommuters and companies conducted for this book found a fairly even split between companies that pay for the equipment in a telecommuter's home and telecommuters who pay.

Obviously, it works out best for you if the employer pays. But if it won't, and you don't own the equipment you'd need, you'll have to buy it yourself. This may well be an investment you'd be willing to make, however, in order to telecommute. Your costs may be offset by the savings you'd realize from not commuting, or eating lunch out, or maintaining a work wardrobe.

Would You Make a Good Telecommuter?

With the practical issues resolved, it's time to look inward, at whether telecommuting would be right for you personally. Companies with formal, established telecommuting programs will help you analyze this. The procedures will be set. Companies such as Pacific Bell and U.S. West take great pains to prepare potential telecommuters for the telecommuting life. Through briefing sessions, they tell them what to expect and what they'll need to prepare for. But most companies with telecommuters do not have such programs.

Self-motivation. More than anything, telecommuters must be self-motivated. With no taskmaster nearby, they must drive themselves. Some people find it motivating to work with other people nearby who are also working. Without that, their own productivity drops. If you are like that, think twice about telecommuting. "If you are not self-motivated it will not work," says experienced telecommuter Charlotte Purvis. "I'm going to work whether anyone is looking at me or not." Many professionals already work this way, so it may not be much of a leap for you. But telecommuting certainly tests self-motivation.

Independent work. Also, consider your relationship with your supervisor. How much hand-holding is necessary in your job? How much contact do you have with your supervisor in the course of performing your duties each day? If the contact is regular, if things requiring assistance regularly crop up, would a phone call handle them, or would you need to be there?

Hard work. Be prepared to work hard, probably harder than you did at the office. Your employer will be watching closely for any signs of a drop in quality or productivity. Such signs would cause your boss to rethink telecommuting.

One telecommmuter who works for a Colorado-based company says that when telecommuting it's not unusual for him to work two or three hours straight without taking a break (as he'd do in the office). If you really like your job, working this hard won't be difficult. Without your job to propel you, there will be a tendency to slack off.

Dianne Breen, the telecommuting newsletter editor from Georgia with two small children at home, likes her work and naturally wants to please her boss. But she also has to prove that she can do her job from home. "I don't want to blow what I know is a good thing," says Dianne. "So I do what it takes: I'll get up at four-thirty just to have a quiet time to write; I'll miss prime-time TV for a month at a time; and I'll go through my day doing two things at once (editing copy while eating, reading background material while the baby's playing in the tub, making business calls while cooking)." In short, telecommuting is not a way to get out of doing a job you dislike. Rather, it's a way of doing a job you like better.

A job you like. Having a job you care about and want to do well also helps you fight the distractions that go with the territory. If you find your work boring, you will be easily distracted. These distractions can be everywhere, Dianne says. "Friends call and want to do something or come over; children want your attention; your favorite TV show beckons; you know you could read just one more chapter of your book and no one would ever know."

Organization skills. To work from home effectively you also have to be well-organized. In an office there are routines that help organize your day. The trip to work itself, lunchtime, the regular meetings—the things that occur every day at a set time. At home, a lot of those cues are missing. You'll have to set your own parameters for your working day. You can start when you want, end when you want, and break when you want.

This freedom comes at a price. Before pushing to telecommute, review the drawbacks discussed in Chapter 3.

Motives. Finally, consider your motives in wanting to telecommute. Are you looking to work less? Be honest. If you are, by telecommuting you could shorten your life in your current job. The important thing is to evaluate telecommuting with your eyes open.

The Right Employer

Now that you know what you are getting into, let's consider finding the right employer. There are two types of telecommuting arrangements: informal and formal.

Formal telecommuting programs. Formal telecommuting is the kind that's set up as part of a program, established after careful planning, often with a consultant's help. Examples of companies with formal telecommuting programs include U.S. West, JCPenney, and The Travelers. Employees have been carefully screened, questionnaires filled out, managers briefed, measures of the program's effectiveness plotted.

Unfortunately, formal programs are rare. Don't rule them out, but don't be too tempted by their lure. For one thing, even though a company may have a formal telecommuting program, it's still your immediate supervisor who decides whether or not you may participate.

Guerrilla telecommuting. The good news is that the other kind of telecommuting, the informal kind, is prevalent. Informal telecommuting, also called guerrilla telecommuting, means working out a casual arrangement with your immediate boss to work from home, perhaps regularly. To keep red tape in check, higher-ups in the organization often do not even know about guerrilla telecommuting. Even the personnel department may be in the dark. If telecommuting works for the company as an informal effort, often there's no need to formalize it.

While there are no exact figures available, Jack Nilles, the consultant who coined the term *telecommuting,* once surveyed *Fortune* 500 companies to determine their use of telecommuting. The answer varied depending on with whom he spoke. Almost always the official line was "We have no telecommuting program." But when Nilles questioned the rank and file, he discovered hordes of telecommuters. In fact, Nilles speculates that nearly all *Fortune* 500 companies have telecommuters. "Any company that has mid-level or professional people with personal computers at home has telecommuters," says Nilles. "They have figured out that it's possible to take work home on occasion and do it from there."

If so, why the secrecy? Consider it from the company's point of view. Establishing a formal corporate program takes an upper-level policy decision. If telecommuting were officially sanctioned, long lines of would-be telecommuters would encircle the personnel office. Worse than that, managers would face touchy situations as they tried to explain why some people could telecommute while others could not. (How do you tell an employee that he's not trustworthy enough for such an arrangement while Joe or Phyllis is?) Keeping it informal lessens risk all around. If it doesn't work out, the damage is minimal. But if a formal program flops, the embarrassment becomes public. No one wants that.

Other concerns: Unions are generally against telecommuting. While some organizations, such as the County of Los Angeles, went full steam ahead because they felt the unions couldn't stop their programs, other organizations prefer not to tangle with them.

Finally, another reason some companies don't acknowledge telecommuting is that they feel it gives them an edge in recruiting new employees or retaining old ones. They prefer not to broadcast it to their competitors.

Telecommuting Screening Survey

The Telecommuting Screening Survey used by the Southern California Association of Governments can help you think about your job, your employer, and yourself in terms of telecommuting. It also forces you to consider practical issues, such as whether your home would be a good place to work. In any event, it should help you sort out all the issues involved with telecommuting.

TELECOMMUTING SCREENING SURVEY FOR EMPLOYEES

1. Does your job permit you to telecommute, at least part of the time, and do you wish to telecommute?

    ( ) Yes   ( ) No

2. The following three groups of characteristics relate respectively to your work, yourself, and your manager. Please rate each characteristic as either low, medium, or high. If you have more than one manager, please place the initials of each manager in the appropriate blanks under "Manager Characteristics" and answer each question for all your supervisors.

WORK CHARACTERISTICS

L	M	H	
___	___	___	Amount of face-to-face communications required
___	___	___	Ability to "clump" required face-to-face communications into predetermined time periods
___	___	___	Degree of telephone communications required
___	___	___	Amount of interface with databases not on the PC
___	___	___	Amount of time spent working at terminal or PC
___	___	___	Availability of quantitative measures for assessing performance (how many "widgets" produced)

——— ——— ——— Clarity of objectives for a given work effort

——— ——— ——— Autonomy

——— ——— ——— Ability to control and schedule work flow

——— ——— ——— Amount of in-office reference material required

——— ——— ——— Amount of physical access to special resources required

——— ——— ——— Ability to "clump" in-office reference/resource requirements into predetermined time periods

——— ——— ——— Amount of concentration required

——— ——— ——— Need for physical security and data

EMPLOYEE CHARACTERISTICS
L   M   H

——— ——— ——— Need for supervision, frequent feedback

——— ——— ——— Quality of organization and planning skills

——— ——— ——— Self-starting

——— ——— ——— Importance of office input to work function

——— ——— ——— Initiative in requesting input when needed

——— ——— ——— Motivation derived from work itself

——— ——— ——— Motivation derived from prospect of promotion

——— ——— ——— Discipline regarding work

——— ——— ——— Reliability concerning work hours

——— ——— ——— Computer literacy level

——— ——— ——— Desire/need to be around people

——— ——— ——— Level of company experience

——— ——— ——— Degree of experience in current assignment

____ ____ ____ Need for scheduling flexibility due to family responsibilities

____ ____ ____ Potential for friction at home if telecommuting

MANAGER CHARACTERISTICS

L   M   H

____ ____ ____ Positive attitude toward telecommuting

____ ____ ____ Trusts employee's ability to telecommute

____ ____ ____ Organization and planning skills

____ ____ ____ Ability to establish clear objectives

____ ____ ____ Provides formal feedback regularly

____ ____ ____ Flexibility

____ ____ ____ Ability to communicate

____ ____ ____ Product-oriented rather than activity- or process-oriented

3. Considering the nature of your job, how much would you want to telecommute?

( ) Less than 1 day/month   ( ) 2 days a week
( ) 1 day/month   ( ) 3 days a week
( ) About once every 2 wks   ( ) 4 days a week
( ) About once a week   ( ) All the time

4. Would you prefer telecommuting?

( ) All day
( ) Only part of the day, commuting in nonpeak periods
( ) Some of both

5. What kinds of work would you expect to do while telecommuting? (Check as many as apply)

( ) Writing/typing   ( ) Talking on the phone
( ) Word processing   ( ) Send/read electronic
( ) Data management   mail
( ) Computer programming   ( ) Meeting people

(   ) Administrative   (   ) Other (please list):
(   ) Graphics/layout   _____
(   ) Research/reading   _____

6. Given the amount of telecommuting you want to do and the kinds of work you would do while telecommuting, what equipment/services would you need that you do not currently have? (E.g., computer, printer, modem, additional phone line, software, desk, filing cabinets)

_____

_____

_____

7. Do you have children at home all or part of the normal working day?

(   ) Yes, all day   (   ) Yes, for part of the day
(   ) No

8. Do you have a spouse or other adult at home all or part of the normal working day?

(   ) Yes   (   ) No

9. For the amount of telecommuting you plan to do, do you have adequate space in the home to dedicate to working?

(   ) Yes   (   ) No

10. Would you be interested in the possibility of working from a satellite location near your home (e.g., in your local City Hall)?

(   ) Yes   (   ) No

11. What is your total commute time (to and from work)? _____ mins.

Working as a Telecommuter: Suggestions for Job-Hunters

Tracking Down Employers

Because most telecommuting is done informally, it's best not to seek a job as a "telecommuter." You should not go into a job interview and explicitly ask about working from home (unless, of course, they suggest it from the start— as happened to Dale Lewallen during his interview with *PC Week*). Looking at it from the company's viewpoint, why should they pay you, a virtual stranger, to work from home? Instead, you should work toward taking your current job home (at least occasionally). All experts agree that you need to work for a company first (at least six months) before you can broach the subject of working from home. By the time six months have passed, you know them and they know you.

Job leads. If you are now in the job market, you may want to use the listings in this book to approach employers who you know have telecommuters with the idea of eventually working for them from home. But it's best to use the listings to generate ideas, not as an end in themselves. For example, you'll notice that several newspapers are listed. If none is close by, contact your local paper. It may operate in the same way. Many use electronic publishing systems, such as Atex, which make sending in copy from a remote site simple. You could check with someone who works for the paper to get a feel for how open it is to reporters or other employees working from home.

To track down possible employers, use other resources as well. Read the books, contact the organizations, and so on, certainly; but also use the resources others may not be as likely to tap, such as those in Chapter 10. For instance, one couple, seeking advice on working from home and how to go about it, used CompuServe's Working From Home Forum. They posted a message on its electronic message board asking forum members for advice. This novel approach brought quick feedback from people who really had something to say on the subject.

Even the most conventional sources can bear fruit. It's now possible to discover want ads in trade journals or even local newspapers advertising for people to work at home. These ads are for jobs that are otherwise traditional. A recent *Publisher's Weekly* ad for an editor/writer for a business textbook publisher, for example, specified all the normal things (detail-oriented, top-flight skills, and the like). But, it added, the person "may work at home."

Increasing your odds. To boost your odds, concentrate your job search in areas where the prospects for telecommuters are known to be good. Right now, while there are pockets of telecommuting everywhere, there's one boom area: California. Such employers as the State of California, the City of Los Angeles, the County of Los Angeles, and large private companies such as Pacific Bell and GTE of California are listed in this book.

Aside from California, other areas to consider are the State of Washington and Washington, D.C., where an extra-high concentration of knowledge workers and the federal government's fresh interest in telecommuting combine to create many opportunities.

If you have the freedom to look anywhere, pick a place with a low unemployment rate. "In an economy such as ours, those places that are doing well (low unemployment rate) will be more receptive to telecommuting, because competition for good workers is tighter," says John Hassett, MultiLink's vice president. Monthly employment statistics from the Bureau of Labor Statistics include unemployment rates for many areas.

Keep an open mind when plotting your search. Companies that you'd think would use telecommuters (hi-tech firms) may surprise you. While leading-edge companies do have telecommuters (note the many computer companies and other hi-tech firms among the company listings), others are dead set against it. One Silicon Valley computer manufacturer, asked about its telecommuting policy, said it had none. "We are quite traditional in our approach to the work force," reported the manufacturer. So much for stereotypes.

Other hints: Except for those with formal programs, going with a large company is not always the best route. Large companies are often saddled with bureaucracy. Change can be difficult; the red tape can discourage even the most progressive managers. Manufacturers Hanover, for example, had to end its pilot telecommuting program because it was actually too successful. Continuing would have meant getting human resources involved and mounds of red tape. Rather than wage a war to see telecommuting through, the company's telecommuting sponsors ended the program.

Downsizing, another plague of large companies, can stop telecommuting cold. That's what happened to programs at The Hartford and Public Service Company of New Mexico. Downsizing often makes a company retrench and stick close to the basics (at least for a while). So does a buyout or merger.

Prospective telecommuters may be better off approaching companies that have been through a downsizing already, since they might be safe from another one for a while. Smaller companies also may be less susceptible to some of the traumas that can hit large ones.

Stay abreast of companies that are expanding into telecommuting. More do so all the time. For example, when contacted about possible telecommuting programs at her company, the personnel manager for

Industrial Indemnity, a California-based financial services company, said "Our company does not provide for any work-at-home programs, but I am very interested in telecommuting for my claims examiners."

Working for Entrepreneurs

Aside from established employers, consider working for an entrepreneur. Thanks to the entrepreneurial craze of the 1980s, there are millions of one- and two-person businesses. As they grow, they will look to hire more employees. The idea is to track down entrepreneurs who would be open to telecommuting.

Many entrepreneurs now use telecommuting technology (modems, fax machines, PCs) to give their businesses an edge. These are the entrepreneurs you need to locate and approach. Entrepreneurs are already open to the idea of employees working out of their homes. Often, they work out of their own; expanding into bona fide office space to accompany more employees is costly, so hiring telecommuters makes sense.

Chapter 6 includes a few entrepreneurs who have expanded to where they now hire telecommuters (among them TechProse and Janal Communications). An example of another entrepreneur who may soon be in the market for telecommuters is Martin Schiff, whose business, Custom Data Solutions, is based in Florida. Custom Data does custom programming, training, support, and sales. Martin's clients span the state of Florida (and the country), and he communicates with many of them by modem. Martin says he uses "remote support" even with his local clients to give them better response time and save them money (he charges for travel time).

At this writing, Custom Data's only employee is Martin Schiff, but Martin anticipates he'll soon need additional employees. At that time, he said, "I would have no objection (in fact I would encourage it) if they wanted to telecommute." In short, keep tabs on entrepreneurs through sources such as the CompuServe Working From Home Forum and view them as potential employers.

The Independent Contractor Route

Rather than working as a salaried employee, consider setting up shop for yourself as an independent contractor. Freelance writers often work this way. Telecommuting—specifically, using a modem to transmit articles and correspond with editors—would give you an true for computer publications, a thriving segment of magazine, trade journal, and book publishing.

Tom Johnson, founding editor at *MacWEEK,* says that when the magazine began in 1987 "We refused to work with any writers who didn't have a modem and an MCI account (for electronic communications)." *MacWEEK* still works that way. Expertise and prior writing credits count, sure, but if you know how to "modem-in" your work you may demonstrate enough technical know-how to get assignments for such publications.

There are drawbacks to life as an independent contractor—no benefits being the chief one. The company listings in Chapter 6 specify for each company whether telecommuters are salaried employees or independent contractors. Also included is a discussion of working as an independent contractor.

Working as a Telecommuter: Convincing Your Current Employer

If you are now working and like your job well enough to want to do it from home, broach the subject of telecommuting with your existing employer. Presumably, your boss knows you can do the job and do it well. He trusts you; he doesn't think you might try to dupe him by arranging to work at home so you could goof off, pursue your own hobbies, or work for someone else. The key to success is preparation. You may get only one real shot at making your case. If you come across poorly initially, you may never be able to bring up the subject again.

Preparing to Make Your Case

Before you meet with your employer, consider how you will position your argument. Be prepared for some resistance. You'll be suggesting something that is out of the ordinary. It's possible your manager won't even know what telecommuting is. Even if she does, you can't expect her to know its advantages and disadvantages (especially for the company). Consultant Gil Gordon says the predominant attitude you are likely to encounter is skepticism, but not rejection.

When preparing for your meeting, Dennis Acebo, Business Development Manager for GTE, suggests: "Put your thinking cap on and think like an executive. They see the benefits of telecommuting as being benefits for the individual, not for the company. They don't consider the soft benefits of telecommuting such as lessening an employee's commute."

The lesson here is that, as nice a person as your supervisor may be, why should he let you work from home unless you can show that it is in the company's interest? So center your appeal around the money the company will save by letting you telecommute. As much as we'd like to think that employees really mattered and altruism is real, "it's strictly financials that drive corporate America," according to Pacific Bell manager Carol Nolan.

Productivity above all. The key argument to make is that by working from home you will be more productive. Your greater productivity translates into money savings for your company. "One thing people listen to is expanded productivity," says John Hancock's Barry Trask. "Keep trying to hang your hat on it. The development of the technical skills required for telecommuting will benefit any employer or employee."

Your claim that working at home will increase your output is not far-fetched. Although her cubicle or office may be larger, your boss works in the same environment you do. She puts up with the same distractions, the commute to work, the ringing telephones, and so forth. It's likely that she takes work home at nights and on weekends and has seen firsthand how much work you can get done at home. In discussing productivity, cite incidences when your commute, or something else related to the fact that you work in an office, cost you time on the job. For example, "Last Thursday I lost two hours when a semi jackknifed in front of me; when I got to work I was so frazzled it was a while before I could get down to work."

Keep in mind that as you make your case, your history with the company is working either for you or against you. If you have a reputation as someone who gets the job done with minimal supervision, then making your case will be easier. If, however, you have a reputation as someone who works no harder than he has to (or are an unknown quantity because you are new to the company) then it may appear that you want to telecommute in order to work less.

Other savings to the company. In addition to boosted productivity, there are other ways telecommuting can save your company money. If telecommuting involves a lot of people who work from home more than they do from the office, it reduces the need for office space and other worker amenities such as restrooms and parking facilities. It also lessens demand for equipment, even electricity. Consultant Gil Gordon estimates the typical metropolitan firm spends from $4000 to $6000 per employee for office space. While the cost savings from these factors may be small at first, they'll build quickly as telecommuting spreads.

Fleming LTD, telecommuting advisers to the State of California and other employers, has compiled the following figures to show how telecommuting's savings can add up for an employer:

TELECOMMUTER AT HOME 2 TO 3 DAYS PER WEEK

PERSONNEL FACTORS	BENEFIT-SAVINGS
Productivity (quantity)	$3,000
Productivity (quality)	$1,000
Recruiting-training-retention	$1,000
Absenteeism	$1,000
FACILITIES	
Office space	$1,800
Parking	$ 200
Annual total per employee	$8,000
$8,000 x 100 telecommuters	$800,000

Figures based on annual salary of $20,000, productivity increase of 20 percent, reduced personnel costs of 10 percent, parking @ $500 per year reduced by 40 percent and use of central office facilities of 150 square feet @ $30 per square foot rent per year reduced by 40 percent.

Aside from the kind of savings recounted here, the State of California found that the dollar impact of reduced sick days taken by its telecommuters was almost as high as money saved due to increased production.

Telecommuting as a perk. In addition to the money it saves, employers who make telecommuting a policy also find it's an effective recruiting tool. The strength of this argument hinges on the business you are in and the unemployment rate where your business is based. For some positions (say a writer's job at a newspaper such as *The New York Times,* or a prestigious magazine such as *Newsweek,* employers have their pick of applicants, and recruiting is no problem.

But even within the same profession, some positions go begging. For example, technical writing jobs can be hard to fill. Finding someone with specialized knowledge who also can convey information clearly is not easy.

Telecommuting also works as an incentive to help retain employees who might otherwise leave. Admittedly, you may not feel comfortable pointing out this benefit. You don't want to suggest that you'll leave if not permitted to telecommute, so the best way to get this benefit across is to distance yourself from it. For example, think about the people who recently left the organization and their reasons for doing so. Might offering them the chance to telecommute have kept any of them on board? For example, did anyone leave solely because a spouse got transferred? Even in the case of a valued employee who received a better-paying position with another company, telecommuting might have kept that person with the company. By pointing out some cases where telecommuting might have helped your company retain a valued employee, you make the case of its retaining powers without hitting too close to home.

Benefits to you. After you've presented the benefits to your employer, you can mention the benefits to you. These alone would not convince a company to try telecommuting. Most employers recognize the value of happy employees, however, so you should still mention them.

Even soft benefits that obviously benefit you more than the employer can be cast so they appear as boons to your employer. Take the ending of your commute. You could point out that often telecommuters use the time they save by not commuting to get more work done. Also, freed from the headaches of commuting and the need to wind down from the morning ordeal (again, just how much of an ordeal this is would depend on your personal situation), telecommuters have more energy to do a good job.

Stress that the increased flexibility would allow you to work when your performance is at its peak, not just when the clock says you should, regardless of your energy level and motivation at the time. With a more flexible schedule, you may find it easier to accommodate overtime. Or, freed from some of your childcare/eldercare worries, you can give your job your best effort. You'll no longer automatically have to miss a day's work to nurse a sick child.

The softest benefit of all is probably the most important from the telecommuter's viewpoint—the fact that telecommuters find they are happier. This too is a boon you should distance yourself from when making your pitch. But if your commute is always a hassle, for example, your manager may know this anyway, and figure out for himself that ending this worry would make you happier. Any manager knows that happier people are easier to manage.

Chapter 2 looks at telecommuting's benefits from the employee's viewpoint. You might want to reread this to refresh your memory of them.

What to Expect During the Meeting

Go into the meeting ready to address (in a nonthreatening, friendly way, of course) any pre-existing notions your boss may have about telecommuting and what it may mean to a company. Here are some of the concerns your boss is likely to have and some guidelines for addressing them:

BOSS: Isn't a home primarily for doing household-type chores or just relaxing? When I think of employees working at home I think of people making phone calls between laundry loads.

YOU: During working hours my home will become a place of work. The chores will wait until I've put in my day's work. I already have a home office set up.

BOSS: How do I know that you'll actually be working? Here I can see you, but at home you could be gardening or reading the newspaper. How would I ever know?

YOU: I'll still be responsible for getting the same work done. If you want, at first I can give you weekly progress reports showing clearly what I've accomplished. If I'm not getting the work done you'll know that soon enough.

BOSS: How about your phone calls? And suppose there's a staff meeting? Won't you be out of touch with the office?

YOU: I'll still come in for meetings; those are usually scheduled anyway. As for my phone calls, I've already discussed that with Bill and he said he'd take messages for me while I'm out. I can always return calls from home and just keep track of the expenses.

BOSS: But won't setting you up as a telecommuter cost the company a lot of money?

YOU: Well, the way I see it, the only things I'd really need are a computer, and perhaps a modem for sending files back and forth. The company already makes laptops available; I could use one of those. And modems now cost less than $150, an expense I'd absorb. I'd only ask for the everyday office supplies I'd normally require on-site.

BOSS: I'm a little uncomfortable with letting proposals and some of the other documents you work with out of the office. How do I know they'd be as safe at your home?

YOU: During working hours, my home office would be off limits to neighbors, friends, even my family. Outside of those hours, records will be secured just as they would be if they remained here.

BOSS: What if you get hurt while you are working for the company at home? Would we be liable? Do the worker's compensation laws apply to home-based workers? For example, if you lift your computer and injure your back in the process, it seems likely we would be responsible. But how about if you plug in your PC and for some reason get an electric shock? Or, suppose you fall down the steps en route to your basement office?

YOU: Well, I know the worker's compensation laws vary from state to state. I've checked the law for our state and there's a provision that applies to home-based workers. I'll do what I can to minimize hazards. For example, my work space is separate from my living space. But as my employer, you'd be free to inspect my home office, since your liability would extend to that area.

BOSS: If I let you telecommute, everyone will want to do it. Pretty soon I'd be the only one at the office.

YOU: You always remain in charge, and in control of the amount of telecommuting going on. If you sense your control diminishing, you can tighten the reins. Besides, not everyone would even want to telecommute. Some workers, for example, would miss the social aspects of office life.

Trust. Your boss may not express all the concerns just covered, but any boss will be concerned about whether a telecommuter will still get the job done. Yet, as anyone who's worked in an office knows, being there doesn't mean that you are actually working. But to much of corporate America this doesn't matter. They need to know that the right number of warm bodies are there. As one manager of a top telecommunications company put it, "When our people get to work in the morning they don't sit down and get right to work. They go down to the cafeteria and eat breakfast. But they are still here. That's what the corporation wants."

Pacific Bell has a lot of people who telecommute only part time. One reason is that upper-level managers like to see their employees when they walk around. Even at a progressive company like PacBell, there is a lot of bureaucracy. "A person is a thing that belongs to the company" is its unstated belief.

It boils down to trust. Your relationship with your boss enters into this heavily. If your boss knows you and trusts you will get the work done whether you are on-site (and therefore in his sight) or not, then perceived loss of control may not be a stumbling block for you. You should have a feel for this already.

When you discuss with your supervisor what will be expected from you once you start working off-site, establish firm goals and deadlines. Telecommuting consultant Lis Fleming feels this is something that's sometimes neglected. Unfortunately, if goals and expectations are not nailed down before telecommuting gets under way, it may be too late. Once the employee is off-site, this is more difficult to do.

Precedence. Easing your way greatly will be the employer listings in this book. Photocopy the listings for companies in your field. The knowledge that this has been done before and that it's working out should go a long way toward making your boss feel easier about allowing it at your company. You may hear "If it's good enough for Apple Computer, DuPont, and AT&T, then perhaps we should give it a try."

Remind your boss that remote work forces existed long before the term *telecommuting* was ever coined. For example, many companies have salespeople either in remote offices or working from home, with a manager based in a central site.

On the whole, once companies try telecommuting, they find it works out well for both the company and its telecommuters, and they become advocates of it. This is difficult for an employer to get a feel for, of course, before getting into it, so it's going to be difficult for you to convey. The employer listings may help here if your boss is willing to make a call or two to speak with a manager who's had firsthand experience with managing telecommuters.

Consultant Gil Gordon says it's the people issues that make this work, rather than the technology issues. Above all, he says, it's important to get across to managers that telecommuting is:

1. Nothing really new.
2. Nothing really scary.
3. Something that can be managed in a way and at a pace that lets people remain comfortable with it.

Signing a Telecommuter's Agreement

One way to allay concerns all around is to offer to sign a Telecommuter's Agreement. Organizations that have formalized telecommuting typically use such agreements to spell out what constitutes telecommuting, the nature of the arrangement, and compensation and liability issues. For example, the Southern California Association of Governments' Telecommuter's Agreement, on which the following sample agreement is based, covers worker's compensation and liability issues in detail. It also covers many other issues that enter into a telecommuting arrangement. Offering to sign such an agreement may ease your employer's concerns.

TELECOMMUTER'S AGREEMENT

Telecommuting, the use of telecommunications technology to transport information, rather than people, to and from the workplace, is an arrangement that the company may choose to make available to some employees when a mutually beneficial situation exists. Telecommuting is not a formal, universal employee benefit, but rather an alternate method of meeting the needs of the company.

Since it is not assumed that employees have a right to telecommute, the arrangement can be terminated any time it is determined that company needs are not being met. Similarly, employees do not have an obligation to telecommute and may return to the conventional office arrangement if they wish to withdraw from the telecommuting project.

When a telecommuting arrangement is implemented, the following conditions will apply:

- Employee salary, job responsibilities, benefits, and company-sponsored insurance coverage will not change due to participation in the telecommuting project.
- The amount of time the employee is expected to work will not change due to participation in the telecommuting project.
- For the purpose of defining the employee's job tour period during which the employer has liability for job-related accidents or illnesses and during which worker's compensation laws apply, it is understood that the employee's work hours will conform to a schedule agreed upon by the telecommuter and his/her manager.
- If a schedule has not otherwise been agreed upon, the employee's work hours while telecommuting are assumed to be the same as before beginning to telecommute.
- Any changes or extension to the above-mentioned schedule with respect to worker's compensation coverage must be reviewed and approved by the employer in advance.
- Since the employee's home work space will be considered an extension of the company work space, the company's liability for job-related accidents will continue to exist during the understood and approved job-tour hours.
- A designated work space should be maintained by the telecommuter at the alternate work location. Worker's compensation liability will be limited to this work space as opposed to applying to all areas of the home.
- As this liability will extend to accidents which may occur in the alternate location, the employer retains the right to make on-site inspections of this work area to ensure that safe work conditions exist.
- On-site visits by the employer may also be made for the purpose of retrieving equipment and other company property in the event of employee illness or termination.
- Any hardware or software the company purchases remains its property. Products developed while telecommuting for the company become its property.
- Company-owned software may not be duplicated except as formally authorized.
- Restricted-access materials (such as payroll) shall not be taken out of the main office or accessed through the computer at a remote location.

- Company equipment in a remote office shall not be used for personal purposes.
- The company will not purchase furniture or answering machines for telecommuters.
- The company will not provide custom-calling services, second phone lines, printers, or personal computers to telecommuters.
- On a case-by-case basis, the company will consider partially reimbursing an employee for monthly service charges on a second telephone line and/or custom-calling services. Reimbursement, if approved, will be proportional to the amount telecommuted (one day a week telecommuting gets 1/7th of the bill reimbursed, and so on). This applies only to the service charges; the usage charges for, e.g., a second line, are dealt with below.
- Supplies required to complete assigned work at the alternate location should be obtained during one of the telecommuter's in-office visits. Out-of-pocket expenses for supplies normally available at the company will not be reimbursed.
- The company will not reimburse the employee for supplies such as computer paper, floppy disks, and cables.
- The company will reimburse the telecommuter for 60 percent of all company-related telephone calls.
- Expenses not specifically covered above will be dealt with on a case-by-case basis, taking into account the reasonableness of the expense, other expenses reimbursed for the same employee, and the overall budget for the project.
- Telecommuting is not to be viewed as a substitute for child care. Telecommuters with preschool children are expected to have someone else care for the children during the agreed-upon work hours.
- Individual tax implications related to the home work space shall be the responsibility of the telecommuter. It is possible, under some circumstances, to deduct expenses of a home office, but a tax expert should be consulted first.

Note that this agreement seems a bit skewed in the employer's favor. To its credit, it clearly says that benefits remain in effect. The amount of time the employee is expected to work also stays the same.

I accept the conditions of this agreement.

_____

(Employee signature)

_____

Date

_____

(Company representative signature)

_____

Date

_____

These are important points since in a few (rare) cases, employers have expected more work from telecommuters, but at less pay and a loss of benefits. The worker's compensation coverage provisions also seem fair. The right to inspect the employee's work site may seem extreme, but it's something that other employers with telecommuters ask for as well.

In other cases, you may be able to improve on some of the provisions stated here. These include:

Equipment. The agreement says you can't use the company's equipment for other projects. That seems extreme. While it wouldn't be fair to use company-supplied equipment to run a business out of your home, using it for an occasional freelance project does not seem unreasonable.

Expenses. Employees are only compensated for 60 percent of all company-related phone calls. Why not 100 percent?

Schedule. The employee has to specify what hours he will be working if they will differ from the normal working hours. At first blush that requirement seems to remove one of telecommuting's major boons: the chance for a flexible schedule. However, the agreement allows the employee to determine his own hours intially; it also implies that changing hours is possible.

Final Advice from an Old Hand

Software writer Diane Yeager-McIntosh has telecommuted for three separate employers, in each case convincing the employer to let her work that way. Some of the arguments she recommends that prospective telecommuters use to convice their current employers to let them give telecommuting a try include:

I will get more done.
How about a trial period?
I will trade the change in lieu of a raise.
I will quit.
I will have more time for overtime.
How about a part-time period?
(You will save on clothes, gas, etc.)

Start Slow

Your switch to working from home should occur gradually. Paul Andrews, a reporter for the *Seattle Times* who's telecommuted for years, suggests that telecommuters ease into this way of working. "Start out on an experimental basis and be flexible to work out the kinks," he says. For example, one day when you have a pressing deadline, ask to work at home where you can give the project the thought and concentration it demands.

At any rate, you'll probably start by working at home a day or two a week, or even every other week. Then, once you've proved it's working out well for you and your employer, you can move to increase that time. But there will be a learning curve for both you and your employer. During that time you should show up at the office fairly often. Remember, telecommuting is not a way of working that most employers are used to yet and you'll have to do a lot of reassuring at first.

If your employer hesitates, ask if he'll let you work from home one day every other week. That's only 10 percent of the time. Or work at night for a few nights or over a weekend and bring well-thought-out professional-looking work into the office. Let your boss know when you did it and how. "Once people see the commitment you are showing and the valuable work you are producing," says John Hancock's Barry Trask, "you just may open some eyes."

Once you've started telecommuting, work to keep the arrangement satisfactory from both your viewpoint and your employer's. As the one who initiated telecommuting the burden for making it successful falls on you. So be alert to signs that it's not working out as well as it could. For example, if you are losing touch with your supervisor or otherwise falling out of the communication loop, act quickly to improve the communication lines.

The Importance of Patience

Telecommuting goes against the grain. It's not something that MBA programs now condone or even acknowledge. Telecommuters must sometimes shop around before finding a boss who will let them work from home. In time, success comes. "There are bosses out there willing to try new things," says Dianne Breen. "Find them and make it worth their while." You may also have to do a little more for a little less. You can always renegotiate once you've proved that you can do the job from home. Telecommuters are trend-setters, and the road is never an easy one if it's not well-worn. But telecommuting's benefits are such that almost all telecommuters would agree it's a road worth taking.

5

75 Jobs for Telecommuters

You've now learned what telecommuting is, its advantages and disadvantages, and how to become a telecommuter. If your job is suited for telecommuting and your company and boss also like the idea, you may be all set. But if roadblocks remain you may want to consider changing jobs or employers, which is where the next two chapters come into play. This chapter discusses the jobs best suited for telecommuting; the next one, in a sense, covers the companies best suited to it.

Why Telecommuting Fits So Many Jobs

There are probably hundreds of corporate jobs you can do from home. Thanks to computers, which allow workers to produce from anywhere, the list gets longer all the time. Almost any white-collar job includes these three stages: research, produce, and present. The fact that so many jobs break down this way makes telecommuting widely applicable.

Step One: Research

The research stage is when you find out what you have to do and gather the materials you need to do it. For the reporter, this includes getting an assignment from an editor and researching the story through interviews and phone calls. For an architect the process starts when the client describes the building he wants designed.

Normally you need to interact with other people during the research stage, and to do this you often need to be at your employer's office. Although for some jobs, such as technical writer or market researcher, computer databases let you do research from a home office as easily as from an office building. This stage is often fairly short.

Step Two: Produce

Next you need to do the work: to produce. The architect designs the building, the reporter writes an article, the programmer creates a program. Most people prefer solitude during this stage. They need the space and peace to concentrate in order to do the best possible job. Consequently, *this is the part of most jobs that's perfect for doing from a home office.*

In this stage, you may need to make a phone call here and there to check a fact or clear something up. Perhaps you'll even need to make a speed run into the office to pick the brain of a co-worker or gather new research materials. But mostly you are on your own. This is often the part of the job that takes the longest.

Step Three: Present

After you've pinpointed the task and completed it, you must present what you've done. Again, what this entails varies with the job. For the data-entry clerk, it may be as simple as dropping off completed forms; the budget analyst may have to make a formal presentation to management. This is usually a brief stage compared to production.

What the Profiles Show

The job profiles that follow describe seventy-five of the best jobs for telecommuting. All are while-collar jobs. In varying proportions each job has these things in common:

1. Does not require much face-to-face interaction.
2. Computers and/or telephones are key tools.
3. Performance is easily measured.
4. Does not often require access to materials at the central work site.

In addition to a description of the job, each profile includes the following:

Salary Range

This number (either a median, average salary, or range) reflects what someone working full time in the job profiled could expect to earn per year. The figures were gathered from the U.S. Bureau of Labor Statistics, trade groups, and published salary surveys. A median salary is a midpoint—half earned less, half earned more. Where ranges are given they are often large, since many factors affect income. These include:

Geography. In 1987, news reporters for the Chicago *Sun-Times* with five years' experience earned a minimum of $45,000; similarly experienced reporters for the Utica (N.Y.) *Observer-Dispatch* only earned $17,500. Part of the variance is due to differences in the prestige and size of the two papers, but the relative cost of living in the two areas also enters the picture.

Type of Company. Several things apply here, including the particular industry, the size of the company, and whether it's a nonprofit or for-profit concern. Some industries, such as utilities, pay better than others. And, generally, the larger the company the better the pay. Nonprofits don't pay as well as for-profit companies. (But for some people, the intangible benefits of working for a museum, for example, compensate for that.)

Experience. The more experience you have, the more money you can command. Accountants right out of school, for example, receive offers averaging $25,830, according to a 1989 survey by the College Placement Council. Yet the median salary for accountants is $32,032, according to the Bureau of Labor Statistics.

Telecommuting Rating

This gives you a quick fix on the job's suitability for telecommuting. The rating takes into account the four factors cited earlier. It also reflects how many companies have people doing that job from home. In addition, it considers what the BLS has to say about the job's prospects. The rationale here is that jobs predicted to show a lot of growth in the next few years will be harder for companies to fill and therefore may use telecommuting as a sign-up incentive.

A programmer's job, for example, requires little interaction and depends heavily on computers. The BLS also predicts a strong demand for programmers through the rest of the century. Finally, twenty-three of the companies listed in Chapter 6 already have programmers who telecommute. So programmer ranks at the top of the list. The job of booking agent, however, is only moderately suitable for telecommuting. Booking agents must spend a lot of time on the road, so that job ranks much lower.

Representative Companies

Each profile also includes, wherever possible, examples of companies where telecommuters work in the profiled jobs. The absence of representative companies does not mean the job is not well-suited to telecommuting. It simply means that none of the companies in Chapter 6 have telecommuters working in those positions. Chapter 6 describes each company mentioned in detail and includes complete contact information.

To get your research started, here are the top fifteen jobs for telecommuters, according to their Telecommuting Rating.

JOB	RATING
Programmer	10.0
Translator	10.0
Software Engineer	9.75
Sales Representative	9.75
Computer Systems Analyst	9.50
News Reporter	9.25
Sportswriter	9.25
Public Relations Professional	9.25
Technical Writer	9.0
Desktop Publisher	9.0
Stockbroker	9.0
Freelance Writer	8.75
Data-Entry Clerk	8.75
Lawyer	8.75
Legal Assistant	8.75

ABSTRACTER

Remember reading *Reader's Digest's* condensed books? Someone on the magazine's staff boiled a complete book down to its essence, saving the reader the time and trouble of plowing through the entire work. Abstracters do the same thing but are more likely to distill magazine articles than books. Like the *Reader's Digest* editor, abstracters edit to wring out highlights and essential facts.

Abstracters work mostly for publishers of indexes and other reference tools. Their work is now largely done on computers. Once trained, an abstracter does not need to work with others; all that's needed is the material to be abstracted and the computer into which the abstracter feeds the finished abstract.

Many of the abstracters who telecommute work as independent

contractors. While this means they must arrange for their own insurance and other benefits, it also means they set their own hours and work for as many employers as they want.

Salary Range: $25,000–$50,000

Representative Companies: Information Access Company; UMI/Data Courier

Telecommuting Rating: 7.5

ACCOUNTANT

Electronic Services Unlimited, a New-York based company that tracks telecommuting closely, rates accountant as one of the top twenty-five jobs for telecommuters.

Computers are now a necessity for these number-crunchers. Accountants often work alone and need to concentrate intensely, which makes this a good job for telecommuting. There are also times when they can count on working overtime (tax season). The extra hours telecommuting adds to the day (by ending commuting) would come in handy then.

Growth in the financial sector will spell increased demand for accountants. A boom in demand for their services will give accountants more leverage and make it easier for them to cut telecommuting deals.

Accountants already have a history of working from home, anyway; roughly 10 percent of accountants are self-employed.

Salary Range: $32,032 (median)

Representative Companies: Southern California Association of Governments; Wendy's International, Inc.

Telecommuting Rating: 8.5

ACTUARY

Actuaries have the best all-around job, according to the *Jobs Rated Almanac* (see Chapter 10). To earn this rating, the actuary's job was pitted against 249 others, considering such factors as stress level, environment, outlook, physical demands, and security.

Actuaries usually work for insurance companies. They determine probabilities based on statistics. If you want to know the chance of an unmarried twenty-five-year-old single white male getting in a car accident over the next year, an actuary can tell you. The answers to such questions determine insurance rates.

Actuaries use computers extensively to do their jobs (number-crunching is still what computers do best). The fact that the job prospects for this occupation are excellent (projected growth rate of 52 percent through 1995) also makes it a good job for telecommuting. Like accountants, actuaries can probably work out a deal that includes telecommuting, since employers are hungry for their services. Also working in their favor is the insurance industry's acceptance of telecommuting.

Salary Range: $25,070–$59,950

Telecommuting Rating: 8.0

ADVERTISING COPY WRITER

Copy writers come up with those clever lines that sometimes, perhaps because we hear or see them so often, we can't seem to get out of our heads. For this they are paid quite well. But the work isn't easy. Like other writing professions, the copy writer has to be able to concentrate. While some find the hubbub, colors, and chitchat of an ad agency inspiring, others prefer to mull over ideas at home. At least occasionally.

Unfortunately, there's been a shakeout among advertising firms, and competition in this field has really heated up. Translation: You may have to take whatever job you can get and really prove yourself before you can hope to telecommute. But even in these times, it shouldn't be difficult for a valued copy writer to make a case for working at home.

Salary Range: $18,000–$54,000

Telecommuting Rating: 7.0

ADVERTISING REPRESENTATIVE

Newspapers, magazines, and television stations all depend on advertising revenues to survive. The ad rep's job is to track down new advertisers and service existing ones. The nature of the job, of course, varies with the medium and its size. For example, someone who sells space in a weekly newspaper has fewer national accounts than someone who sells ads for *The New York Times*. But there are always aspects of the job that are the same. Ad reps track down new leads by scouring the competition to see who's advertising. They also stay abreast of new businesses opening in their territories. There's a lot of telephone work, which makes this job well-suited for telecommuting. Ads must be pitched, prices quoted, meetings set up—all of which can be done on the phone. Computers come in handy for managing and keeping track of accounts. The ambitious newspaper sales rep may even use desktop publishing equipment to lay out ads for clients.

Newspapers, which are among the biggest users of telecommuters, would seem a good place to pitch your services.

Salary Range: $23,000 (median for newspaper sales reps.)

Telecommuting Rating: 7.5

ARCHITECT

Architects ultimately design buildings, of course, but this process breaks down into three steps. First, the architect meets with the client to get a feel for the type of structure intended. They discuss the available budget, what the building should look like, and its purpose. Then the architect disappears for a while to come up with the preliminary drawings (the stage that's well suited to telecommuting). After the drawings are approved, the architect may oversee construction and work with building contractors to ensure the final product adheres to the plans.

Architects increasingly use computers as design tools (Computer-Aided Design, or CAD). During the construction stage, architects may need to be on the phone a lot to contractors and suppliers. There is some travel during this stage also.

So far, most of the salaried architects who telecommute work for state and local governments.

Salary Range: $15,000–$67,200

Representative Company: California State Department of General Services

Telecommuting Rating: 8.25

AUDITOR

Auditors verify the accuracy of numbers for evidence of fraud and waste, which makes them among the least popular people around. Government employs many auditors, as do business and industry.

Computers take much of the tedium out of the auditor's job, which requires great concentration. After reviewing the numbers, the auditor presents his findings in a report to management.

Given the need for concentration, the report writing, and the reliance on computers, this is a good job for part-time telecommuting.

Salary Range: $21,000–$46,000

Representative Companies: County of Los Angeles; the Federal Government

Telecommuting Rating: 8.0

BANK OFFICER

Also known as financial managers, bank officers prepare budget estimates, solicit new business, or work to expand a bank's present business. Part of their work also involves approving and extending lines of credit. Banks employ a large number of female workers, which has something to do with their interest in telecommuting.

NCNB Corporation and First National Bank of Chicago are featured in this book. Both started telecommuting programs to attract and retain female workers. Both programs work. The employees see telecommuting as a way to extend maternity leaves and still collect paychecks. But more than that, they like working for institutions that help them balance work and family demands. NCNB, in particular, has received a lot of media attention due to its innovative personnel policies. It's likely that other banks will follow its lead and allow telecommuting.

Salary Range: $19,620–$56,680

Representative Companies: First Chicago Corporation; NCNB Corporation

Telecommuting Rating: 7.5

BOOK AUTHOR

In the competitive field of writing books either as a sideline or full time, authors welcome anything that gives them an edge. Increasingly, telecommuting, especially the ability to send a publisher a manuscript electronically, fits in that category.

Currently, some authors use electronic databases when researching their books; others chat with fellow authors or agents by electronic mail. After the research is done, computer-savvy authors can (and should—it's much easier) word-process their information into book form. The final step is to send it electronically to their publishers.

Publishers find information that's in electronic (as opposed to paper) form easier to work with since it can be fed directly into their electronic publishing systems without rekeying. This saves an expensive step in the production process. It also reduces errors and speeds the process.

Not all publishers are set up to receive manuscripts electronically but some are, and that's reason enough to look into it. "The easier you make a publisher's job the more likely they are to use you," says author John Everett. John, an information broker and co-author of a book on the subject, *Information for Sale,* never met his co-author. The collaborators sent each other chapter drafts back and forth by CompuServe.

For more information on submitting manuscripts electronically, see the latest edition of *Writer's Market,* a yearly publication that describes magazines, book publishers, and other markets where writers can sell their wares. Its descriptions of book publishers mention whether computer submissions are acceptable.

Salary Range: $3,070–$98,400 (few authors write books full time)

Representative Companies: See *Writer's Market*

Telecommuting Rating: 8.5

BOOKING AGENT

Booking agents find work for entertainers, primarily nightclub performers. These acts come and go with fashion, but in the southern New Jersey area, for example, variety bands and specialty acts for hotels such as harpists and strolling violinists are now popular. While booking agents spend a lot of time speaking face-to-face with club owners (personal contact is very important in this business) they are also on the telephone a lot.

Agents scan newspapers and other information sources for leads— usually clubs that have just started using live entertainment. They then make telephone calls to follow up on those leads. They also use the phone to maintain client contacts. But the telephone is "just a vehicle to get you in the face of the club owners," says one New Jersey agent. "In fact, if they don't see your face you are history." Like a sales representative's job, booking agents are out of the office a lot. But there is no reason that when they are in the office they can't also be at home.

Salary Range: $50,000 (average)

Telecommuting Rating: 7.0

BOOKKEEPER

Bookkeepers keep track of a company's business transactions by entering accounts-receivable and accounts-payable data into a computer. Sophisticated software packages make this job much easier.

At some companies, bookkeepers also prepare and mail out invoices. Bookkeepers may also be asked to prepare special financial reports. Both tasks are well suited to computers. There is also a lot of telephone work involved in the job. Bookkeepers often respond to customers' inquiries about their bills. Finally, for a bookkeeper, the need to concentrate is extremely important; even small mistakes can prove very serious.

About one in four bookkeepers works part time, so there are a lot of precedents for flexible working arrangements. Because the Bureau of Labor Statistics predicts that job prospects for bookkeepers will only be fair through the rest of the century, its Telecommuting Rating is fairly low.

Salary Range: $13,917–$26,160

Telecommuting Rating: 7.0

BUDGET ANALYST

Budget analysts have the ultimate number-crunching job. They research, analyze, and develop budgets. Those who work for large companies are likely to be part of a separate budget department. Those who work for smaller companies may work more as accountants or controllers than analysts. Bottom line: Budget analysts are paid to boost profits. Therefore, in addition to working on budgets they try to find ways of improving efficiency.

Typically, budget analysts report to senior management and offer advice on annual budgets (a key part of the job). To prepare for this, they do research that includes defining company objectives, examining past budgets, and identifying current economic trends.

They do need to meet with managers when gathering information for their reports and when presenting their finished reports and estimates. But for the step that falls in the middle, budget analysts spend a lot of time alone working with numbers. Theirs is a computer-intensive job where financial software packages are now as important as the calculator once was. Knowledge of these packages makes the budget analyst more marketable.

Salary Range: $22,000–$40,500

Representative Company: State of California Franchise Tax Board

Telecommuting Rating: 7.5

CHIEF EXECUTIVE OFFICER

People who run companies have a lot of face-to-face meetings with others, so—admittedly—telecommuting is not for every CEO. However, some aspects of the technology fit in well with the CEO's lifestyle. First, a CEO has the freedom and resources to arrange for telecommuting. He can outfit a limo with a laptop computer and cellular modem, a fax machine, and (naturally) a car phone. These Portable Executives, as *Business Week* calls them, are becoming more and more common.

One such executive is Egil Juliussen, who actually runs three companies: StoreBoard, Inc. (Dallas), which tracks computer sales; Workstation Laboratories (Phoenix), which rates computers and workstations; and the Computer Industry Almanac, a who's who of the computer world (see Chapter 10). Juliussen works from his home, located at Lake Tahoe on a mountain ridge 7400 feet above sea level. Although the howling of the coyotes at night took some getting used to, he appreciates the splendor and wonder of his mountaintop office.

Would Juliussen recommend this to other CEOs? "Depends on the company," he says. "If there is a lot of people interaction, telecommuting won't work." But for Juliussen, telecommuting works out just fine. Because his companies are in the information business, with a fax machine and computer/modem hook-up he can monitor them from anywhere. Also, they are all small: Workstation has only three or four people, all of whom hold high-level jobs. And in the case of Computer Industry Almanac, the only employees are Juliussen and his wife, Karen.

Salary Range: $1,128,854 (1988 average, including bonus, as reported in *Business Week)*

Representative Companies: Personal Computer Support Group (PCSG) Inc.; Workstation Laboratories

Telecommuting Rating: 8.0

CITY MANAGER

City managers are appointed by local city, county, or town councils to run local governments. They spend a lot of their time consulting with experts on ongoing city projects, meeting with citizens, and visiting public facilities.

The office work that comes with the job makes it suitable for telecommuting. This includes reviewing budgets and filling out proposals for state and federal grants earmarked for the local government. In larger cities, city managers have more personnel-related responsibilities.

City managers have long work weeks—forty to sixty hours—and must be on call for emergencies. While some taxpayers might object to their officials working solely from home offices, part-time telecommuting is certainly possible. Now that local and state governments in California and elsewhere are experimenting with telecommuting, more city managers should get the chance to try it.

Salary Range: $31,000–$114,000

Telecommuting Rating: 7.0

COLUMNIST

Unlike news reporters, columnists don't face the pressure of daily deadlines; they have to produce a column two or three scheduled days a week. Another difference between the two jobs is that columnists inject opinion into their articles, and "wishes and whims," according to Baltimore *Evening Sun* columnist Jack Kelly. (Reporters must be objective.) Columnists also dig up their own material. For these reasons, "peace and quiet is more important to a columnist," says Kelly, whose column focuses on old and traditional things in Baltimore. Jack Kelly typically works from home in the mornings and gets to the newspaper around noon. He gets twice as much work done at home as he does at the newspaper.

Columnists are among the best-paid employees at newspapers. They are the stars. Most should have no trouble arranging to telecommute.

Salary Range: $12,000–$50,000+

Representative Companies: Baltimore *Evening Sun;* Detroit *Free Press*

Telecommuting Rating: 8.0

COMPUTER SERVICE TECHNICIAN

Computer service technicians keep expensive computer equipment in good operating order. Some install equipment as well as service it. To pinpoint problems, technicians run diagnostic tests. By the nature of the job, computer service technicians often work independently. Technicians usually have assigned accounts and are responsible for ordering parts, keeping inventory, and filling out expense reports and time reports. They essentially run their own minibusinesses. All these tasks add up to a job that can be done at least part time from home.

Formerly, the most important part of the job, repairing and servicing equipment, had to be done at the user's site, but that's no longer always true. Now, technicians can sometimes diagnose problems from afar using powerful portable computers to link up to the remote computer by the phone lines.

Since many computer facilities operate around the clock, technicians often handle emergency repairs outside normal working hours. Being able to work from home makes the job much easier, especially when a repair call comes in at 4:00 A.M.

Salary Range: $26,676 (median)

Representative Company: Prime Computer

Telecommuting Rating: 8.5

COMPUTER SYSTEMS ANALYST

Systems analysts help companies computerize their businesses from scratch or enhance existing computer systems. The first thing an analyst does is determine the nature of the problem. This often requires on-site visits and is the part of the job that's obviously not well suited to telecommuting.

After pinpointing what needs to be done, the analyst plans the system, using mathematical models and cost accounting. Analysts often work on projects in teams, but in many cases (as John Hancock's Barry Trask has learned) they find they can do this part of the job alone.

Following the design phase, the analyst prepares for the client a report that explains the details of the planned system. Finally, assuming the plan is approved, the analyst prepares a cost benefit analysis and designs forms for data collection.

Barry Trask says his job is computer- and communications-oriented anyway. Because systems analysts sometimes work evenings and weekends to meet deadlines and often have the equipment they need to work from home, they can ease into telecommuting.

Computer systems analysts score high on all three measures: forecasted growth, prevalence of the job among the surveyed companies, and overall suitability for telecommuting, hence its high Telecommuting Rating.

Salary Range: $28,000–$72,840

Representative Companies: General Telephone of California; John Hancock; Lanier Business Products; Sears; US West

Telecommuting Rating: 9.5

CONSULTANT

Consultants offer companies expertise that they may not have available in-house, on an as-needed basis. About half of all consultants are self-employed; a few specialize in advising companies about telecommuting (see Chapter 9). Yet there are also organizations that employ hundreds of consultants.

Consultants work with data: they collect it, review it, and analyze it. Any of this can be done from a home office, especially if the client is computerized.

Drafting plans, of course, can be done from anywhere. It's significant that the part of the consultant's work that requires face-to-face meetings (the initial problem assessment) is the least time-consuming.

Salary Range: $34,944 (median)

Representative Companies: Digital Equipment Corporation; Interactive Systems Corporation; Psychological Services, Inc.

Telecommuting Rating: 8.0

COPY EDITOR

Copy editors are the watchdogs of the publishing world. They dot I's and cross T's, but largely they ferret out lapses in the rules of grammar. Like other people who work with words, they sometimes use computers.

The Writing Edge, which advertises its services on the Delphi online service, offers professional writing assistance and copy editing by fax and electronic mail. You send them that thorny proposal outline, or sketch for a new brochure, and they send the finished prose through the phone lines to your computer. You then feed it straight into your electronic publishing system. What could be neater? More and more copy editors will work this way in the future.

Salary Range: $12,400–$41,300

Representative Companies: Globalink Language Services; Newsbytes News Service; Phillips Publishing

Telecommuting Rating: 7.75

CORRESPONDENT

Correspondents, like other reporters, gather and disseminate news. They are even more likely to telecommute, however, because they may work from distant cities or even foreign countries located far from the mother ship. Sometimes, especially for large publications covering major cities such as London, there are enough correspondents in a city to justify office space. More often, correspondents are on their own, hence the need for a home office.

Many journalists covet these bureau jobs for the freedom they offer and the chance to live and work in a foreign country, so competition for them is keen. Your best chances for employment are with one of the wire services, such as Associated Press or United Press International, both of which maintain more than 100 bureaus. Many newspapers have at least one bureau.

Salary Range: $25,168–$63,333+

Representative Companies: Detroit *Free Press;* Newsbytes News Service; United Press International (UPI)

Telecommuting Rating: 8.5

COST ESTIMATOR

Cost estimators predict the costs involved in upcoming manufacturing or construction projects.

Estimators first review blueprints and other documents associated with the job. Next they meet with the architects, engineers, and other professionals involved to choose machinery and other necessary equipment. After gathering this data the estimator retreats to an office (a home office would work out well) to come up with the actual calculations. This includes preparing a parts or materials list and determining the labor hours involved. This is all detailed work that calls for telephones for fact checking and data gathering and computers for performing the key calculations.

Construction estimators visit construction sites, while manufacturing estimators visit factory floors, but both still spend most of their time in offices. During bidding for contracts the pressure increases; telecommuting would be a way to offset some of that pressure.

Salary Range: $18,000–$96,000

Telecommuting Rating: 7.25

CRITIC

Critics work strange hours: they report on openings, premieres, and debuts, which typically occur at times most people have off (evenings and weekends). A critic who telecommuted could write the story right after the event (or with cellular modems *at* the event) without going back to the office. Also, like other journalists, critics must stay abreast of trends and the beat they cover. Computer research would help there.

Like the job of columnist or correspondent, reporters work up to a critic's post. The latitude that comes with it has to be earned—something that applies to a lot of telecommuting jobs.

Salary Range: $35,000–$100,000

Representative Company: Baltimore *Evening Sun*

Telecommuting Rating: 8.0

CUSTOMER SERVICE REPRESENTATIVE

Customer service representatives spend a lot of time on the telephone. They have little need for the resources associated with most offices (copiers, fax machines, and the like), relying instead on just a few basic references.

JCPenney has had homeworkers taking customer catalog orders since 1981. Thanks to its telecommuting program, the company can control its staffing levels, not always easy during peak ordering seasons (like Christmas). Penney has telecommuting customer service reps in eight of the company's sixteen telemarketing centers.

Other customer service representatives work for utilities. While the telephone companies are among the most active supporters of telecommuting, energy companies have been slow to move into it.

Salary Range: $15,600–$24,000

Representative Companies: JCPenney; Prime Computer, Inc.

Telecommuting Rating: 7.5

DATA-ENTRY CLERK

Today a data-entry clerk is among the most "location-independent" of jobs, thanks to computers—it does not matter where it's done as long as it gets done. Rosenbluth Travel, for example, a Philadelphia-based travel agency (and one of the country's largest), has moved forty data-entry jobs out of the city to Linton, North Dakota.

Data-entry jobs and telecommuting don't always mix. Some employers don't want confidential information (payroll data, for instance) outside company premises. This is also an area where some telecommuters have had bad experiences. Eight data-entry clerks at California Western States Life Insurance Company sued their employer over the quotas it imposed. Yet the cottage keyer program at Blue Cross/Blue Shield of South Carolina is one of telecommuting's true success stories.

Data-entry workers should be able to find work as telecommuters, especially if they don't mind working as independent contractors. Insurance companies, utilities, and other companies that generate a lot of paperwork would be the best to approach.

If not for the job's poor forecasted growth rate, the Telecommuting Rating for data-entry clerk would be among the very top.

Salary Range: $12,000–$20,000+

Representative Companies: Appalachian Computer Services; California State Department of General Services; Meckler; University Graphics, Inc.

Telecommuting Rating: 8.75

DATABASE ADMINISTRATOR

Databases are collections of facts arranged in a form suitable for computers. Just about all businesses have internal databases. Their contents vary with the type of business. Most universities, for example, have alumni databases, which may contain details on year of graduation, major, past pledges, address, and place of employment. Database administrators design these databases, decide what they'll contain, and oversee their use.

Like many professional-level jobs, there is a planning and strategizing part to this work, which makes it good for telecommuting. Database administrators often have the computers and other tools they need to telecommute.

Database administrators are often managers. But they don't have the same concerns that other managers who telecommute have about losing control over their staffs, because they usually have programmers reporting to them. And with all the programmers who now telecommute, it's possible that database administrators and their entire crews will work from home, communicating through electronic mail and the telephone.

Salary Range: $27,000–$47,000

Telecommuting Rating: 8.25

DESKTOP PUBLISHER

Desktop publisher is among the new professions made possible by computers that this chapter profiles (another is information broker). Desktop publishers produce professional-quality publications using laser printers, special software packages, and, often, Macintosh computers.

Here's how the desktop publisher works for TechProse, a company profiled in Chapter 6. A client sends the desktop publisher text for a newsletter by modem. The telecommuter lays out the text and prepares galleys using a software package such as Ventura Publisher. The telecommuter then faxes copies of the galleys to the customer for final approval.

Desktop publishing is a growing area that is currently especially attractive for entrepreneurs.

Salary Range: $15,000–$60,000

Representative Companies: Continental Communications Agency, Inc.; Direct Data; TechProse

Telecommuting Rating: 9.0

ECONOMIST

Economists work primarily for colleges and universities and the federal government. They analyze the allocation of scarce resources that go into the production of goods. They advise businesses, insurance companies, and associations. Many economists work by themselves; a few work as part of teams. Report writing is a key part of an economist's job.

Computers help in every aspect of the job. Desktop publishing aids the report writing since the reports often feature graphs and charts.

Economists also rely on computers to develop mathematical models and sampling techniques. Economists who work as teachers in colleges and universities often have a lot of flexibility in their work schedules. Balancing out their teaching is research, administrative work, and consulting, all of which can be done from a home office.

Salary Range: $34,996 (median)

Telecommuting Rating: 7.75

EDITORIAL WRITER

Unlike news reporters, who may not have the time, editorial writers must ponder and carefully weigh their words. The editorials they write reflect the opinion of their newspapers. The ability to concentrate that comes with working from a home office would greatly benefit editorial writers.

Most editorial writers spend a lot of time reading news and commentary articles to keep fully informed. In fact, junior editorial writers (a position more likely available at larger newspapers) may do nothing but research for more senior writers.

Your chances of telecommuting as an editorial writer are quite good. The tough part is getting this job in the first place. The editorial writer's job requires years of seasoning.

Salary Range: $26,780–$47,372+

Representative Company: Baltimore *Evening Sun*

Telecommuting Rating: 8.0

EDUCATIONAL CONSULTANT

This job takes several forms, depending on the company. At Multi-Link, a company that offers teleconferencing training courses, Charlotte Purvis' title is Director of Educational Services. She helps companies learn how to conduct teleconferences, which bring people separated by many miles together for "telephone meetings." The fact that she telecommutes not only works out well for her but also helps the company sell the technology. Charlotte, in essence, proves that it works by showing that you can do business remotely.

Lanier Business Products employs educational consultants who help clients learn to use applications software packages. They work from home when learning how to use new software packages, tough work under the best of circumstances. Other consultants work for on-line database companies, helping new database users learn the ropes of going on-line. To do this they actually train them on-line.

Salary Range: $29,224 (median)

Representative Companies: Lanier Business Products; Multi-Link

Telecommuting Rating: 7.75

EDUCATIONAL SOFTWARE WRITER

Computer-aided instruction is a booming business, with hundreds of courses now available on computer diskette. Ranging in price from under $50 to hundreds of dollars, they can teach you the basics of telecommunications, how to use a local area network, or how to search databases. Taking a course this way is the next best thing to being in a classroom, and sometimes it's preferable since students can pace themselves.

Software writer Diane Yaeger-McIntosh works from home for a company called STS, developing packages for Addison-Wesley, Random House, and other clients. She talks with her boss on the phone three times a week, "sometimes twenty." Aside from her computers, the only things she needs to develop "courseware" are textbooks and her boss' rough outline of what the final product should look like.

Salary Range: $23,000–$32,000+

Telecommuting Rating: 8.0

ELECTRONIC NEWS EDITOR

News editors for electronic database services such as Dow Jones News/Retrieval sift electronic and published information for article ideas. They then use word processing packages to prepare the short, snappy, *USA Today*-type articles that are easily read from a computer screen. From there, the article often goes to a managing editor for further processing. A computer is mandatory for just about every part of this job.

Already, some electronic news editors telecommute. They work often for computer-related publications such as *Newsbytes,* a newsletter available on several on-line services. Since electronic news editors use telecommuting technology themselves, they write about it with authority.

Opportunities in this field are now scarce, but they'll increase as more people add modems to their computers and use videotex services to stay informed.

Salary Range: $16,000–$38,000+

Representative Companies: Newsbytes; Phillips Publishing Inc.

Telecommuting Rating: 7.75

FREELANCE WRITER

Tom Johnson, a freelance writer for the electronic age, hasn't sent a paper manuscript in at least two years. Former start-up editor at *MacWEEK* (a computer magazine), Tom also spent a year in El Salvador as a reporter for *Time*. He now works as an electronic freelancer for a variety of magazines, including the *Time-Life* publications.

The PC-equipped freelancer who can send his work directly into a company's electronic publishing system has an edge over competitors who use typewriters instead of terminals. Typewritten manuscripts must still be keyed into a computer—a step that's unnecessary when the work arrives electronically.

As a freelance writer, your best prospects for work as a telecommuter are publications already attuned to its wonders, such as computer magazines or other computer-related companies. Any company, however, that uses an electronic publishing system to produce press materials, company reports, specifications, and the like, is a prospect.

Salary Range: $24,000–$48,000

Representative Companies: Phillips Publishing; *MacWEEK*

Telecommuting Rating: 8.75

FUNDRAISER

Fundraisers plan programs to raise money for charities and other causes such as Big Brothers. To make their pitches they write letters and brochures, make phone calls, and visit potential donors. The goal is to persuade people to give money by explaining the virtues of the organization or cause they represent. Fundraisers may also organize volunteers and coordinate special events to raise money.

This is a communications-related job that depends heavily on telephone work and writing skills. Computers come in handy for maintaining donor lists and getting background information that fundraisers may use for their pitches. The hi-tech fundraiser may tap directories (many of which are available electronically) to locate potential contributors. Using tools like computer databases will become more important to fundraisers in the 1990s, as the competition for corporate contributions heats up.

Many fundraisers work for nonprofit organizations. A few work as freelancers.

Salary Range: $51,000 (average salary for hospital-based Director of Development position)

Telecommuting Rating: 8.5

HEART SPECIALIST

Thanks to fax machines, heart specialists can occasionally work from home or even the golf course. Heart specialists spend a lot of time reviewing electrocardiograms and traveling back and forth to hospitals in the process. But with fax machines, the EKGs can now go to the doctor. A nurse or technician can photocopy the EKG, then fax it to the heart specialist, wherever he happens to be. He can then review it, jot down his comments, and fax it back.

Some heart specialists already "operate" this way. Louisville's William Comer is one. Dr. Comer carries his portable fax machine around in a canvas bag so he can review electrocardiagrams from the office, his home, or wherever, according to the Louisville *Courier-Journal*. The newspaper reports that Comer also uses the portable fax to send in patient prescriptions to the nursing staff. By use of the fax instead of the telephone the nurse gets a printed copy of the order, reducing the possibility of mistakes.

Even with fax machines it's hard to imagine heart specialists working away from hospitals more than a couple of days a month, which explains the low Telecommuting Rating.

Salary Range: $187,900 (1987 average)

Telecommuting Rating: 6.75

ILLUSTRATOR

"Telecommuting is an essential part of my business," says freelance illustrator Dan Swan. "I could not be competitive without it."

Here's how illustrators like Dan use telecommuting to get an edge. A typical job might be to prepare a logo or graphic for a brochure or instructional manual. The client sends an idea of what he wants to your fax machine. You then use a scanner to feed the image into your computer so you can call it up on your screen to serve as a template. You prepare the artwork on the computer, then fax the proof to the client. When it's approved, you send the computer file, by modem, to a service bureau for a high-quality printout. Or you can send the file straight to your client.

Admittedly, not many illustrators now work this way. "But they'd be silly not to," says Dan. "I can turn a job around in ten minutes. Others can't compete with that speed." In addition to quick turnaround, as an illustrator telecommuting can increase your reach and potential markets.

Dan Swan is sold on telecommuting, and there's no reason why other illustrators, especially freelancers, can't walk the same path. "Telecommuting allows me to work where I live, forty miles west of Chicago, pay lower rents, and yet provide near-instantaneous service to my clients," says Dan.

Salary Range: $23,570–$50,964

Representative Companies: *MacWEEK;* University Graphics, Inc.

Telecommuting Rating: 8.0

INDEXER
Anyone who's saved time looking for that elusive bit of information ("I know it's in here somewhere!") by turning to an index can appreciate the indexer's work.

Indexers work for publishers, most often book publishers and reference-work publishers. Many work as freelancers and independent contractors. Indexers rarely need to consult with others when they do their jobs. Computers make their painstaking work easier, but mostly they need a quiet environment in which to concentrate.

Indexers who would like to telecommute should have no problems landing work. In addition to the companies listed below, contact book publishers (listed in *Literary Market Place*) or the National Federation of Abstracting and Indexing Services (NFAIS), a trade group based in Philadelphia.

Salary Range: $25,000–$45,000

Representative Companies: The H. W. Wilson Company; Information Access Company; NewsBank, Inc.

Telecommuting Rating: 8.25

INFORMATION BROKER

Information brokers are researchers for hire. Sometimes called freelance librarians, they work on given tasks on a fee-paid basis. Large companies sometimes hire information brokers when the company librarian is on vacation. Small companies that have only occasional research needs also hire information brokers.

Most information brokers use computer databases extensively for research. They also supplement computer research with the old-fashioned manual kind, conducting telephone and personal interviews as necessary.

Surprisingly, while many information brokers use computers, modems, and fax machines, many of their clients do not. John Everett, author of *Information for Sale* and one of the country's best-known information brokers, says he's yet to have a client ask for on-line (either electronic mail or computer-to-computer) delivery of search results. "I could do it, but I haven't had the request, and I don't plan to market it heavily anytime soon," John says.

Salary Range: $30,000–$35,000 (average)

Telecommuting Rating: 8.5

INSURANCE CLAIMS REPRESENTATIVE

Claims representatives investigate claims, determine settlements resulting from these claims, and authorize payments. This is a job that depends heavily on telephones. For example, when investigating claims, claims representatives have to interview witnesses and others involved in the incident.

Working from home can be part of the claims representative's lot from the beginning. Large insurance companies often train their novice adjusters by home study courses and sometimes also use these courses for more advanced training. After the training, claims reps often work from home when work loads are heavy or when preparing their annual reports.

Ninety percent of claims representatives work for insurance companies. As industries go, the insurance industry has been among the most receptive to telecommuting.

Salary Range: $25,012 (median)

Telecommuting Rating: 7.75

JUDGE

Here's an example of an occupation that you wouldn't think would go well with telecommuting. The State of California's telecommuting pilot, however, includes several administrative law judges. While judges still need to be in courtrooms to hear cases, they also have a lot of background reading and report writing to do. They can easily do these kinds of things from home. Judges also advise counsel and examine evidence. Some may also establish rules or procedure for questions the law does not now address.

Salary Range: $78,700–$108,400

Representative Company: California State Department of General Services

Telecommuting Rating: 7.0

LAWYER

Like some other professionals, lawyers have traditionally worked from their homes. With the rise in the number of large law firms and the grouping together of law practices to cut costs, more lawyers have joined the briefcase brigade and become commuters. Now, thanks to telecommuting, lawyers can have the best of both worlds. They can still work for that prestigious firm paying that equally prestigious salary, but they can do it from home.

When lawyer Fred Wilf telecommutes, he uses on-line communications to trade draft documents with clients and other lawyers, to search legal databases, and to market his services informally on electronic information services ("Gee, that's an interesting question of law that you pose!"). Lawyers can also telecommute when working on large projects such as drafting a patent or a pleading.

Few lawyers now telecommute. One reason is that lawyers who work for law firms may need to circulate in order to drum up business. They like to be where the clients are—for example, around courthouses. Also, the technology is fairly new, and "Lawyers don't have much time to focus on new technology," says Paul Bernstein, another lawyer who works from home. Bernstein, who has his own practice, uses MCI mail (an electronic mail service) and fax extensively. Bernstein says that other lawyers may possibly arrange to telecommute, depending on the power structure at their firms. A lawyer for more than twenty-five years, Bernstein says young lawyers should be realistic about their chances of becoming telecommuters. "As a young lawyer, you can't convince anyone of anything. As an older person, it's a question of prenegotiating your deal."

Law firms may be conservative, but lawyers can look forward to good job prospects through the rest of the century. This, along with work that's well suited for telecommuting and a good showing among the company profiles, makes for a high Telecommuting Rating.

Salary Range: $30,000–$122,000

Representative Companies: AT&T; California State Department of General Services; Lipton, Famiglio, and Elman

Telecommuting Rating: 8.75

LEGAL ASSISTANT (PARALEGAL)

Like lawyers, whether legal assistants can telecommute depends on what they happen to be working on and for whom they work. Legal research, for example, certainly lends itself to telecommuting. A legal assistant can gather information (case citations and excerpts) by electronic database and modem the results to lawyers at the main office.

If the job at hand is mundane (such as filling out court forms) the paralegal may need materials from the law office. But even these kinds of tasks may soon be done from home. Thanks to new software now available, forms can be filled out electronically, then transmitted by modem to the office, where they are printed out.

Lawyers are conservative, which may be why few legal assistants now work at home. But, as more lawyers begin telecommuting, perhaps their staffs will follow suit.

Salary Range: $21,892 (median)

Representative Companies: McGuire, Woods, Battle, and Boothe; State of California Franchise Tax Board

Telecommuting Rating: 8.75

MARKET RESEARCH ANALYST

Market researchers gather and analyze information to help businesses make informed decisions before launching new products or repositioning old ones. On-line databases are a great help here. Demographic databases contain the latest census data. Other databases contain information about products and summaries or the full text of journal articles. Electronic databases can also be a help when doing primary research. A market research analyst could post a message about a possible new software product on a CompuServe bulletin board, then wait for feedback to appear in his electronic mailbox. Firms such as New York City's TechProse already operate this way.

Market research analysts also have to perform mathematical and statistical calculations, tasks with which computers help.

Salary Range: $30,900–$61,680

Representative Companies: LINK Resources Corporation; Pacific Bell Telephone; Weyerhauser; TechProse

Telecommuting Rating: 8.25

MEDICAL RECORDS TECHNICIAN

This is an example of a job that's becoming more location-independent thanks to computers. Medical records technicians update patient records. A crucial part of their job is evaluating these records for completeness and accuracy. While most work for hospitals, many now work for health maintenance organizations.

This job requires a good deal of concentration and attention to detail, since these records are used not only for billing purposes but also to decide on a course of treatment. The need for careful attention to detail is becoming only more important as health care providers move toward faster bill turnaround and more detailed analysis of patient records.

The modern home office, with the quiet and access to equipment that now comes with it, fits in well with how this job is evolving.

Salary Range: $18,100 (average)

Representative Company: University of Wisconsin, Center for Health Sciences

Telecommuting Rating: 8.25

NEWS REPORTER

Reporters spend about half their time gathering information. While this often requires face-to-face meetings, a lot of information-gathering is done by telephone. The other half of the job is spent writing up the story. "This is the part of the job that can be done just as easily and efficiently from home," says Paul Andrews, a Seattle *Times* reporter who telecommutes.

In the early 1980s, reporters popularized laptop computers, using them to file stories from the field. Many more reporters work this way today. Now, at conferences, there are always computer rooms set up for the convenience of journalists with laptops. Reporters also carry them aboard planes, trains, buses, and cars. "A plane ride from London to the East Coast (about seven hours) gives you enough time to finish your story," says *Time's* Dick Thompson.

Many reporters already telecommute, although they may not call it that. Reporters have a lot of freedom and are not expected in an office all day anyway. They have clear goals that must be met. Often the attitude is that as long as the story is done by deadline it doesn't matter where it's done. This is among the best jobs for telecommuters.

Salary Range: $11,000–$53,100+

Representative Companies: Baltimore *Evening Sun;* Detroit *Free Press;* Digital News; Gannett; *Orange County* (CA) *Register;* The Seattle *Times*

Telecommuting Rating: 9.25

OPERATIONS RESEARCH ANALYST

Operations analysts help organizations determine the best way of doing things. Their work involves problem solving and applying mathematical principles to organizational problems. They work in areas such as inventory control, personnel, forecasting, resource allocation, product mix, and distribution systems. The exact nature of the problems they ponder varies by industry. An operations research analyst who works for a hospital, for example, might come up with ways of scheduling admissions or managing patient flow.

Like many of the jobs described here, there is an information-gathering part of this job, where operations analysts pick the brains of managers and others with something to say about the problem at hand. This is best done at the work site. Once they collect all the facts, however, analysts sift them to determine the best solution. That's best done in a quiet yet productive environment. The final stage, where the operations analyst presents findings to management, would again require a trip to the office.

Salary Range: $35,100 (median)

Representative Company: Wendy's International, Inc.

Telecommuting Rating: 8.0

PATHOLOGIST

Part of the new branch of telemedicine, which also incorporates teleradiology, "telepathologists" examine specimens long-distance. They provide technical expertise that a smaller facility may lack, but they may do it from far away.

Where the specimen is located there's a remote-controlled light microscope attached to a video camera. At the remote site (where the doctor is) there's a monitor and computer work station. The doctor tunes in the specimen on the remote monitor, then discriminates between malignant and benign tumors.

Science fiction? Hardly. The Mayo Clinic now has a telemedicine-services link between its facility in Rochester, Minnesota, and a clinic in Jacksonville, Florida. It provides high-quality health care to remote areas where such services may not otherwise be available. As with radiologists, pathologists are more likely to work from a health facility than from their homes. But once the equipment is in place, there's no reason why they couldn't work from home.

Salary Range: $124,600 (1987 average for pathologists)

Telecommuting Rating: 6.75

POLLSTER

Pollsters sometimes get to ask people the kinds of question that most people wouldn't have the nerve to ask even their best friends. But it's an interviewer's job to ask questions. Many use telephones and the mails, but a surprising amount of opinion research is done face-to-face. After the interviews are finished, pollsters help tabulate the results. They code and categorize responses to speed tabulation. They may also help prepare statistical summaries. Some survey companies set up their field managers (pollsters who worked their way up the ranks) with complete home offices.

Two of the largest survey research firms, the National Opinion Research Center and Gallup Polls, have telecommuters working for them. (Gallup's telecommuters only work sixteen hours per month, so that company is not included in Chapter 6). With more than 2000 survey research firms in the United States, it's likely others also use telecommuters.

Salary Range: $11,440–$35,000

Representative Company: National Opinion Research Center

Telecommuting Rating: 7.5

PROBATION OFFICER

Probation officers monitor the activities of adult and juvenile offenders. They may also determine who handles a particular case: the court or another agency. Paperwork is a big part of this job. For example, probation officers prepare a social history of the offender for the court. They also write reports on the probationers for whom they are responsible. In the County of Los Angeles, probation officers used to dictate their reports into tape recorders. The tapes were later sent to a transcription service. As part of its telecommuting pilot, the county set up probation officers at home with a software package that lets them prepare their reports remotely and modem them in. With city, state, and federal governments heavily into telecommuting, probation officer may become a better-than-average job for telecommuting.

Salary Range: $20,440–$43,600

Representative Companies: City of Los Angeles; County of Los
    Angeles

Telecommuting Rating: 8.25

PROFESSOR

Through Connect Ed, a program run by the New School for Social Research in New York City, you can earn a graduate degree without setting foot in a classroom. Instead, you fire up your computer and "attend" class whenever you have time. So, instead of putting in a long day and then heading across town to the college campus, you learn at your leisure. The professor uploads the lesson on the school's bulletin board. Similarly, students upload their assignments to the teacher. Interaction isn't as spontaneous as in a classroom, but it still takes place. Professors and students can enjoy a dialogue on-line.

A new breed of electronic professors who work from home run these electronic classrooms. These jobs are rare, but telelearning is growing steadily.

Aside from these programs, traditional professors such as Alberto

Galofre, an associate dean at St. Louis University School of Medicine, telecommute part time. Dr. Galofre communicates every evening from home using a software package that lets him send and retrieve information from his PC at work. He also works entirely from home an average of one day a week. Those days he'll access his office computer, chat with his staff at their own work stations, and download letters, memos, or other information. He also accesses his calendar to see what appointments he has for a given day.

Dr. Galofre thinks that in the future he'll telecommute even more. "I see a day when I may need to come to the office only one or two days a week since I could handle most of the work, including talking to students, staff, and faculty from my home. This of course depends on meetings and other events that need my body!"

For now, Dr. Galofre says that few other professors work this way, due largely to the same mindset that keeps many corporate employees in office buildings. "I believe the mental framework is still there that you *must* come to work, to work! This is perhaps the most important barrier because technically I have shown it is possible for professors to telecommute."

Professors face very poor job prospects through the year 2000, according to the Bureau of Labor Statistics, due to sharply declining college enrollments.

Salary Range: $35,152 (median)

Telecommuting Rating: 7.0

PROGRAMMER

When a programmer works alone on a project, says telecommuter Jesse Levine, "programming by modem is a snap." Once the programmer knows what his boss or client has in mind and settles on what the program should do, the programmer then goes off and programs it. "The company does not care at all where I do the actual work," says Levine.

Because of the inherent solidarity of the job, many programmers now telecommute at least part time. Aside from the usual advantages, for programmers telecommuting has special benefits. For example, programmers must often tap into company computer resources (which they can do remotely). Telecommuters can set their own hours, which means that programmers can work when there's less demand on company resources. Less demand translates into quicker response time when running software programs.

Of course, there will be some projects that require interaction with other programmers. Then telecommuting gets trickier. But it can still be done if the part the programmer is working on is sufficiently independent.

The only thing standing in the way of widespread telecommuting among programmers is the fact that some companies now contract out programming work to offshore programmers. For rudimentary programming jobs, using foreign programmers saves a company a lot of money. As long as this trend continues, there will be less demand for U.S. programmers, meaning that cutting telecommuting deals may get difficult.

Of the 100 companies profiled in Chapter 6, twenty-three have working for them programmers who telecommute. These are not all computer companies either, as the list of representative companies shows. High demand for programmers, the best showing among the company profiles, and the job's suitability for telecommuting earn it the highest possible Telecommuting Rating.

> Salary Range: $23,000–$48,000

> Representative Companies: Allstate Insurance Company; California State Department of General Services; City of Fort Collins (CO); Control Data Corporation; Data General Corporation; General Telephone of California; Lift, Inc.; Travelers Corporation; Worldwide Church of God

> Telecommuting Rating: 10.0

PSYCHOLOGIST

Many traditional "patient-on-the-couch" psychologists work from their homes. But now, even psychologists who work for companies (industrial and organizational psychologists) sometimes work from home.

Organizational psychologist Cheryl Mahaffey of Psychological Services, Inc. finds telecommuting makes a lot of sense. She not only saves three hours of commuting each day, she also gets to spend more time with her children and at her house, which rests on a cliff overlooking the Pacific.

Cheryl's company is a consulting firm that specializes in testing and evaluation services, mostly for the human resources departments of large companies. It only matters that her clients can reach her—whether or not she's in an "office" isn't important. And, when meetings are scheduled, she always travels to the client's office. Some clients don't expect physical availability at all.

Salary Range: $26,936 (median)

Representative Companies: Digital Equipment Corporation (DEC); Psychological Services, Inc.

Telecommuting Rating: 8.0

PUBLIC RELATIONS PROFESSIONAL

A PR professional's business is "linking up with resources," says Ron Solberg, a PR pro who regularly uses on-line services for research and communications. "We either send information or receive it." PR professionals formerly relied on telephones for this; many now use computers. In fact, telecommuting "fits right in with the way most of us do business," Ron says.

Telecommuting among PR professionals is not pervasive, but it is growing. To maximize your chances for work as a telecommuter in this field, contact PR firms that specialize in computer or other hi-tech accounts (such as Hi-Tech Public Relations, listed in Chapter 6). Check *O'Dwyer's Directory* for listings of PR firms and their clients. Also, contact the Public Relations Society of America's Communications Technology Committee and the PRSIG, an active electronic meeting place for PR professionals, available through CompuServe.

Salary Range: $39,413 (median)

Representative Companies: AT&T; EasyCom, Inc.; Hi-Tech Public Relations, Inc.; NCNB Corporation; MultiLink Incorporated; South Coast Air Quality Management District

Telecommuting Rating: 9.25

PURCHASING AGENT

Purchasing agents buy goods, services, and materials for organizations. Like any careful shopper, a purchasing agent shops around to get the best deal. They use computers to keep track of inventories, so they know when it's time to place an order. They may also use computers to keep information about various suppliers such as bidders' lists and records of past performance. Occasionally, purchasing agents leave the office to meet with suppliers. Other times they must be on-site to discuss custom-made products with other employees.

Purchasing agents often work for small companies with fewer than five employees. Some, however, work for large businesses and agencies, which can have more than 100 agents. This profile of who purchasing agents work for matches the profile of the types of employers (small and large, but not often medium-sized) most likely to use telecommuters.

Salary Range: $25,896 (median)

Telecommuting Rating: 6.75

RADIO ANNOUNCER

When one of United Press International's key news anchors was laid up after a hip replacement, UPI set him up with an office at home rather than lose his valuable services. UPI rented a leased telephone line of broadcast quality from AT&T. UPI also gave him a computer so the main office could feed his copy to him. As he spoke into the phone, his broadcasts traveled from his home in Alexandria, Virginia, to UPI's radio station at its headquarters in Washington, D.C. From there it was broadcast to his nationwide audience. His listeners never knew the difference.

Actually, according to UPI's David O'Ziel, it's not that unusual for radio announcers to broadcast from their homes. Howard Cosell, says O'Ziel, as an anchor for ABC Sports, broadcast from his home.

Whether or not radio anchors can arrange to work from home has much to do with their pull and reputation. Working at home would work out best for news anchors or other radio announcers who can gather news by computer. Other announcers—disc jockeys, for example—require the kind of equipment ordinarily found only in radio stations.

Salary Range: $8,400–$60,000

Representative Company: United Press International

Telecommuting Rating: 6.75

RADIOLOGIST

A friend studying to be a radiologist first told me about a new breed of radiologist who works remotely—the teleradiologist. Computer technology allows technicians to send CT scans or MRIs (Magnetic Resonance Images) across phone lines to radiologists at remote locations. Because these images are already digitized, transporting them this way is a snap.

The image the remote doctor receives, however, is not quite as sharp as what he'd see if viewing the image in person. Studies are under way to look at whether discrepancies between what the remote doctors and local doctors see are serious. One such study found "clinically significant discrepancies" in 14 of 897 cases (1.6 percent). But even those can remedied by retransmitting enlarged shots of areas of special concern.

Sending images remotely is also done fairly routinely from hospital to hospital. Sometimes teleradiology is used to send images from a medical center that does not have a full-time radiologist to another facility that does have one. The radiologist there reviews the images on a TV screen.

Few radiologists work this way and only a subset of those do it from home, but technology makes it an option for the future.

Salary Range: $180,700 (1987 average)

Telecommuting Rating: 7.0

REAL ESTATE AGENT

Real estate agents give advice on buying and selling homes. Many agents have offices both at home and at their employer's headquarters. Real estate agents often work from home because they work odd hours. Much of what they do—show houses, close deals—occurs outside regular business hours, since that's when the clients are available.

Real estate agents deal with an amazing amount of data. To stay abreast of the housing market in their areas they tap multiple listing services, which describe properties for sale. In many cases these services are now available on-line. An agent accesses the data with a computer and modem like any other database. Other on-line services give details from property sales.

Agents also keep careful records of past sales, mortgage rate information, and listings. The savvy agent may also have his own database of information regarding past, present, and prospective clients.

Salary Range: $26,780 (median)

Representative Company: Thyng Associates

Telecommuting Rating: 8.25

RECORDS MANAGER

Records managers design systems for storing, accessing, and otherwise handling company records. These records range from engineering drawings and specifications to employee records. A records manager begins his job by visiting the site to interview records users to learn about the ways in which they use records and what their record handling needs are. He takes measurements of the site and gets a feel for the physical requirements of the records.

From that point records managers need the quiet of an office to design the system. They may use a computer to lay out any forms they design for records handlers to use. A computer also comes in handy for writing the finished proposal. When this is done, records managers return to the site to discuss their system with management and get it up and running.

Salary Range: $20,000–$40,000

Telecommuting Rating: 7.75

REGISTERED NURSE

Registered nurses as telecommuters? Yes, and it's becoming more common. Many nurses, dissatisfied with the shift work and long hours associated with hospital work, want to use their training in other ways. Some have managed to do this. They work for insurance companies as medical reviewers, verifying that operations and other medical procedures were justified. Some work from home. While medical reviewers do nothing to alleviate the current shortage of nurses, they find the pace much more to their liking.

Expect to see more opportunities for nurses to leave hospitals for jobs as medical reviewers as pressures on employers to keep spiraling health costs down continue.

Salary Range: $21,000–$38,500

Representative Companies: Blue Cross/Blue Shield of South Carolina; Companion HealthCare

Telecommuting Rating: 7.75

RESEARCHER

The image of the relentless researcher hunched down over dusty tomes in some wood-and-leather campus library may be appealing, but that's no longer the way to do business. Today researchers often gather information with computers, dipping into one of the more than 4500 computer databases now available. Researchers also gather information by telephone, something else just as easily done from a home office. Face-to-face interaction is sometimes needed, but only rarely.

Picture this scenario: A researcher for a furniture manufacturer must write a report on the market for home office furniture. One of the first things our hypothetical computer-savvy researcher does is solicit information and interviews through a message on CompuServe's Working From Home Forum message board, an electronic gathering place for people who work from home. While waiting for responses, he searches databases to find articles, forecasts, and statistics on market size. He downloads these to a floppy disk to be read at his leisure (remember our 1990s researcher has never left his home).

Later, he checks CompuServe and finds several people have responded to his message. He drops them electronic notes to arrange for in-depth telephone interviews. Still later, he'll combine this information with findings from the articles he's read, word-process the results, and send the finished report to his employer.

This scenario is not fiction. Many researchers already work this way.

Salary Range: $18,000–$30,000

Representative Companies: EasyCom, Inc; DuPont; The RAND Corporation

Telecommuting Rating: 8.5

RESERVATIONS AGENT

Reservations agents and clerks help people plan trips by furnishing information on destinations, accommodations, and rates. They also make and confirm reservations.

Almost all reservations agents use computers to retrieve information quickly and easily. Reservations agents also spend a lot of time on the phone. Unfortunately, about 75 percent work for airlines, which are not big boosters of telecommuting. Part of the problem may be that agents and clerks often belong to unions, many of which are against their members working from home. Reservations agents who work for smaller travel agencies have the best chances of telecommuting. But even large travel agencies are coming around. Philadelphia's Rosenbluth Travel shifted some of its clerical positions to the Farm Belt to save on office rentals and labor charges and reduce turnover. These workers, then, are off-siters. The next step would be for Rosenbluth to set up home offices for its clerks.

Salary Range: $21,996 (median)

Representative Company: Best Western International, Inc.

Telecommuting Rating: 7.5

SALES REPRESENTATIVE

This is one of the best jobs for telecommuting. Sales representatives already have a history of working from home. Because they travel a lot and their territories may be far from their employer's office, home offices make sense. Also, their work is easily measured. When a sales representative does not perform well the company's revenues reflect it.

Several parts of the sales representative's job can be done from a home office. Pinpointing sales leads, for example, requires little more than a telephone and prospect list. A computer would also come in handy here. Many directories, for example, are available electronically. So are the Yellow Pages for every town and city in the United States. Sifting these sources electronically takes a fraction of the time it takes to do so manually. Sales representatives also use their home offices for setting up appointments, taking orders, answering customers' questions, and handling the paperwork that comes with the job.

While the Bureau of Labor Statistics predicts the demand for all sales-rep jobs will be high into the next century, the prospects for sales jobs in the computer industry are the best. This is good news for people who want to telecommute, because these companies are among the most likely to use telecommuters.

Considering the number of sales reps who work from home already, the bright outlook for this job, and the number of times it came up during the company survey, sales rep ranks among the best jobs for telecommuting.

Salary Range: $25,636 (median)

Representative Companies: AT&T; Digital Equipment Corporation; Farallon Computing, Inc.; GE Plastics; United Press International (UPI); W. W. Norton & Co.

Telecommuting Rating: 9.75

SECRETARY

Whether or not a secretary's job is suitable for telecommuting depends heavily on the employer. No two secretaries' jobs are alike. For example, some secretaries also act as receptionists and therefore could not telecommute. But most secretaries do a lot of typing, scheduling, phone answering, and handling correspondence, which they could just as easily do from home.

Secretaries' jobs are also fairly stressful; they sometimes face demands from all directions (ringing phones, boss' and other workers' requests, guests). The privacy and quiet of a home office might be especially welcome here.

The best companies for a secretary to approach about telecommuting are those that already have a lot of people working from home. Small businesses and even entrepreneurs are also good prospects.

Salary Range: $16,224 (median)

Representative Company: California State Department of General Services

Telecommuting Rating: 6.75

SOCIAL WORKER

Social workers help families deal with overwhelming problems. Many work for the government, in social agencies. Others work in the private sector for community and religious organizations, hospitals, nursing homes, and home health agencies. Specialists abound in this profession. Some social workers specialize in child welfare, others the aged, and still others in assisting hospital patients. A few social workers now even specialize in organ transplant procurements.

Much of a social worker's job requires face-to-face talks with clients. But there is also a lot of behind-the-scenes work that can be done from a home office. Case management, where a social worker assembles a package of services to aid a client, requires a lot of telephone calling and paperwork. Computers would aid in data management—maintaining records on clients and information about agencies and other useful resources.

Salary Range: $21,996 (median)

Telecommuting Rating: 7.5

SOFTWARE ENGINEER

"Telecommuting is ideal for a software engineer," says telecommuter Michael Trigoboff. "You're away from interruptions and you can structure your environment just the way you want it (lighting, music, temperature) without bothering anyone else." Software engineers, like programmers, usually work alone anyway and don't really need other people around "except when they want to take a break and hang out for a while." Michael, who now works for himself, also worked at home for a company. "I used to go in twice a week for meetings, and that was enough to coordinate my work with the rest of the team," he says. "I was on the phone a lot, but my physical presence wasn't really needed most of the time."

Engineers of all types are excellent candidates for telecommuting. The companies listed below employ engineers of one type or another who telecommute. See Chapter 6 for the details.

Salary Range: $37,596 (median salary for all engineers)

Representative Companies: California State Department of General Services; Data General Corporation; Digital Equipment Corporation; Farallon Computing, Inc.; Hewlett-Packard; Hughes Aircraft; Personal Computer Support Group (PCSG), Inc.; Washington State Energy Office

Telecommuting Rating: 9.75

SPEECHWRITER

Few politicians and corporate executives are as good at managing words as they are at managing people. Enter the speechwriter. While this job can be a thankless one (few people publicly acknowledge the efforts of their speechwriters), it generally pays well.

It's also well suited to telecommuting. Writing a speech takes a lot of research. Fortunately, computers take a great deal of drudgery out of that research. Many computer databases, for example, focus on news. Just about every major newspaper is available electronically, as are all major magazines and trade journals. Speechwriters can sift many thousands of articles for the information they need in mere seconds.

Computers help with the writing part too. Word processing packages and outlining programs don't make writing fun, but they do take a lot of the drudgery out of it.

Speechwriting is often part of another professional's job, typically the public relations director. But large companies may have people on staff who do nothing but write speeches. Once they prove their value, they should be able to work from home. Since speechwriters are likely to work for top managers, who are often out of the office anyway, they wouldn't miss much if they worked from home.

Salary Range: $30,000–$90,000

Representative Company: Equitable Life Assurance

Telecommuting Rating: 8.25

SPORTSWRITER
As with other reporters, there are two parts to a sportswriter's job: gathering the news (researching) and reporting (writing it for publication). Like other writers on a newspaper, sportswriters have a lot of latitude.

Many sportswriters now use laptop computers to write their stories from stadiums. And with cellular modems entering the market, they don't even have to work from the press box anymore. They can type away right from the sidelines.

Salary Range: $11,000–$53,100+

Representative Companies: Baltimore *Evening Sun;* Detroit *Free Press*

Telecommuting Rating: 9.25

STOCKBROKER
Computers have decentralized the business of monitoring stocks, bonds, and securities. Thanks to the many on-line services available from respected names such as Telerate, Quotron, and Dow Jones, anyone with a personal computer and modem can get the same stock information from the exchanges that office-based brokers get.

Many stockbrokers work in New York City and other large cities—places where commuting gets more difficult all the time. Their offices are frenetic, their pulses run high (remember the movie *Wall Street?*).

Contrast this with the image of the casually attired stockbroker chatting on a cellular phone from his greenhouse while his laptop (located on his patio table) pulses with the latest stock prices.

Salary Range: $13,734–$170,040

Telecommuting Rating: 9.0

TECHNICAL WRITER

Technical writers transform technical information, such as documentation, into brochures, user manuals, or other publications for general audiences. It's one of the higher-paying of the writing professions. It's also one of the areas most likely to grow.

Many technical writers use computers not only to create publications but also to review in-house documentation and research external databases. They already work for the types of companies most likely to hire telecommuters: hi-tech firms. They frequently work independently. They sometimes confer with specialists (such as engineers) on technical points or with graphic artists when their publications are in the layout stage. Often this is done with just a phone call.

Technical writers often have defined tasks and deadlines that have to be met. These are two characteristics of a job that make it suitable for telecommuting.

A good way for technical writers not currently employed to break into part-time telecommuting is to work through "body shops." These special employment agencies keep a flock of writers on their rolls to handle temporary assignments. (Check your Yellow Pages under Employment Contractors.) If you work from home for a company that develops a full-time opening, perhaps you can change your part-time telecommuting assignment into one that's more permanent.

Salary Range: $27,196 (median)

Representative Companies: *Digital News; MacWEEK;* Meckler; Phillips Publishing, Inc.

Telecommuting Rating: 9.0

TELEMARKETER

Selling by the telephone has become a big business, one that's suitable for telecommuting. Because they spend almost all of their time on the telephone, telemarketers can work from anywhere.

Software programs such as TeleMagic, which are designed expressly for telemarketers, make their jobs easier. TeleMagic includes an automatic telephone dialer, a database function for fast information retrieval; a calendar, a notepad, and a basic word processor.

A consideration: Sales people, often gregarious types, may find they miss office camaraderie. In other words, the fact that telecommuters work alone may not appeal to telemarketers, who might actually welcome interruptions.

Companies such as Sitel, Inc., are moving telemarketing jobs out of large cities to the Midwest, where workers are plentiful. The Midwest's central location also means that phone charges will be low. Sitel has already moved 500 jobs into small communities such as Breda, Iowa, a farming community hit hard by the agricultural slump of recent years. Other companies have moved telemarketing jobs to Nebraska and North Dakota. The next step is to move these jobs into people's homes, which some companies are now doing.

Salary Range: $8,320–$50,000

Representative Companies: JCPenney; Remote Control

Telecommuting Rating: 8.5

TRANSCRIBER

If you've watched *60 Minutes, 20/20,* or *NOVA* you've probably noticed that the show's credits include a message inviting you to send for transcripts of the show (For transcripts of tonight's *Nova,* send $3 to Erudition, Box 1213, Pedant, PA). It's likely that telecommuters prepared those transcripts.

A company called Journal Graphics in New York City has transcribers spread across the country. They videotape selected television shows, make an audiotape from the videotape, then transcribe from that. The final product is sent over the telephone lines to Journal Graphics' offices in New York, which fills requests.

Of course, there are other things that must be transcribed besides television shows. But to work full time as a telecommuting transcriber you'd have to work for several companies. It might be best to combine this work with other jobs that can be done parttime from home such as abstracting or technical writing.

Salary Range: $16,000–$25,000 (medical transcribers)

Representative Companies: Journal Graphics; University of Wisconsin, Center for Health Sciences

Telecommuting Rating: 8.25

TRANSLATOR

Want to become a telecommuter? Then read no more. All you have to do is become a translator. Unfortunately, that's no easy task. Mastering another language takes a long time. Still, translator ranks among the top jobs for telecommuters, given the opportunities and how suitable it is for doing from home.

Translators these days have hi-tech setups equal to those of many computer professionals. Thanks to computers, "Gone are the days when translators worked by hand or spent long hours typing out a translation only to find that a better word could have been chosen back on page three of a two-hundred-page translation," says Julia Adams of Globalink Language Services. Globalink works almost exclusively with telecommuters, and now has a force of 850 remote translators. Like many translation companies, Globalink has a short turnaround time on most of its translations, so it can't afford to use the mails.

Most translators work as independent contractors for companies such as Globalink or Berlitz (both profiled in Chapter 6). Paul Danaher, a telecommuting translator based in West Germany, says that many of his customers send him documents stored on diskettes. He translates right over the original and returns a diskette that they can use in their own publishing systems. Like many translators, particularly those in the United States, he also uses a modem to receive and send assignments over the phone lines. "The fact that clients can dump the original into my electronic mailbox and collect the translations the next day *wherever* I am is very important to keeping the client," says Paul.

The lot of the freelance translator is an unusual one; the work is always changing. Danaher one day may translate market letters from West German banks that have to be sent out immediately to English-speaking investors. Another day he may translate opinions on tax law by West German CPA firms for American companies.

"I think most translators will telecommute in the future," Paul says. "More and more customers have their original texts in machine-readable form and welcome the ability to send and receive formatted files." Globalink's Julia Adams thinks the future that Danaher speaks of is here now. "I think it's time we as a society realized that the world has grown much smaller in only a few short years, and that we must begin thinking in more global terms," she says.

Government information about this job's growth prospects is not available. Its top rating reflects the fact that some employers of translators actually insist that their translators telecommute.

Salary Range: $30,000+

Representative Companies: Berlitz Translation Services; Continental Communications Agency; Globalink Language Services

Telecommuting Rating: 10.0

TRAVEL AGENT

Travel agents help people plan trips—offering suggestions on destinations and help arranging transportation, hotel accommodations, and car rentals—an information-intensive profession.

To find the best fares as well as transportation that meets the client's scheduling requirements, travel agents must sift through flight schedules from hundreds of airlines. Helping them do this are computerized reservations systems such as the *Official Airline Guide* and others from American Airlines and Delta. Computer skills figure so prominently into what travel agents do that training in microcomputers is frequently part of their job.

Travel agents have a lot of paperwork. (Don't pity them, though. Visiting hotels and resorts in order to rate them is also part of the job.)

Travel agents can also learn the ins and outs of doing their jobs at home. There are home study courses that cover the basics of the travel industry.

Salary Range: $14,400–$25,200

Telecommuting Rating: 7.75

TYPESETTER

Typesetters prepare text for the printing process. Before computers, the hot type process was common. Individual letters were formed with molten lead; these were arranged into lines of type, then sentences, and finally paragraphs. The equipment associated with this process isn't even manufactured any more. Typesetters are now more likely to use "cold type." Text is entered into a computer, where it is checked for spelling accuracy and aligned (hyphenated and justified). The text is then sent to a typesetter that uses either a cathode ray tube, laser, or photography to create an image on typesetting paper or film.

Forty percent of all typesetters work for newspapers, which are among the heaviest users of telecommuters. Another 27 percent work for commercial printing plants, with the rest working for other printing and publishing operations. Those who work for small printers have the best chance of telecommuting.

Salary Range: $17,056 (median)

Telecommuting Rating: 7.25

URBAN PLANNER

Like economists, urban planners deal with resource allocation: the difference is that urban planners are more future-oriented. They help cities and regions accommodate growth by studying and preparing reports on land use and the types of industries and businesses moving into a community. Most of this is office work, although it may also require periodic visits to examine facilities.

Once this is ironed out, planners estimate the need for housing, transportation, and business and industrial sites. To gather this information, planners may consult other planners, developers, and civic leaders. Aside from this, they frequently use computers to record and analyze information. Most planners work for local governments, which are great supporters of telecommuting. In addition, this profession is booming in California, which is also the hottest area for telecommuting. And many urban planners do consulting on the side, yet another reason to set up a home office.

Salary Range: $17,800–$55,039

Representative Companies: Southern California Association of Governments; South Coast Air Quality Management District

Telecommuting Rating: 8.0

WORD PROCESSOR

Formerly called typists, word processors seem to take on the name of the machine they use to do their jobs—a curious practice (imagine calling carpenters hammers or doctors stethoscopes).

Word processing is well suited to telecommuting. Word processors will likely have to come into the office once or twice a week to pick up work, but completed assignments can be returned on-line. Word processors can produce more at home, where they don't face the constant hammering of office machines. Working in a home office also means that other important factors, such as lighting and how comfortable the chair is, are controllable. Eyestrain and backaches are common problems for office-bound word processors, who may not take the breaks they need.

This is the Information Age, true; nevertheless, job prospects for typists in general are not good. Technology advances have meant that a lot of people who used to turn their typing over to others are now doing it themselves. This will only get worse (from the typist's viewpoint) as optical character recognition technology spreads. The picture is a lot brighter, however, for those typists and word processors who have command of several word processing programs or desktop publishing knowledge.

Salary Range: $13,500–$29,000

Representative Companies: Direct Data; GlobaLink Language Services; Letter Perfect; Washington State Energy Office

Telecommuting Rating: 8.0

While telecommuting has come far, and it represents the best option for many people, it's not right for everyone. Ten jobs that are not yet suitable for telecommuting are:

Pizza deliveryperson	Door-to-door salesperson
Brain surgeon	Firefighter
Airline pilot	Auto worker
Ballet dancer	Mail carrier
Member of Congress	Coalminer

6
100 Companies with Telecommuters

This chapter profiles 100 companies that employ telecommuters. Two types of companies are stressed: the high-profile, *Fortune* 500-type company and companies that employ large numbers of telecommuters. The listings are otherwise eclectic, demonstrating the wide variety of companies that have telecommuters working for them.

How the Companies Were Located

Computer searches were used to locate articles about telecommuting from newspapers, magazines, trade journals, and wire services. Hundreds of sources were scoured, from *The New York Times* to the San Jose (Calif.) *Mercury News*. Other leads came from word of mouth. I followed up on these leads with telephone calls and mail surveys.

Two Types of Companies

Companies that use telecommuters tend to fall in one of two categories: They are either large companies, such as Digital Equipment Corporation and AT&T, or they are small, like MultiLink and Farallon Computing. Few midsize companies appear among the profiles.

Large Companies

Telecommuting comes about with large companies, because of factors relating to their size. First, regardless of the business it's in, a big company has people in many different jobs, including at least some that can be done from home. Almost every large company, for example, has a computer center of some sort. Therefore it probably has programmers or systems analysts—both rated highly in Chapter 5. Also, among large companies, you'll find another important ingredient for telecommuting: the champion. A champion is someone who reads or hears about telecommuting, thinks it's a good idea, and becomes the company's telecommuting advocate. The champion then keeps the idea before management, taking responsibility to see it through. The more employees a company has the more likely it is that a champion will emerge. Champions are needed for formal, structured telecommuting to get under way.

Finally, large companies have large human resources departments. One of their jobs is to see that the company recruits the best people possible. Recruiters and personnel managers are starting to read about telecommuting. Often they learn that telecommuting is a way to attract and keep top employees.

Small Companies

Small companies, with their flexible, freer environments, can implement new ideas quickly. They are fast on their feet. If an idea makes sense, a manager can often move on it without facing loads of red tape. Smaller companies are also likely to see telecommuting as a quick fix to a resources problem. Entrepreneurs, for example, save the cost of renting office space by setting up people in home offices. Finally, individual workers are more accountable for their own work. When there are only fifty or so employees in a company, it's more difficult to coast. People soon find out if you are not doing your share. Each employee is important. Managers who let employees work from home can rest assured that they'll soon know if it is not working out.

How to Use the Profiles

There are three ways to use the company profiles that follow:

As a Source of Job Leads

Few companies allow new hires to telecommute. Companies want to get to know you before they will trust you to work from home for them. A few companies, however, do hire outsiders for telecommuting positions. (In the listings, their names are noted with an asterisk.) In all other cases, assume that the company only allows its existing employees to work from home. You may still want to contact these companies about job opportunities. But you'll have to work there for six months to two years, and prove yourself in the process, before you can hope to take your job home.

Ammunition

If you'd like to telecommute for your current employer, these listings can help you make your case. Many prestigious companies are listed here, companies that don't make a move unless they are sure there's a payoff. List for your manager those companies that are in the same business as your own. That list helps pave your way. For one thing, no company likes to think that others are passing it by. It also gives your boss contacts for further information.

Make up another list of the large, recognizable companies with telecommuting programs. Seeing that IBM, JCPenney, or AT&T has telecommuters goes a long way toward legitimizing the idea.

A Thought Starter

Suppose you are in the market for a new job. In that case, use the listings to get a feel for the kinds of employers who use telecommuters. There are some definite trends among the companies listed. By noting these trends and approaching local companies or others that are similar, you widen your scope. You are no longer limited just to the companies listed here.

Here are some trends to get you started.

Hi-tech companies. There are many computer manufacturers and other computer-related companies listed. IBM, Apple, DEC, Prime, many of the biggest names in computers appear. Telecommunications companies (such as AT&T and Pacific Bell) are also prominent.

These companies employ a lot of engineers, programmers, editors, and others who are in jobs suitable for telecommuting. It's also part of their charter to keep up with emerging technologies, especially computer-related ones. They may even have a vested interest in promoting telecommuting, since telecommuters often use computers. That alone is a good reason for Apple, for instance, to back the concept. Likewise, one reason telephone companies such as US West or AT&T back it is that telecommuters often need extra phone services.

Publishers. You'll find a lot of newspapers and magazines listed here. That's because reporting, editing, writing, and many other publishing jobs are suitable for telecommuting.

Other information-intensive companies. Companies that process a lot of information such as insurance companies (for example Blue Cross/Blue Shield of South Carolina) are prominent.

What the Profiles Show

Each company listing includes complete contact information, including the mailing address and phone number. Also included are:

The Number of Telecommuters

How many people work from home is a measure of the company's commitment to telecommuting. A small number of telecommuters by itself, however, does not mean a small commitment to telecommuting. MultiLink, for example, only has nine telecommuters—but it has fewer than 100 employees, total. It's therefore a much better prospect for would-be telecommuters than The Travelers Insurance Company, which has fifty telecommuters but many thousands of employees.

Positions

The job titles that telecommuters hold are listed.

Telecommuter Status

Some companies pay their telecommuters as independent contractors; others treat telecommuters as salaried employees. That information is included.

Comments

This section includes details on the company's use of telecommuters. For example:

- Why it started using telecommuters
- How telecommuting is working out for the company
- Whether or not it supplies telecommuters with computer equipment
- Propects for telecommuting in the future

Alphabetical Listing of the 100 Profiled Companies

1. Allergan, Inc.
2. Allstate Insurance Company

3. American Express Company
4. Appalachian Computer Services
5. Apple Computer, Inc.
6. AT&T
7. Baltimore *Evening Sun*
8. Beneficial Corporation
9. Berlitz Translation Services
10. Best Western International, Inc.
11. Blue Cross/Blue Shield of Maryland (Medicare Division)
12. Blue Cross/Blue Shield of South Carolina
13. California State Department of General Services
14. Citibank
15. City of Fort Collins
16. City of Los Angeles
17. Companion HealthCare
18. The Compucare Company
19. Continental Communications Agency, Inc. (CCA)
20. Control Data Corporation
21. County of Los Angeles
22. Data General Corporation
23. The Detroit *Free Press*
24. Digital Equipment Corporation
25. *Digital News*
26. Direct Data
27. EasyCom, Inc.
28. E. I. du Pont de Nemours & Co.
29. Equitable Life Assurance
30. Farallon Computing, Inc.
31. The Federal Government
32. First Chicago Corporation
33. Gannett
34. General Telephone of California
35. GE Plastics
36. Globalink Language Services
37. Hewlett-Packard Company
38. Hi-Tech Public Relations
39. *Home Office Computing*
40. Honeywell, Inc.
41. Hughes Aircraft
42. The H. W. Wilson Company

43. Information Access Company (IAC)
44. Interactive Systems Corporation
45. International Business Machines Corporation (IBM)
46. Janal Communications
47. JCPenney
48. Jet Propulsion Laboratory
49. John Hancock Mutual Life Insurance Company
50. Journal Graphics
51. Lanier Business Products
52. Letter Perfect
53. Lift, Inc.
54. LINK Resources Corporation
55. Lipton, Famiglio & Elman
56. *MacWEEK*
57. McGuire, Woods, Battle & Boothe
58. Meckler Publishing Corporation
59. Merrill Corporation
60. MultiLink Corporation
61. National Opinion Research Center (NORC)
62. NCNB Corporation
63. New England Telephone and Telegraph Company
64. NewsBank, Inc.
65. Newsbytes News Service
66. New York Life
67. The Olsten Corporation
68. Orange County *Register*
69. Ortho Pharmaceutical Corporation
70. Pacific Bell Telephone Company
71. *PC Week*
72. PDN Software Newsletter
73. Personal Computer Support Group (PCSG), Inc.
74. PHH Homequity
75. Phillips Publishing, Inc.
76. Prime Computer, Inc.
77. Psychological Services, Inc.
78. The RAND Corporation
79. Remote Control
80. Rockwell International
81. Sears, Roebuck & Co.
82. The Seattle *Times*

83. South Coast Air Quality Management District (SCAQMD)
84. Southern California Association of Governments
85. State of California Franchise Tax Board
86. TechProse
87. Thyng Associates, Inc.
88. Time Inc.
89. Travelers Corporation
90. UMI/Data Courier
91. United Press International (UPI)
92. University Graphics, Inc.
93. University of Wisconsin, Center for Health Sciences
94. US West
95. Washington State Energy Office
96. Wendy's International, Inc.
97. Weyerhaeuser
98. Workstation Laboratories, Inc.
99. Worldwide Church of God
100. W. W. Norton & Company

Allergan, Inc.
Address: 2525 Dupont Drive
        Irvine, CA 92715
Telephone: (714) 752-4500
Number of Telecommuters: 7
Positions: Programmer
Telecommuter Status: Salaried employee
Comments: Allergen, a *Fortune* 500 pharmaceutical company, is a top manufacturer of eye- and skin-care products. A shortage of office space prompted the company to offer telecommuting to some employees more than seven years ago. Telecommuters now work at home several days a week. The "out of site, out of mind" fears that some telecommuters have don't apply here. At least one Allergan telecommuter was promoted.

Allstate Insurance Company
Address: Allstate Plaza South
        Northbrook, IL 60062
Telephone: (312) 402-7141
Number of Telecommuters: See comments

Telecommuter Status: Salaried employee
Positions: Programmer
Comments: One of Allstate's first telecommuters was a systems programmer who, after only eleven weeks with the company, was severely injured in a car accident en route to her new job. To help speed her recovery, her managers arranged for her to work from home three days a week using a "take-home" terminal.

This programmer joined two other Allstate telecommuters. Also programmers, they are both confined to wheelchairs and came to Allstate by Lift Inc. (see entry), a nonprofit organization that finds, trains, and places handicapped individuals with an aptitude for programming. Allstate supplies the needed equipment.

Now other Allstate employees also telecommute as part of the company's research in developing an overall policy toward telecommuting. Some of the things Allstate is exploring are the types of jobs it has that are appropriate for telecommuting, and which home/office schedules are best (for example, three days a week in the office/two days a week at home).

American Express Company
Address: American Express Tower
                World Financial Center
                New York, NY 10285
Telephone: (212) 640-2000
Number of Telecommuters: See comments
Positions: See comments
Telecommuter Status: Not available
Comments: A few American Express employees now telecommute informally. American Express is putting together a more formal program, and it looks as if there will soon be many opportunities for telecommuters at this company. American Express' interest in telecommuting is part of its overall research into work-force options.

*Appalachian Computer Services
Address: P.O. Box 140
                London, KY 40741
Telephone: (606) 878-7900
Number of Telecommuters: 10
Positions: Data entry operator; coding staff
Telecommuter Status: Independent contractor

Comments: A program initiated by management, telecommuters must have typing ability and be willing to work flexible hours. Telecommuters do not receive company benefits; the only benefits are "monetary based on piecework." The company accepts outside applications for telecommuting positions and plans to expand its program.

Apple Computer, Inc.
Address: 20525 Mariani Avenue
        Cupertino, CA 95014
Telephone: (408) 996-1010
Number of Telecommuters: See comments
Positions: See comments
Telecommuter Status: Salaried employee
Comments: Apple is on just about everyone's list of the best companies to work for in the U.S. The youthful brashness (and genius) of its founders, Steve Jobs and Mike Wozniak, still sets the pace at this leading-edge company. "While we don't have a formal telecommuting program," says public relations representative Kate Paisley, "Our technology and culture make telecommuting an option in many cases."

All new employees get an Apple computer for home use. Also, all employees are part the company's AppleLink worldwide electronic network. This means they can instantly communicate with other Apple employees across the hallway or across the world. "The result of this combination," says Paisley, "is that it's very easy to conduct certain types of business from almost any location, even at home."

As another part of its informal telecommuting program Apple says it maintains "flexible relationships" with its employees. "Apple recognizes that not every employee's working needs are the same. At times, working at home may allow an employee to be more productive, creative, or to be there for a sick child. Working at home is arranged on an occasional basis between employees and their managers. All levels of employees may participate, depending on the nature of their job. Since it is so informal, we don't keep track of the number of employees who take part."

*AT&T
Address: 611 W. 6th Street, Suite 1200
        Los Angeles, CA 90017
Telephone: (213) 488-0530

Number of Telecommuters: 70 as part of formal program, "thousands" informally

Positions: Salespeople; project manager; public relations manager; lawyer

Telecommuter Status: Salaried employee

Comments: You'd expect that AT&T, the country's leading telecommunications company, would have telecommuters, and indeed it does. But that's only part of the company's stake in telecommuting. In Los Angeles, where the law requires companies to start ride-sharing and other programs that save car trips into work, AT&T not only has a program itself, it also helps other companies get telecommuting under way.

For itself, AT&T says telecommuting helps it meet the following objectives:

1. To enable its salespeople and project managers to spend more time focused on their customers
2. To increase productivity
3. To better manage time

There are currently two types of telecommuting at AT&T. There is a formal program, where the company has formally endorsed the concept and helps people to work this way, but there is also a good deal of informal or ad hoc telecommuting.

AT&T's Los Angeles headquarters is formally testing telecommuting for the company as a whole. Some seventy people participate in this program. Telecommuters sign a telecommuting agreement that specifies the nature of the arrangement. They also attend orientation training with their managers.

Thousands of other AT&T employees telecommute informally. Many are salespeople who find the quiet environment of a home office handy for drafting proposals, putting bids together, and otherwise managing their accounts. Project managers, who manage the installation and maintenance of large communications projects, find telecommuting beneficial since their jobs are computer-intensive and involve a lot of telephone work and report writing. They can also search AT&T's in-house databases remotely. Some AT&T lawyers also telecommute, researching legal databases from home and preparing legal briefs and cases. Finally, public relations managers telecommute, especially when writing proposals or press releases. New hires can arrange to telecommute if other members of the group they are hired into already work that way. Basically, it's a decision that's up to the employee's supervisor. AT&T expects to see an increase both in the ranks of its own telecommuters and in its efforts to help other companies get telecommuting under way.

Baltimore *Evening Sun*
Address: 501 North Calvert Street
         Baltimore, MD 21202
Telephone: (301) 332-6000
Number of Telecommuters: 10–20
Positions: News reporter; columnist; critic; sportswriter; editorial
         writer
Telecommuter Status: Salaried employee
Comments: The ability to telecommute, says columnist Jack Kelly, "takes some of the stress out of the newspaper business." A wide variety of writers for this paper telecommute. Both reporters and critics, for example, file their stories from home instead of trudging back to the office after a late-breaking story or performance.

Almost anyone who writes for this paper can telecommute; whether or not they do depends more on possessing the necessary equipment than management approval. Like other newspapers, the *Sun* cares more about the work getting done than from where it gets done.

Beneficial Corporation
Address: Beneficial Center
         Peapack, NJ 07977
Telephone: (201) 781-3000
Number of Telecommuters: Unavailable
Positions: Executive vice president; president
Telecommuter Status: Salaried employee
Comments: Top executives at this financial services company have personal computers at home to boost productivity and communicate on a moment's notice. Some employees in the company's data processing department also work from home.

*Berlitz Translation Services
Address: 257 Park Avenue South, 17th Floor
         New York, NY 10010
Telephone: (212) 777-7878
Number of Telecommuters: "Hundreds"
Positions: Translator

Telecommuter Status: Independent contractor

Comments: Berlitz Translation Services is a division of Berlitz International, which also includes the well-known Berlitz Language Centers (schools). The Translation Services division does translating for companies, primarily translating documents into and out of English. It also provides UN-type interpreters and voice-overs for audio productions.

Berlitz does a lot of business; keeping the staff it needed in-house would cost a fortune, given its Manhattan location. Besides, as sales manager David Laube explains, "With microcomputers and telecommunications capabilities there is no need to do that." Says Laube: "Anybody who's serious about being a translator will have a microcomputer and modem."

In fact, one of the first things Berlitz asks prospective translators is if they have a computer and modem. Translators also need to supply their own reference materials, although Berlitz provides materials for special projects. Finally, Berlitz expects its translators to stay current and active in their languages, something professionals in the field probably do anyway.

Berlitz pays its translators, many of whom work full time, on a combination basis of hours worked and volume produced. Their earning potential is excellent: Laube says its home-based translators can earn "from $30,000 per year and up and up."

Best Western International, Inc.

Address: P.O. Box 10203, 6201 N. 24th Parkway
Phoenix, AZ 85064
Telephone: (602) 957-4200
Number of Telecommuters: 30
Positions: Reservations sales agent
Telecommuter Status: Salaried employee

Comments: Best Western's telecommuters work at home, but they are more likely to look out of prison bars than windows. In August 1981, Best Western created a satellite reservations center inside the Arizona Center for Women (ACW). The convicts take calls from people booking reservations. So far, they've handled more than 3 million calls, representing well over $80 million in room reservations.

The Department of Corrections first interviews potential agents. The applicants must type twenty or more words per minute, be sales-

oriented, have a good sense of geography, and must not have a record
of fraud. The agents make the same as other Best Western reservations agents.

Since the program began, Best Western has hired fifty of the 200
inmate participants on their release. (This is nevertheless not the
recommended way to get a job as a telecommuter.)

Most important, the program has worked out well for the inmates.
For some it has meant that they've kept their dignity in an environment that often strips it away.

*Blue Cross/Blue Shield of Maryland (Medicare Division)

Address: 1946 Greenspring Dr.
          Timonium, MD 21093
Telephone: (301) 561-4045
Number of Telecommuters: 4
Positions: Coder/keyer
Telecommuter Status: P/T benefits
Comments: Telecommuters here are called cottage keyers. Only sen-
ior-level keyers can participate. Telecommuters receive part-time
benefits, since the company considers them part-time employees.

Blue Cross/Blue Shield says it has a 50/50 ratio of outside and inside personnel filling these spots. "Our cottage program has proven
very successful," says company representative Helen Shugart. "We
have cottagees who are self-motivated and independent. They have
been flexible to our needs as they arise and provide quality work.
They are happy with the environment they (and we) have chosen
and that is shown by the quality of their work."

Blue Cross/Blue Shield of Maryland is evaluating the program to
make sure it meets company goals. For now, it plans to leave the program as it stands.

Blue Cross/Blue Shield of South Carolina

Address: I-20 at Alpine Road
          Columbia, SC 29219
Telephone: (803) 788-3860
Number of Telecommuters: 150–200
Positions: Keyer; coder; medical reviewer
Telecommuter Status: Independent contractor (plus retirement
          benefits)
Comments: One of the oldest and best-known telecommuting pro-

grams, Blue Cross/Blue Shield of South Carolina's heavy use of cottage keyers was featured on ABC's *Nightline* and covered by the *Wall Street Journal.*

The keyers process claims forms; coders assign code numbers reflecting a particular diagnosis that determines payment. Medical reviewers are registered nurses who review medical records to verify that medical procedures claimed were needed.

Coders and keyers must live within driving distance of the company so they can pick up paperwork weekly. Blue Cross/Blue Shield made certain to mention this, since the publicity has generated calls from would-be telecommuters as far away as Alaska.

The company supplies all equipment and even maintains an in-house staff that helps telecommuters with equipment problems. The company may expand the program, which it says has worked out "great." The error rate for its at-home coders and keyers is almost zero, compared to a rate of 2 percent for in-house people who do the same job. Because they tend to work when they are at their best, those at home produce more than in-house workers, meaning they earn more bonus pay. The company claims this more than makes up for the money they lay out for their health coverage.

Telecommuters' jobs are almost always filled from in-house, and there's a waiting list for such jobs. However, occasionally ("once in a blue moon") the company hires from outside its ranks. The program began in 1978—ancient history for this field.

California State Department of General Services
Address: Telecommunications Division
   601 Sequoia Pacific Boulevard
   Sacramento, CA 95814
Telephone: (916) 324-1739
Number of Telecommuters: 200
Positions: Clerical worker; judge; lawyer; secretary; programmer; engineer; director; manager; architect
Telecommuter Status: Salaried employee
Comments: California's commitment to telecommuting begins at the top, in this case the state government. Its formal pilot program began in January 1988 and is scheduled to run for two years. Managers and employees from more than fifteen state agencies are participating. The pilot encompasses "almost every job you can think of," says its prime consultant, Jack Nilles. (Of the state's 140,000 employees,

more than half are information workers.) The time spent telecommuting varies from one to several days per week.

This is the nation's most carefully planned and data-intensive telecommuting pilot. To gauge the program's cost effectiveness, the state tracks everything from energy consumption to phone bills to productivity. While the state is still collecting data, the pilot reportedly paid for itself by the end of its first year. That is, savings due to increased productivity and a decrease in sick time offset the training and other costs of starting the pilot.

A big reason for the program's success is the careful and extensive training. Through questionnaires, consultants prescreened employees for personal and job characteristics. Extensive training for both participants and their supervisors followed. The biggest names in telecommuting were involved, including Gil Gordon, Jack Nilles, and Joanne Pratt.

The program has gone smoothly; the only problems involved employees who did not go through the formal training. While the pilot ended at the end of 1989, telecommuting among state employees continues and may even increase.

Citibank
Address: 399 Park Avenue
        New York, NY 10043
Telephone: (212) 559-1000
Number of Telecommuters: Not available
Positions: Not available
Telecommuter Status: Not available
Comments: Citibank, the largest commercial bank in the U.S., is part of Citicorp. Citicorp is extremely decentralized, but it encourages its units to use personnel programs, such as telecommuting, that best meet the needs of employees and customers. Citibank does not centrally track these programs.

City of Fort Collins
Address: P.O. Box 580
        Fort Collins, CO 80522
Telephone: (303) 221-6500
Number of Telecommuters: 50+
Positions: Programmer; rideshare coordinator; manager; analyst
Telecommuter Status: Salaried employee

Comments: Located about 65 miles north of Denver, the city of Fort Collins runs one of the best-publicized of the formal telecommuting programs. Would-be telecommuters need only get their supervisor's permission. Asked whether telecommuting was done formally (part of an established program) or informally, a city representative responded "Formal policy—informal institution."

The city has taken full advantage of the PR benefits of its program. For example, it sells a videotape ($25) that explains how telecommuting operates among its employees.

City of Los Angeles
Address: 120 S. San Pedro Street, Suite 600
Los Angeles, CA 90012
Telephone: (213) 485-2866
Number of Telecommuters: 200–300
Positions: Administrator; manager; clerical worker; probation officer
Telecommuter Status: Salaried employee
Comments: In Los Angeles, where the average freeway speed is predicted to drop to 17 miles per hour in the next few years, it's need that drives telecommuting, not worker convenience or preference.

For some time, city workers have had a number of flexible work options to reduce trips in to work. These include compressed work weeks, meaning that employees may choose to work forty hours in four days or eighty hours in nine days. Some city workers have also telecommuted informally. In mid-1989, however, the city government began a far-reaching telecommuting pilot program involving hundreds of workers. City employees at all levels participate, working at home for one, two, or several days a week.

Participants must meet three criteria: their jobs must not demand a lot of face-to-face interaction; they must have a good relationship with their supervisors, who also must agree to the participation; and the worker must want to telecommute (it's a voluntary program).

*Companion HealthCare
Address: 300 Arbor Lake Drive, Suite 800
Columbia, MD 29223
Telephone: (803) 786-8466
Number of Telecommuters: Unavailable

Positions: Medical reviewer
Telecommuter Status: Independent contractor (plus retirement benefits)
Comments: Companion HealthCare is a Health Maintenance Organization (HMO), and subsidiary of Blue Cross/Blue Shield of South Carolina. Medical reviewers, all of whom are registered nurses, review claims to make sure operations and other medical procedures claimed were needed. All have personal computers (with modems) at home, which they use to review claims and produce correspondence related to their work. Whether or not staff members can participate in the program depends on available openings and their desire to telecommute—the option is that available.

The Compucare Company
Address: 12355 Sunrise Valley Drive
    Reston, VA 22091
Telephone: (703) 264-3086
Number of Telecommuters: 6
Positions: Programmer/analyst; product coordinator
Telecommuter Status: Salaried employee
Comments: Compucare provides hospital information systems (software and management services) to health care institutions. Its telecommuters, all company veterans, work at home for various personal reasons. For example, its product coordinator (who keeps track of which customers have which release of the company's product) began telecommuting after her spouse's transfer. "The company did not want to lose her," explains spokesperson Eileen Renaghan, "so we set her up with a home office including an Apple computer, printer, and fax machine." She now works from her home in Ohio and has yet to return to the company's headquarters. Other telecommuters here also work from home full time.

*Continental Communications Agency, Inc. (CCA)
Address: 7120 Hayvenhurst Ave., Suite 205
    Van Nuys, CA 91406
Telephone: (818) 782-4711
Number of Telecommuters: 50
Positions: Translator; desktop publisher
Telecommuter Status: Independent contractor

Comments: CCA is one of the West Coast's leading sources for translation and graphic design services. The company uses telecommunications extensively, which helped it create a worldwide translation network including translators in Europe and North America. CCA accepts outside applications for translator jobs, and the company plans to expand its network of translators.

Control Data Corporation
Address: 8100 34th Avenue, S.
          Bloomington, MN 55440
Telephone: (612) 853-8100
Number of Telecommuters: See comments
Positions: Programmer; analyst; editor; "any job the manager agrees to"
Telecommuter Status: Salaried employee
Comments: Control Data provides computer products and services for business, scientific, and engineering applications worldwide. The company had revenues of $3.6 billion in 1988.

One of the first companies to explore telecommuting, Control Data began a telecommuting project for the disabled in 1978. Dubbed Homework, the program taught disabled people to use computers to work. Eventually, its able-bodied employees wanted a similar program. In response, Control Data developed its Alternative Work Site policy. This permits any manager and any employee to explore a work-from-home arrangement. Control Data is so comfortable with telecommuting that it does not count or monitor the number of people who do it.

Control Data deserves special recognition because it's kept its telecommuting afloat (even expanding it) through hard times. The company reported losing quarters more than once in past years and always seems to be restructuring.

County of Los Angeles
Address: 22 N. Grand Avenue, Room 585
          Los Angeles, CA 90012
Telephone: (213) 974-2631
Number of Telecommuters: 500
Positions: Clerk; probation officer; program monitor; auditor
Telecommuter Status: Salaried employee

Comments: This program, announced in a televised news conference that sparked a rush of calls and letters from would-be telecommuters, came out of nowhere in 1989 to start in record time.

The County of Los Angeles has more than 80,000 employees and is one of the area's largest employers. It moved quickly into telecommuting to address two issues. First, office space was so sparse that although it had money to hire more workers, it had no place to put them. Second, the area's South Coast Air Quality Management District (see entry) mandated that employers devise ways to cut trips to and from work to reduce the area's smog and traffic problems.

Telecommuters receive formal training. They must commit to a core set of hours each day during which they can be reached or agree to return telephone calls within one-half hour. Usually, employees supply their own equipment, although the county will arrange for people who need equipment to purchase it at its discounted rate.

Primarily professional and administrative employees are involved; only a few clerical workers participate. Employees must designate a workplace in their homes that is subject to inspection from the county. For worker's compensation purposes, the county considers the home work space an extension of the employee's work space at the office.

While the county does not generally hire outsiders for telecommuting jobs, it may in the future. Those in difficult-to-fill jobs, such as paralegals, have the best shot at getting hired "off the street" to work from home.

Officials expect that 2000 of the county's downtown Los Angeles workers will work from home within the next five years.

Data General Corporation
Address: 4400 Computer Drive
           Westboro, MA 01580
Telephone: (508) 366-8911
Number of Telecommuters: Unavailable
Positions: Programmer; engineer
Telecommuter Status: Salaried employee
Comments: Data General is a leading manufacturer of computers and computer software. The company has a terminal loaner program. It's designed for employees who want to check their electronic mail over weekends, but some employees also use the terminals to telecommute. Other employees arrange to work at home on an individual basis. These include engineers who want to run programs

from home at night, when there is less demand on Data General's computer resources. A program that takes up to five hours to run during the day can be run from home (remotely linked to the company's computers) in much less time.

Detroit *Free Press*
Address: 321 West Lafayette
Detroit, MI 48231
Telephone: (313) 222-6400
Number of Telecommuters: 6 formally; "dozens" informally
Positions: Columnist; reporter; correspondent; editor
Telecommuter Status: Salaried employee
Comments: Columnists and correspondents work from home almost exclusively; reporters (for the most part) do so occasionally. Two reporters who work from home frequently, though, are the television sports reporter and the outdoors writer.

The TV sports reporter has television sets, the tools of his trade in a sense, lined up in the basement of his house. The outdoors writer, who lives more than an hour away from Detroit in the Michigan woods, seldom comes into the office. Correspondents in countries including Zimbabwe and Canada, as well as Eastern Europe, file their stories by computer and modem.

Digital Equipment Corporation
Address: 146 Main Street
Maynard, MA 01754
Telephone: (508) 493-5111
Number of Telecommuters: "Thousands"
Positions: Sales and service representative; technical and engineering staff member; consultant
Telecommuter Status: Salaried employee
Comments: Since fall 1987, members of Digital's Corporate Organizational Consulting group have piloted telecommuting for the company as a whole. The group advises Digital managers on effective organizational change and growth. Roughly fifteen of the group's thirty members (largely behavioral scientists) have what Project Leader Grace Boynton calls "home offices." They use these offices to "think, create, communicate, and work with electronic data," Dr. Boynton says.

Employees at Digital's Orange County, California, Sales and Service Center now also telecommute. Finally, members of Digital's technical and engineering staff (numbering in the thousands) have computer equipment at home and "have the latitude to work at home whenever they want to," says Boynton. In fact, "Telecommuting is something that's being done informally all over the company."

*Digital News
Address: 33 West Street
          Boston, MA 02111
Telephone: (617) 482-8470
Number of Telecommuters: 8
Positions: Writer; editor; reporter
Telecommuter Status: Mixed (see comments)
Comments: Digital News is a biweekly publication that covers equipment manufactured by Digital Equipment Corporation. Its circulation approaches 80,000. Half of its telecommuters receive company benefits; others get no medical insurance or retirement benefits. *Digital News* accepts outside applications for telecommuting jobs.

Direct Data
Address: 1215 Francis Dr.
          Arlington Heights, IL 60005
Telephone: (312) 253-7303
Number of Telecommuters: 26
Positions: PPCO (Professional Personal Computer Operator)
Telecommuter Status: Independent contractor
Comments: When she took over Direct Data, entrepreneur Rosalin Dano was facing a problem that will confront many of us. She cares for her ninety-year-old father-in-law in her home, and says that "although he is in good health, I prefer the flexible scheduling of my own business to aid me in balancing my work career with my family responsibilities."

Actually, a friend of Dano's started Direct Data, which provides services such as word processing and desktop publishing. But marketing problems kept her from making a go of it. "I then asked her if I could use her idea and she consented," says Dano. The company now employs one full-fledged telecommuter and a network of twenty-five independent subcontractors, each of whom runs and owns her own business.

As Dano recently told the Chicago *Tribune,* working at home has changed her life: "I'm no longer on double-time as are many other women who work full time at the paycheck job and at the homefront job."

EasyCom, Inc.
Address: 411 South Sangamon, Suite 5A
Chicago, IL 60607
Telephone: (312) 243-2074
Number of Telecommuters: 2+
Positions: President; researcher
Telecommuter Status: Independent contractor
Comments: EasyCom is a public relations firm that uses computers extensively for on-line research and communications. Ron Solberg, EasyCom's president, is also the System Operator (SysOp) for CompuServe's public relations forum and the chair for the Public Relations Society of America's Communications Technology Committee.

E. I. du Pont de Nemours & Co.
Address: 1007 Market Street
Wilmington, DE 19898
Telephone: (302) 774-1000
Number of Telecommuters: Not available
Positions: Researcher; engineer; sales representative
Telecommuter Status: Salaried employee
Comments: DuPont has quite a few telecommuters, says principal consultant George Palmer. There is no set program here. Whether an employee telecommutes depends on whether or not he has the necessary equipment and a "need to do it." Most of the company's salespeople telecommute, as do engineers and researchers. Telecommuters keep in touch with the office through electronic mail.

Equitable Life Assurance
Address: 787 7th Ave.
New York, NY 10019
Telephone: (212) 554-1101
Number of Telecommuters: Unavailable
Positions: Speechwriter; other
Telecommuter Status: Salaried employee
Comments: Equitable had a formal telecommuting pilot program that involved managers and programmers. The pilot program ended, but informal telecommuting continues. An employee arranges to

work at home by getting a department manager's approval. A speechwriter who telecommutes instead of braving Manhattan traffic each day has a fax machine and personal computer set up in his home.

*Farallon Computing, Inc.
Address: 2201 Dwight Way
          Berkeley, CA 94704
Telephone: (415) 849-2331
Number of Telecommuters: 8–10
Positions: Engineer; regional sales representative
Telecommuter Status: Not available
Comments: Farallon makes a product called PhoneNET, which connects Apple Macintosh computers with computer networks. Founded in 1986, the company has already racked up an impressive record: PhoneNET connects over half of all networked Macintoshes.

The Farallon engineer who telecommutes developed PhoneNET and gets to more or less call his own shots. The regional representatives have no choice but to telecommute since they are not located on Farallon's premises. Farallon plans to use more telecommuters as it moves into other geographical areas.

The Federal Government
Address: Office of Personnel Management
          1900 E Street, NW
Washington, DC 20415
Telephone: (202) 632-5491
Number of Telecommuters: See comments
Positions: Auditor/examiner; other (see comments)
Telecommuter Status: Salaried employee
Comments: The federal government has a long history of using homeworkers. That should continue since opportunities for telecommuters who want to work for the government will open up considerably in the coming years.

The General Services Administration and other federal agencies now let some employees work at home instead of in the office. In many cases, the agency made these arrangements for employees who would otherwise be on a leave of absence but whose services it still needed.

Another area where the federal government has explored working at home is the employment of disabled workers through the Rehabilitation Research and Training Center Program (RRTC) at George Washington University. Unfortunately, federal funding for the RRTC project ended in 1979, even though the program produced positive results. Finally, federal auditor/examiner personnel, including federal credit union examiners, routinely spend most of their time at various sites but have their offices in their homes.

Beyond these examples, "interest in work-at-home opportunities for federal employees, including disabled workers, is increasing," says Paul T. Weiss of the General Services Administration. The President's Council on Management Improvement (PCMI) now sponsors a Flexible Workplace Project. This will pilot-test flexible workplace arrangements (including work-at-home) for federal employees governmentwide. The General Services Administration and the Office of Personnel Management co-chair the project, now in its pilot phase.

For more information, contact the Federal Job Information Center or the Office of Personnel Management in the region where you'd like to work.

First Chicago Corporation
Address: One First National Plaza
            Chicago, IL 60670
Telephone: (312) 407-2023
Number of Telecommuters: 5–10
Positions: Project manager; manuals analyst; compensation analyst; programmer analyst
Telecommuter Status: Salaried employee
Comments: This is a large Midwestern bank, which in 1988 reported a net income of more than $500 million. First Chicago's telecommuting program is now more than five years old. The bank originally saw telecommuting as a way for new mothers to extend their maternity leaves. First Chicago has a well-thought-out program with definite eligibility requirements. For example, participants must have:

- Minimum of two years employment at the bank
- Minimum of one year reporting to current manager
- Performance ratings of 4 or better on last two reviews

Benefits for telecommuters are determined by standard eligibility requirements. "Our program works well because we keep paperwork to a minimum and view the manager/subordinate relationship as the key to its success."

Gannett
Address: 1100 Wilson Boulevard
        Arlington, VA 22209
Telephone: (703) 284-6000
Number of Telecommuters: Unavailable
Positions: Reporter; other
Telecommuter Status: Salaried employee
Comments: Gannett publishes newspapers, including *USA Today,* and owns several television stations. Employees can arrange to telecommute at their managers' discretion. Most work from home only occasionally. However, disabled employees or women on extended maternity leaves may work from home for several weeks at a time.

General Telephone of California
Address: 1 GTE Place
        Thousand Oaks, CA 91362
Telephone: (805) 372-6000
Number of Telecommuters: 70+
Positions: Programmer; systems analyst
Telecommuter Status: Salaried employee
Comments: Telecommuting at GTE stretches back to the 1984 Summer Olympic Games, held in Los Angeles. GTE initiated telecommuting among its employees in response to the city's request that companies reduce commuting by its employees.

After a hiatus, GTE recently began a formal program again; roughly seventy people now participate. Many other GTE employees telecommute informally.

*GE Plastics
Address: 214 7th Street, Suite 401
        Parkersburg, WV 26102
Telephone: (304) 424-5411
Number of Telecommuters: 100+
Positions: Salesperson; administrative assistant; programmer analyst; manager; vice president
Telecommuter Status: Salaried employee
Comments: GE Plastics, which manufactures chemicals and plastics products, was originally owned by Borg-Warner. After General Electric bought it, the company's use of computers and other technology really took off, and so did telecommuting. For example, all members

of the sales force have microcomputers at home. Many people use electronic mail and portable computers as part of their jobs.

The sales and sales support staff is part of a formal telecommuting program. Others telecommute informally. While the company expects its salespeople to telecommute, programmers, engineers, and even administrators and advertising staff members can also arrange to work at home—it's up to their managers. In some cases, GE Plastics supplies the software/hardware necessary for telecommuting; other employees purchase their own PCs.

It's interesting that many students who interview with the company right out of college ask for the right to work at home. They come from technical disciplines and used microcomputers in their college dorms; therefore they are used to working at home. Depending on the job, new employees can sometimes arrange to telecommute.

*Globalink Language Services
Address: 9990 Lee Highway, Suite 510
         Fairfax, VA 22030
Telephone: (703) 359-6273
Number of Telecommuters: 850 (approximately)
Positions: Translator; editor; word processor
Telecommuter Status: Independent contractor
Comments: Translators are prime candidates for telecommuting, and this translation company is at the forefront of the technology. While the requirements are steep (translators must supply their own equipment and they receive no benefits since Globalink does not consider them company employees), many opportunities are available. Globalink says telecommuting speeds turnaround time and has let it greatly expand its network of translators. "We work with a large number of freelance translators and prefer those with computer, modem, and fax machine."

Hewlett-Packard Company
Address: 3000 Hanover Street
         Palo Alto, CA 94304
Telephone: (415) 857-1501
Number of Telecommuters: See comments
Positions: UNIX engineer; other (see comments)
Telecommuter Status: Salaried employee
Comments: With more than 80,000 employees and revenues topping

the $8 billion mark, Hewlett-Packard is not only one of the country's largest companies, it's one of its most admired. In the office equipment and copier area, a *Fortune* poll found that H-P ranked just behind IBM and Digital Equipment (and ahead of Apple). Among engineers, H-P is the most admired company.

H-P is an example of a company that has no formal telecommuting program but still has people telecommuting informally. In H-P's case, usually these are people who can wrangle special deals (for example, UNIX engineers) because their skills are in great demand.

Hi-Tech Public Relations
Address: 444 DeHaro Street, Suite 207
San Francisco, CA 94107
Telephone: (415) 864-5600
Number of Telecommuters: 3+
Positions: Writer, account executive; corporate strategist
Telecommuter Status: See comments
Comments: Hi-Tech Public Relations is among the top PR agencies specializing in hi-tech accounts. The company pays some of its telecommuters as independent contractors; others are salaried.

Home Office Computing
Address: 730 Broadway
New York, NY 10003
Telephone: (212) 505-3580
Number of Telecommuters: See comments
Positions: Editor; other editorial staff (see comments)
Telecommuter Status: Salaried employee
Comments: A magazine for people who work at home, both telecommuters and entrepreneurs (see Chapter 10). One of the magazine's senior editors telecommutes from his home in Massachusetts and writes about it in his monthly column. Other people stay home for a day or two a week when working on certain projects. The magazine is "increasingly flexible about who works where and when," wrote editor-in-chief Claudia Cohl in the June 1989 issue.

Honeywell, Inc.
Address: Honeywell Plaza
Minneapolis, MN 55408
Telephone: (612) 870-5200

Number of Telecommuters: See comments
Positions: Diverse work force specialist; other (see comments)
Telecommuter Status: Salaried employee
Comments: Honeywell, a *Fortune* 500 giant, has more than 78,000 employees. Telecommuting is done informally and work-at-home arrangements are not reported to any central office. Each division establishes its own policy about telecommuting at this very decentralized company. Those "eligible" range from the disabled to new mothers.

Hughes Aircraft

Address: P.O. Box 45066
          Los Angeles, CA 90045
Telephone: (213) 568-7200
Number of Telecommuters: Unavailable
Positions: Engineer; programmer
Telecommuter Status: Salaried employee
Comments: Hughes has many professional-level employees, and the company recognizes that programmers and engineers, in particular, need an atmosphere conducive to creative work. Therefore there are no limits placed on working at home. The policy here is not "institutionalized"; it's up to the employee's local manager.

Hughes provides the computer equipment, budget permitting. The company's credit union has also provided interest-free loans to employees buying computers.

The H. W. Wilson Company

Address: 950 University Avenue
          Bronx, New York 10452
Telephone: (212) 588-8400
Number of Telecommuters: 3–4
Positions: Indexer
Telecommuter Status: Not available
Comments: Remember the *Reader's Guide to Periodical Literature?* As a student you probably used this green book to locate magazine articles for research papers. H.W. Wilson produces the *Reader's Guide,* and many other reference books for libraries.

Several Wilson indexers work from home, from Connecticut down to Georgia. Typically, these are people who left the company but who wanted to continue indexing. They had experience in crucial areas and, rather than lose them, Wilson let them telecommute. Telecommuters receive publications to index by Federal Express and use the company's on-line service, Wilsonline, to stay current on company practices.

In the abstracting and indexing field, Wilson's closest competitor is Information Access Company, which also has telecommuters.

Information Access Company (IAC)
Address: 362 Lakeside Drive
          Foster City, CA 94404
Telephone: (415) 378-5110
Number of Telecommuters: 15
Positions: Indexer; indexer-editor; abstracter; abstracter-editor
Telecommuter Status: Salaried employee
Comments: IAC is one of the leading producers of electronic databases and indexes. Its products include *Magazine Index, Trade and Industry Index,* and *Computer Index.* These are research tools that reference articles from magazines and trade journals. (The well-known *Reader's Guide to Periodical Literature* is *Magazine Index's* main competitor.)

IAC first saw telecommuting as a way to keep employees who would otherwise leave the company to pursue other interests or stay home for other reasons. Now IAC also views telecommuting as a perk for top performers. Before they can arrange to telecommute, employees must work in-house for one to two years. From the program's start, IAC gave its telecommuters the same benefits as its in-house people. Also, IAC sets performance goals for its homeworking indexers that are 20 percent above what on-site indexers must produce.

*Interactive Systems Corporation
Address: 2401 Colorado Ave.
          Santa Monica, CA 90404
Telephone: (213) 453-8649
Number of Telecommuters: 5
Positions: Sales manager; consultant; principal member of technical staff
Telecommuter Status: Salaried employee
Comments: Interactive Systems Corporation is a software distributor with approximately 200 employees. Whether or not new employees may telecommute depends on personal circumstances and the skills

they bring to the company. "If the company feels the prospective employee's expertise is needed but he or she is unable to commute because of distance we will consider him for the job."

International Business Machines Corporation (IBM)
Address: Old Orchard Road
          Armonk, NY 10504
Telephone: (914) 765-1900
Number of Telecommuters: See comments
Positions: See comments
Telecommuter Status: Salaried employee
Comments: With more than 220,000 employees in the U.S. and revenues topping $50 billion, IBM is arguably the most admired company on the face of the earth. No wonder: Against ever-increasing pressure from foreign competitors, IBM still prospers.

IBM has no formal telecommuting program, but its newly liberalized personnel policies make working at home an option for some employees. It announced its new work-at-home program as part of a package of a new "work flexibility" program. Simultaneously, IBM extended its personal leave of absence program to three years and liberalized its flextime program.

IBM announced the program in light of the changes it saw in the work force—more working women, dual-career couples, single parents, and people opting for second careers thanks to generally longer lifespans.

IBM's work-at-home program is in a pilot stage. The program is available only at certain locations, which are test cases for the entire company. Participating employees must come into the office once a week to submit work and get new assignments.

As far as personnel policies are concerned, as IBM goes, so goes the rest of corporate America. Thus the significance of its new work policies cannot be overestimated.

Telecommuting's grapevine reports that some IBM employees informally telecommute outside these new programs. Officially, however, IBM says that employees may only work at home if they are unable to regularly come in to the office each day.

*Janal Communications
Address: P.O. Box 271
          Fort Lee, NJ 07024

Telephone: (201) 947-9839
Number of Telecommuters: 3
Positions: President; public relations associate
Telecommuter Status: Independent contractor
Comments: Janal specializes in public relations services for hi-tech firms. Company president Daniel Janal uses on-line services extensively to research and send and retrieve files. One of the company's associates works out of Topeka, Kansas. Another works out of her house in San Francisco. Associates upload their materials to Compu-Serve, where Janal retrieves them at his leisure. Janal Communications has been in business since 1986 and expects to expand its staff.

JCPenney
Address: 100 N. Corporate Drive
　　　　　Brookfield, WI 53005
Telephone: (414) 792-5525
Number of Telecommuters: 200+
Positions: Customer service representative
Telecommuter Status: Salaried employee
Comments: JCPenney has one of the country's oldest and largest telecommuting programs. Telecommuters, located in six of the company's sixteen telemarketing centers, take calls from people ordering from the company's catalog. To be eligible to telecommute, employees must have worked in the center at least one year and must "have good working habits and exceed standards." Do Penney telecommuters get the same benefits as its in-house people? "Absolutely," says program manager Carl Kirkpatrick. "Same hourly rate and the same benefits."

Penney thinks highly of its telecommuting program, which has sharply reduced employee turnover. It's also meant the company no longer has to worry about having enough telemarketers available during peak periods (such as holidays).

Jet Propulsion Laboratory
Address: 180-200 4800 Oak Grove Dr.
　　　　　Pasadena, CA 91109
Telephone: (818) 354-4103
Number of Telecommuters: 20
Positions: "Any job that can be done in this mode"
Telecommuter Status: Salaried employee

Comments: Telecommuting is an option for employees recovering from medical procedures.

John Hancock Mutual Life Insurance Company
Address: John Hancock Pl.
  P.O. Box 111
  Boston, MA 02117
Telephone: (617) 421-6000
Number of Telecommuters: 3
Positions: System designer; systems analyst
Telecommuter Status: Salaried employee
Comments: At Hancock, telecommuting is largely due to the efforts of one supervisor—Alex Malcolm. Malcolm supervises a group of computer specialists who create and develop strategic computer systems. He believes it makes sense to let people work where they will be the most comfortable and productive. Telecommuting here evolved naturally. Members of Alex's staff already had computer terminals at home with modems to hook into Hancock's central computer. "We quickly learned that we could be more productive at home— away from the telephone and normal office distractions," says Alex. "It also allowed us to work in more natural rhythms."

Any member of Alex's group can work at home if the analyst thinks it will boost productivity. Alex doesn't think he would hire someone off the street to telecommute if she was only interested in working from home. He says it could happen, though, if her skills and the job warranted it.

Aside from Malcolm's group, Hancock has no general telecommuting policy, although there may be pockets of telecommuters here and there. But Malcolm expects Hancock's telecommuting program to expand. Mostly, however, New England conservatism reigns here, except for one Alex Malcolm.

*Journal Graphics
Address: 267 Broadway
  New York, NY 10007
Telephone: (212) 732-8552
Number of Telecommuters: 13
Positions: Transcriber
Telecommuter Status: Independent contractor
Comments: If you've ever watched a news program or talk show that

invited you to send in $3 or so for a "transcript of tonight's show," there's a good chance telecommuters working for Journal Graphics prepared them. Journal Graphics now provides the transcripts for forty-two television shows including *20/20, Phil Donahue, The Oprah Winfrey Show,* and *60 Minutes.*

Its transcribers live in Hawaii, New York, Seattle, and Washington, D.C., and usually specialize in one show. To prepare a transcript, they first videotape the program. From the videotape they make an audiotape and prepare a transcript from that. It takes roughly four times as long to transcribe a show as it does to watch it.

Journal Graphics sometimes looks to hire transcribers in other cities. This usually happens when a television show for which it produces transcripts airs earlier in that city than it does anywhere else. An example is *The Oprah Winfrey Show,* which airs in the mornings in Chicago but afternoons everywhere else. By having a Chicago-based transcriber, Journal Graphics can fill rush orders for the show that much sooner.

Telecommuters here work as freelancers. They are paid per show transcribed on a flat rate. They must be able to type 80 words per minute and pass a spelling test and another test that measures general awareness of current events.

Lanier Business Products
Address: 2310 Parklake Drive
Atlanta, GA 30345
Telephone: (404) 270-2000
Number of Telecommuters: 120
Positions: Systems analyst; educational specialist
Telecommuter Status: Salaried employee
Comments: Lanier has an informal policy permitting working from home with a manager's approval. Systems analysts have personal computers at home and occasionally work there when testing new software packages. Educational specialists, who teach courses in the use of microcomputers, sometimes learn new software packages at home. "We value our employees, and recognize that it's possible to get more done at home," says manager Lori Day.

Letter Perfect
Address: 4205 Menlo Drive
Baltimore, MD 21215

Telephone: (301) 358-8973
Number of Telecommuters: 11
Positions: Word processor; typist
Telecommuter Status: Independent contractor
Comments: Letter Perfect is a small company that's in an information-intensive business, which makes its climate perfect for telecommuting. Such companies rarely get the publicity that the *Fortune* 500 companies with telecommuters do.

Letter Perfect sells mailing lists, and produces two monthly newsletters: *People on the Move in Maryland* and *New Business Listings in Maryland.* All but one of its homeworkers are independent contractors. The other is an in-house employee who is no longer able to regularly come into the office. She is paid on a per-hour basis.

Lift, Inc.,
Address: 350 Pfingsten, Suite 103
            Northbrook, IL 60062
Telephone: (312) 564-9005
Number of Telecommuters: See comments
Positions: Programmer
Telecommuter Status: Salaried employee
Comments: Lift, Inc. is different from the other companies included in this book in that it does not directly employ telecommuters. Instead, Lift trains, hires, and then places computer programmers with severe physical disabilities, such afflictions as polio, cerebral palsy, and blindness.

While some of Lift's clients can commute using public transportation or with the help of attendants, others work from home. Still, telecommuters must be on-site at least once a week to get assignments, review work with their supervisors, attend staff meetings, and communicate with others on their teams. The only requirement is that applicants be relatively stable medically and have a high degree of computer aptitude.

Since 1975 Lift has worked with 132 computer programmers. It has placed 92 of these with such corporate clients as Allstate Insurance Company, Mutual of New York, AT&T, Bank of Hawaii, Walgreen Company, Time, Inc., and Quaker Oats. As Lift's brochure puts it: "If your company is typical, you have an urgent need for competent, dependable computer professionals. If the price/performance is competitive, do you really care if your employee is in a wheel chair?"

LINK Resources Corporation
Address: 79 Fifth Avenue
New York, NY 10003
Telephone: (212) 627-1500
Number of Telecommuters: 7+
Positions: Manager; research associate; writer; sales representative; president
Telecommuter Status: Salaried employee
Comments: Here's a company that stands behind what it preaches. LINK is one of the top market research firms in the electronic information field. When it bought Electronic Services Unlimited, a company specializing in telecommuting research and publishing, it moved briskly into telecommuting. Prospective telecommuters should contact this company, not only because it employs telecommuters but also because it carefully tracks the whole work-at-home movement. Ask for information on its research in this area (be warned: The complete studies are expensive and are geared to big companies that want to sell to the work-at-home market).

Obviously, there's big money to be made in selling computers, fax machines, furniture, and the like to people who work from home. For its 1987 "National Work-At-Home Survey," Link charged $10,000 just for the report's executive summary, six reports of the customer's choice, and follow-up telephone consults. This wasn't even the complete package!

Lipton, Famiglio & Elman
Address: 201 North Jackson Street Box 546
Media, PA 19063
Telephone: (215) 565-4730
Number of Telecommuters: 2+
Positions: Lawyer
Telecommuter Status: Salaried employee
Comments: At least two members of this law firm telecommute during off hours and occasionally during regular working hours. They also use computers and modems to research court cases and communicate with other lawyers. Attorney Fred Wilf, for example, goes online to trade messages and documents with clients.

*MacWEEK
Address: 301 Howard Street, Suite 1500
San Francisco, CA 94105

Telephone: (415) 243-3500
Number of Telecommuters: See comments
Positions: Writer; editor; graphic artist
Telecommuter Status: Both independent contractors and salaried
    employees
Comments: While many magazines, and especially computer publications, accept manuscripts sent by computer and modem, *MacWEEK* may stand alone as the only one that works solely with freelancers who submit stories electronically. Its freelancers must also use a specific electronic mail service—MCI's.

MacWEEK's reasoning is that filing electronically gives the writer more time. With on-line communications, "Writers can file stories six hours before they are due," explains Emily Brower, *MacWEEK's* resident on-line guru. *MacWEEK* also believes that since it is a computer publication (it covers Macintosh computers), its writers should use the technology.

In addition to its freelance writers, some of the graphic artists *MacWEEK* works with also submit electronically. Finally, *MacWEEK* staff members occasionally work at home, especially when it's hard to get things done in the office.

MacWEEK was designed to be self-sufficient from the start. It always relied on desktop publishing, for example, so that layout and pasteup work could be done in-house. The same goes for receiving manuscripts on-line instead of by the "U.S. Snail." Emily Brower: "The idea from the beginning was to have people send things electronically."

McGuire, Woods, Battle & Boothe
Address: One James Center
        Richmond, VA 23219
Telephone: (804) 775-1199
Number of Telecommuters: 3
Positions: Legal assistant
Telecommuter Status: Independent contractor
Comments: This is a small telecommuting program that's run informally. Telecommuters are considered hourly employees. There are no special requirements that telecommuters must meet; selection is on a case-by-case basis.

*Meckler Publishing Corporation
Address: 11 Ferry Lane West
        Westport, CT 06880

Telephone: (203) 226-6967
Number of Telecommuters: 35–40
Positions: Editor; writer; keystroker
Telecommuter Status: Independent contractor
Comments: A small publishing company specializing in books and journals about computer databases, CD-ROMs, and other products of the information age. Its telecommuters are far-flung and eclectic. For example, the editor of a journal for information professionals *(Database Searcher)* lives in California. Stringers from Holland and Japan send Meckler's staff details on the CD-ROM market in their respective countries. An "army" of in-house Meckler employees stands ready to receive these data feeds. About ten minutes before he is ready to transmit, the telecommuter calls the in-house staff person to set up the feed.

Meckler plans to add many more telecommuters in the future. "The beauty of telecommuting for us, as a small publisher," says company president Alan Meckler, "is that it lets us expand without adding staff."

Merrill Corporation
Address: 1 Merrill Circle
St. Paul, MN 55108
Telephone: (800) 328-6830
Number of Telecommuters: 4
Positions: Editor; programmer; project manager
Telecommuter Status: Salaried employee
Comments: This is a financial printing firm that first got into telecommuting when it wanted to hire a consultant based in northern Illinois. Rather than take a chance on not being able to hire him, it tentatively gave telecommuting a shot. Merrill liked the results so well it now has other telecommuters.

MultiLink Incorporated
Address: One Market Street
Lynn, MA 01901
Telephone: (617) 595-7577
Number of Telecommuters: 9
Positions: Public relations coordinator; director of educational services; regional sales manager
Telecommuter Status: Salaried employee
Comments: MultiLink provides the technology and training compa-

nies need to set up "phone meetings." Such teleconferences let scattered participants "attend" the same meeting by dialing a central number (even by car phone). In October 1985 the company created the Director of Educational Services position and specifically designed it for a telecommuter.

MultiLink makes it a point to give its telecommuters all company benefits, from profit sharing to insurance. Salaries are also the same. MultiLink plans to keep its telecommuting ways intact: "We are uninhibited when it comes to the use of telecommuters," says company founder and executive vice president John Hassett.

The company has some interesting approaches to its business with implications for telecommuters. Like telecommuting, the technology behind teleconferencing is advanced enough to be used much more than it is. Human factors (reluctance, mostly) hold it back. MultiLink admits that there's something lost when meetings are held electronically (the communication that's spurred by eye-to-eye contact). Therefore the MultiLink operator conducts a rollcall at the start of each meeting. The company also stresses the use of visuals at meetings. It suggests handing out not only pie charts but also biographical sketches, including photos, of the meeting participants. This way people can visualize who they are talking to.

*National Opinion Research Center (NORC)
Address: 1155 East 60th Street
          Chicago, IL 60637
Telephone: (312) 702-1200
Number of Telecommuters: 84+
Positions: Director; office of field coordination and management; district manager; divisional field manager; data processing staff
Telecommuter Status: Salaried employee
Comments: NORC is a nonprofit company specializing in survey research—it surveys people about their feelings on important social issues. Affiliated with the University of Chicago, it is the oldest organization of its kind. NORC's surveys cover topics such as drug and alcohol use, the effectiveness of government programs, and the use of doctors and hospitals.

In a way, NORC has always had telecommuters. Its field managers, who manage, train, and hire the company's 1000 interviewers, have worked from home since the company began more than fifty years ago.

The field managers are spread throughout the U.S. These managers and their immediate supervisors make up the bulk of the organization's telecommuters. Others (central office staff) telecommute part time, but this is usually due to special circumstances such as new mothers who prefer to work part time after the birth of their babies. Other senior staff members, however, also work from home part time.

NORC's telecommuters get the same benefits as its nontelecommuters. Even field managers who only work part time receive benefits, at a rate proportional to hours worked. NORC provides district managers and district field managers with all necessary equipment, including computer work stations, answering machines, telephones, and sometimes fax machines. It spends roughly $3000 to set up a typical home office. Field managers now only get an answering machine and telephone, but work stations for them are coming.

NORC wants to expand its telecommuting program. The company accepts outside applications for telecommuting positions, but they must start with an interviewing assignment and work their way through field management ranks. Field managers have an average of ten years' experience at NORC.

NCNB Corporation

Address: One NCNB Plaza
         Charlotte, NC 28255
Telephone: (704) 374-5000
Number of Telecommuters: 40
Positions: Vice president; public relations specialist
Telecommuter Status: Salaried employee
Comments: The Wall Street Journal, USA Today, Business Week, and *Family Circle* have all carried articles on the innovative work options available to NCNB employees.

With assets of more than $30 billion, NCNB is the largest bank in the Southeast. Nearly 70 percent of its 13,000 employees are women. The company instituted a "select time policy" after a 1986 survey found nearly a third of its employees wanted to work fewer hours to better care for their families. Select time lets people who care for dependents work at home part time. To participate, employees must have been with the bank for at least one year and have satisfactory employment records.

The policy has worked out well for NCNB. Just having it has helped the bank recruit key people. It's also helped reduce turnover;

prior to the program 2500 employees left each year. Now that rate is much lower.

New England Telephone and Telegraph Company

Address: 99 High Street, Room 705
            Boston, MA 02110
Telephone: (617) 743-9800
Number of Telecommuters: 5+
Positions: Marketing specialist; controller; course developer
Telecommuter Status: Salaried employee
Comments: New England Telephone's telecommuting pilot program ran from June 1988 to May 1989. The program involved disabled employees and others who needed to work from home to care for relatives. One participant, for example, was a marketing specialist whose son had been in a car accident. To avoid taking a leave of absence to care for him, she asked to work at home. The pilot worked so well that New England Telephone's Flexible Work Arrangements Committee suggested it implement telecommuting as corporate policy.

New England Telephone anticipates that employees with special needs will continue to telecommute. They'll be joined, however, by other employees who meet the program's qualifications. These include a self-motivated and self-paced way of working, and a manager who is flexible enough to agree to manage from afar.

The company also has other flexible working arrangements including flextime, compressed time, and job sharing. Boston's traffic congestion and the construction it spurred first inspired the company to create flexible work arrangements.

*NewsBank, Inc.

Address: 58 Pine Street
            New Canaan, CT 06840
Telephone: (203) 966-1100
Number of Telecommuters: 21
Positions: Indexer; proofreader
Telecommuter Status: Independent contractor
Comments: A publishing company that produces current affairs reference services, NewsBank has used home-based workers since the 1970s. On the average, telecommuters work twenty to twenty-five hours per week. They must come into the office twice a week to pick up and drop off materials and attend occasional meetings.

Telecommuters go through a three-month training program to learn the company's way of indexing and how to use personal computers. They now use floppy disks to transmit information, but modem delivery is coming. NewsBank provides all equipment (currently IBM clones) to its telecommuters.

The company does accept outside applications for work-at-home positions, and even places newspaper ads for these jobs. NewsBank expects its freelancers to be committed to the company and to the job. "You have to have a work ethic to do this."

*Newsbytes News Service
Address: 822 Arkansas Street
        San Francisco, CA 94107
Telephone: (415) 550-7334
Number of Telecommuters: 12
Positions: Editor; reporter; bureau chief
Telecommuter Status: Unavailable
Comments: Newsbytes, the largest independent computer industry news service in the world, covers the week's most significant microcomputer and consumer technology news. Some fifty-two magazines, newspapers, news sources, and on-line systems worldwide republish its stories.

The Newsbytes News Service consists entirely of a network of home offices—twelve in all—based in the following metropolitan areas: San Francisco, Los Angeles, Atlanta, Washington, D.C., London, Brussels, Tokyo, Toronto, Singapore, Kuala Lumpur, Malaysia, and Sydney, Australia. Telecommuters all, each files his or her reports electronically (once a week, on Fridays) to editor Wendy Woods, who works from San Francisco. Then she edits, formats, and uploads the complete weekly news service to three major on-line systems—GEnie, NewsNet, and the Quantum computer services. From there it's disseminated to more than forty-five other media worldwide, including magazines, newspapers, in-house newsletters, and electronic bulletin boards. Having been in operation since 1983, the system works well, with all reporters enjoying their autonomy—although editor Woods says "I sometimes get frustrated about my inability to face off with them in person when I have problems with their writing!"

The correspondents, most of whom are actually bureau chiefs, are permanent part-time employees. Newsbytes is a partnership, with

Wendy Woods majority owner. "We certainly would like to hear from computer industry reporters who wish to participate," says Woods.

New York Life
Address: 51 Madison Avenue
New York, NY 10010
Telephone: (212) 576-7844
Number of Telecommuters: 200+
Positions: Programmer/analyst; actuarial associates
Telecommuter Status: Independent contractor
Comments: New York Life is the fifth largest insurance company in the U.S. Its formal telecommuting program is one of the most wide-ranging. Started by management, originally it encompassed at-home programmers as part of a pilot project. Now, telecommuting is both formal and informal, in that office workers can also telecommute. Telecommuters must have worked in-house for New York Life and be computer literate. "The technology is making this a relatively easy thing to do," says project manager Robert Dattler. "The administration and control is the tough part. We are very careful about who we would pay to work at home."

*The Olsten Corporation
Address: One Merrick Avenue
Westbury, NY 11590
Telephone: (516) 832-8200
Number of Telecommuters: 160
Positions: "On-call coordinator"
Telecommuter Status: Salaried employee (full-time employees only)
Comments: Olsten provides home health care services to people recovering from hospital procedures who need further medical care. The company also provides nurses to hospitals that are short-staffed. Olsten must be available to its customers twenty-four hours per day. To meet that requirement, its "on-call coordinators" answer calls from doctors who need nurses or from health care professionals looking for work or guidance in deciding the care a patient needs. The on-call coordinators who work from home handle the odd shifts (after five on weekdays, and weekends). People with the same job also work in-house for the company and take calls that come in during

regular business hours. Training, which takes place at the local Olsten office, is an important part of this job.

This is not a computer-based position—the only equipment required is a telephone. Olsten says it will always have on-call coordinators working from home, since most states insist that companies
like Olsten have employees on call.

Orange County *Register*
Address: 625 North Grand Avenue
           Santa Ana, CA 92701
Telephone: (714) 835-1234
Number of Telecommuters: 10–20
Positions: Entertainment reporter
Telecommuter Status: Salaried employee
Comments: While several categories of reporters telecommute here
(among them parents with sick children), as a group it's the entertainment reporters who do so regularly. The entertainment industry
is a source of a lot of news for this Santa Ana-based newspaper (located about sixty miles from Los Angeles). Reporters who drive to LA
to cover entertainment stories, however, can face rush-hour commutes of up to two and a half hours, making telecommuting a near
necessity for stories to be filed on time.

Reporters arrange to telecommute with their immediate editors.
No one telecommutes full time here: There's "always a feeling you
have to put in a personal appearance," is how one reporter put it.

Ortho Pharmaceutical Corporation
Address: US Route 202
           P.O. Box 300
           Raritan, NJ 08869
Telephone: (201) 218-6000
Number of Telecommuters: 5
Positions: Statistician; programmer; data processing personnel
Telecommuter Status: Salaried employee
Comments: Telecommuting will soon greatly expand here. From
1987 to 1988 Ortho ran a pilot telecommuting program. The pilot
was tremendously successful, with all of the telecommuters and their
supervisors reporting increased productivity. Since then, employees
have telecommuted on a more informal basis.

Ortho expects to enact a formal telecommuting policy to give its employees the option of telecommuting "in appropriate circumstances." This bodes well for telecommuting, since Ortho is part of *Fortune* 500 giant Johnson & Johnson.

Pacific Bell Telephone Company
Address: 140 New Montgomery Street
  San Francisco, CA 94105
Telephone: (415) 542-9000
Number of Telecommuters: 1500
Positions: Engineer; manager; programmer; analyst; forecaster;
  marketing planner
Telecommuter Status: Salaried employee
Comments: Pacific Bell's name is synonymous with telecommuting. PacBell is the largest of the Bell operating companies; it handles residential and business telephone traffic for all of Southern California and its outlying areas. PacBell first explored telecommuting in 1984, when the Olympic Organizing Committee asked local business to help redistribute traffic. In May 1985 it launched a formal telecommuting pilot program that began with seventy-five work-at-home telecommuters and twenty-two working from satellite offices. From the start, PacBell wanted to prove any job could be done from home.

Until recently, PacBell considered telecommuting experimental. The program has since grown into one of the largest of its kind. Now, at the discretion of the supervisor, any manager can telecommute. PacBell's work-at-homers are spread throughout California. And it still has satellite offices, located in San Francisco and Woodland Hills.

PacBell has carefully monitored and evaluated its program. Its survey of participants found a whopping 96 percent were satisfied with telecommuting. With each change in management, the program's status is jeopardized, yet it always continues. "We can't afford not to continue doing it," says PacBell manager Carol Nolan, herself a former telecommuter. Pacific Bell has packaged its telecommuting program and may sell the set of procedures to other companies.

*PC Week
Address: 800 Boylston Street
  Boston, MA 02199
Telephone: (617) 375-4000
Number of Telecommuters: 7

Positions: Senior technical analyst; product analyst; executive editor

Telecommuter Status: Salaried employee

Comments: Telecommuting allows this weekly computer newspaper to draw from the best technical talent available. Most of its telecommuters review computer software and hardware, an area that it's now stressing. While no reporters work from home, the executive editor does. Telecommuters are based in San Francisco, Los Angeles, and Denver.

What's unique about telecommuting here is that almost everyone who telecommutes never worked in the company's offices. Most were hired the way technical analyst Dale Lewallen was: Dale didn't find out until the interview that his new job was home-based.

PDN Software Services
Address: P.O. Box 42538
　　　　　Cincinnati, OH 45242
Telephone: (513) 831-6799
Number of Telecommuters: 1+
Positions: Reviewer
Telecommuter Status: Independent contractor

Comments: This is a small publishing company that produces a newsletter called *PDN Software Newsletter.* The publication reviews software programs that are distributed as shareware (freely distributed, requiring a small fee only if the program is regularly used). The company now has five reviewers working for it on a freelance basis and another who formally telecommutes.

Telecommuting is new to PDN. It is now wrestling with some of the same problems that plague larger companies with telecommuters. For example, it is trying to work out an equitable compensation method. PDN says it plans to increase its use of telecommuters "on an experimental basis."

*Personal Computer Support Group (PCSG), Inc.
Address: 4540 Beltway Drive
　　　　　Dallas, TX 75244
Telephone: (214) 404-4030
Number of Telecommuters: 5
Positions: Director; engineer; programmer
Telecommuter Status: "Individually negotiated"

Comments: PCSG develops hardware and software products for IBM microcomputers. The owners work from home almost exclusively. The company also has a programmer working out of Pennsylvania, a hardware engineer based in California, and a part-time programmer who is a student at Berkeley. Other programmers will work from home occasionally.

Equipment allowances and benefits are individually negotiated with each telecommuter. All staff members use the company's electronic bulletin board to pass messages and computer files to each other.

PCSG says it will always have telecommuters. "Programming is a solitary occupation," says company spokesman Phil Mayes. "There are days when all you need is a machine." Mayes says PCSG would accept applications from outsiders who wanted to work from home, particularly for programming or engineering jobs.

PHH Homequity
Address: 249 Danbury Road
      Wilton, CT 06897
Telephone: (203) 834-8500
Number of Telecommuters: 2
Positions: "Can be any employee"
Telecommuter Status: Salaried employee
Comments: PHH Homequity is a relocation company that helps corporations set up transferred employees and their families in their new locations. Telecommuters here are people who are recovering from illnesses or who for some other reason cannot come to work.

Phillips Publishing, Inc.
Address: 7811 Montrose Road
      Potomac, MD 20854
Telephone: (301) 340-2100
Number of Telecommuters: 5–10
Positions: Editors; freelance writers
Telecommuter Status: Both independent contractors and salaried
      employees
Comments: Phillips Publishing publishes twenty-five separate newsletters on high-technology topics. Telecommuters work on the staffs of *Telephone News, Fiber Optic News,* and *Mutual Fund Investing.*

Phillips offers telecommuting as a perk. It's usually initiated from the bottom up, with the editor or writer asking permission to work from home. Everything is kept flexible. Some telecommuters work at home full time, others only part time. Telecommuters often use both personal computers and fax machines, and may either use their own equipment or the company's. Phillips would like to expand its use of telecommuters. "That way we can keep good people happy," said a company spokeswoman.

Prime Computer, Inc.
Address: Prime Park
    Natick, MA 01760
Telephone: (508) 655-8000
Number of Telecommuters: 100
Positions: Secretary; manager; customer service representative
Telecommuter Status: Salaried employee
Comments: An informal telecommuting program involving about 100 people, spanning several types of jobs across several departments from marketing to corporate communications to manufacturing.

Telecommuting at Prime has to be justified. Would-be telecommuters fill out a "device request" to get a terminal for home use. Once approved, they can use it as needed. Examples where telecommuting has been arranged for include women on maternity leave and managers working on performance reviews.

Among Prime's most frequent telecommuters are its customer service representatives, whom a company spokesman called "modern day minutemen of high tech." By telecommuting, these employees can analyze problems from their homes whenever they occur. This spares them 4:00 A.M. drives into the office. Another telecommuter works just on the company telephone directory. With 12,000 employees at Prime, it's easy to see why this task comprises someone's whole job!

Psychological Services, Inc.
Address: 100 N. Broadway, Suite 1100
    Glendale, CA 91210
Telephone: (818) 244-0033
Number of Telecommuters: 3
Positions: Senior consultant; senior analyst; director of consulting
    services
Telecommuter Status: Salaried employee

Comments: Psychological Services is a consulting firm specializing in testing and evaluation, mostly for large companies. The company's move from downtown Los Angeles to the San Fernando Valley triggered its telecommuting program.

Cheryl Mahaffey, Psychological Services, Inc.'s Director of Consulting Services, had wanted to telecommute ever since her children were born. Her reasoning: A consultant's job here rarely requires being in the office. The company's move to Glendale gave Mahaffey and another consultant the chance to try telecommuting. They set up offices at home, complete with separate phone lines and computers with modems.

Right now, telecommuting is an option reserved for senior people—those holding mid- to upper-level positions.

The RAND Corporation
Address: 1700 Main Street
    P.O. Box 2138
Santa Monica, CA 90406
Telephone: (213) 451-6913
Number of Telecommuters: See comments
Positions: See comments
Telecommuter Status: Salaried employee
Comments: Trivial Pursuit question: What do the initials RAND stand for? RAND (an acronym for Research and Development) is the original think tank. It was established in 1946 to look into the future of air power for the U.S. Air Force (Project RAND). The private, nonprofit institution now employs more than 1000 people.

Nowadays, RAND researches many different areas: criminal justice, demographics, foreign aid, and conflict resolution. It is also a perfect example of a company with an informal attitude toward telecommuting. "We deal in information," says public information director Amanda Gaylor. The company's researchers (42 percent have Ph.D.'s; 32 percent have master's degrees) have a great deal of individual freedom, and working at home is a part of that. "This is a very free environment," says Gaylor.

*Remote Control
Address: 514 Via de la Valle, Suite 306
    Solana Beach, CA 92075
Telephone: (619) 481-8577

Number of Telecommuters: 50
Positions: Telemarketer
Telecommuter Status: Independent contractor
Comments: "Telemarketing is the number-one job in the world that's overlooked and underutilized," says Michael McCafferty, Remote Control's president. The company produces a software product called Telemagic, which helps salespeople keep track of their prospects. Besides being a fan of telemarketing, McCafferty is also big on working from home, since that's where he wrote the original Telemagic program.

Telemarketers sell the company's product and must have sales experience and previous microcomputer experience. Remote Control accepts outside applicants for these positions. McCafferty's advice to prospective telecommuters: "Try it, it's great!"

Rockwell International
Address: 4311 Jamboree Road
        Newport Beach, CA 92658
Telephone: (714) 833-4600
Number of Telecommuters: Unavailable
Positions: Manager
Telecommuter Status: Salaried employee
Comments: Rockwell has equipped managers in its sales, marketing, and engineering departments with personal computers and modems, so they occasionally can work from home. Managers in marketing and sales requested this originally to promote better communication with other Rockwell offices worldwide.

Sears, Roebuck & Co.
Address: Sears Tower
        Chicago, IL 60684
Telephone: (312) 875-2500
Number of Telecommuters: Unavailable
Positions: Systems analyst; personnel manager; vice president
Telecommuter Status: Salaried employee
Comments: Like so many other large companies, Sears has no official policy permitting working from home, yet it's done informally. Systems analysts, who develop computer systems for the company, have microcomputers and modems at home. Others work at home to tap into Sears' computer resources or concentrate on special projects.

Sears also has some employees who work part time and others who job-share.

Finally, a former Sears executive is overseeing a program called Over the Rainbow. This will provide for a thirty-six-apartment facility for disabled individuals. The apartments will be built with working at home in mind. The complex is scheduled to be ready by September 1991.

The Seattle *Times*
Address: Fairview Avenue North and John Street
    P.O. Box 70
    Seattle, WA 98111
Telephone: (206) 464-2360
Number of Telecommuters: See comments
Positions: Reporter; editor; technical services personnel
Telecommuter Status: Salaried employee
Comments: "The *Seattle Times'* official policy neither encourages nor discourages home/work," says telecommuting reporter Paul Andrews, "but the company has been quite accommodating in helping employees who want to transmit stories." Paul Andrews, for example, has telecommuted five years, and now works from home ten to fifteen hours per week.

While Andrews suspects that telecommuting will expand at the Seattle *Times,* he knows of no agenda: "It depends largely on how much interest employees have in expanding work-at-home options." Ahhh, if only employees generally had that much power to call the telecommuting shots!

South Coast Air Quality Management District (SCAQMD)
Address: 9150 Flair Drive
    El Monte, CA 91731
Telephone: (213) 572-6200
Number of Telecommuters: 15–30
Positions: Public information specialist; air quality specialist; other
Telecommuter Status: Salaried employee
Comments: This is a pilot program scheduled to run from July 1989 through July 1990. Telecommuters receive a transportation subsidy, which the company gives employees who get into work without using their cars (typically it's employees who carpool or bicycle to work who get the subsidy).

This is a modest entree into telecommuting. Telecommuters work from home either one day a week or one day every two weeks. Yet this may still represent as much as 25 percent of their time, since many employees were already on a compressed work week of four ten-hour days.

Telecommuting is defined loosely. Some employees use computers; others do not. Those who already have personal computers can use their own equipment if they choose; SCAQMD also provides equipment by a lending-library approach. Employees spanning all divisions take part in the pilot.

Like other pilots, there is a lot of paperwork involved, all aimed at determining the pilot's effectiveness. Telecommuters fill out monthly reports detailing their expenses and the money saved by eliminating trips to the office.

The agency is the force behind Regulation XV, a law designed to improve Southern California's air quality. Specifically, the law says that companies with 100 employees or more must submit a trip-reduction plan to cut down on car trips in to work. Part of the plan calls for companies to appoint a transportation coordinator responsible for implementing the plan. Companies that neglect to submit plans face fines and their executives could receive jail terms.

The fifteen to thirty telecommuting participants were chosen from an initial list of 600 employees who asked to participate in the pilot. How SCAQMD went about paring the list is interesting. It shows what the competition for telecommuting jobs can be like, and what some employees must go through to become telecommuters. To narrow its list, SCAQMD had the would-be telecommuters fill out a screening survey, detailing their work habits and personality traits. Their supervisors also had to fill out surveys. Following that, if the employee still seemed a good candidate, the materials went to a division director and finally to that person's boss. These executives, along with someone from the company's personnel office, formed a Telecommuting Advisory Council (TAC), which had the final word on who would participate. The TAC used a weighed set of criteria to further pinpoint the employee's eligibility for the pilot. It considered seven factors, assigning points to each. These included costs, commute length, number of days per week requested to telecommute, data security risks, whether or not children are at home, whether or not a spouse or other adult is home during the day, and whether or not a home office is available.

Southern California Association of Governments
Address: 600 S. Commonwealth Ave., Suite 1000
          Los Angeles, CA 90005
Telephone: (213) 739-6789
Number of Telecommuters: 15
Positions: Planner; accountant; department director
Telecommuter Status: Salaried employee
Comments: SCAG began its pilot telecommuting program in 1986 to gain experience with telecommuting that it could pass on to companies and government agencies in the state. Because of the high concentration of information workers at the agency it seemed a logical choice for the pilot program. The program, a ringing success, achieved the following benefits for the participants and the agency:

- Higher productivity (employees worked at peak times)
- Less sick time (due to less stress and more flexibility)
- Employees better able to handle needs (greater flexibility in their schedules)
- Cost savings (due mostly to less commuting)

Telecommuters get extensive training, including an orientation. The supervisor's support is considered crucial to the effort. SCAG plans to expand its program, so it can ultimately reduce trips to and from the office by 20 percent.

State of California Franchise Tax Board
Address: P.O. Box 550
          Sacramento, CA 95812
Telephone: (916) 369-4966
Number of Telecommuters: 13
Positions: Programmer analyst; administrative assistant; lawyer; legal assistant; procurement analyst; PC coordinator; budget analyst; accounting analyst; legislative clerk
Telecommuter Status: Salaried employee
Comments: Given its relatively small size, this telecommuting program wins *The Telecommuter's Handbook* award for including the greatest variety of positions! Telecommuters must be experienced in their positions to take part in the program. The Franchise Tax Board, one of several state agencies participating in the State of California's pilot telecommuting project, plans to eventually expand into satellite offices.

*TechProse

Address: 370 Central Park West, Suite 210
New York, NY 10025
Telephone: (212) 222-1713
Number of Telecommuters: 7+
Positions: President; market researcher; programmer; desktop publisher; secretary
Telecommuter Status: Independent contractor
Comments: One of the most interesting companies featured, and possibly the only one of its kind (but probably not for long), TechProse does electronic marketing for companies. It finds new audiences for products and services using electronic mail and fax. For example, TechProse will run electronic campaigns. A staff member will shoot out a message on an electronic bulletin board, inviting people to place an order for a product by dialing an 800 number with their modem. The TechProse employee captures all the replies, then feeds them to the client. The advantage from the clients' viewpoint is that all the leads are prequalified—it knows that the respondees have modems and know how to use them.

TechProse may also start a fax service whereby it will regularly tap databases of interest to a client and fax it the results. The company's clients include CitiBank, *Business Week,* and *MacWORLD.*

Secretaries and market researchers pick up the company's electronic mail, send mail, prepare reports, and handle other basic telecommunications jobs. TechProse also has a lawyer associated with the company who works with operators of electronic bulletin boards. Programmers write programs for the company and then park them on the company's electronic bulletin board. "As long as my people do their work I don't care where they do it from," says president Sarah Stambler.

*Thyng Associates, Inc.

Address: P.O. Box 5055-398 Essex Street
Beverly Farms, MA 01915
Telephone: (508) 921-0612
Number of Telecommuters: 6–7
Positions: See comments
Telecommuter Status: Limited benefits (see comments)
Comments: A financial services company that counsels banks, insurance companies, real estate investment trusts, pension trusts, real es-

tate owners/developers, and architects/engineers. Thyng Associates also does real estate development and construction and property management.

All of the company's technical people regularly telecommute—working from home, planes, and airports. (The company does not use titles; all of its telecommuters inspect real estate projects—land, construction sites, renovations, and completed buildings.) Telecommuters are retained as subcontractors who pay all their own taxes. The company covers group medical and dental insurance and has previously furnished limited partnerships gratis. Telecommuters' salaries, according to company spokesman Scott Thyng, are generally two to four times those of in-house people.

Thyng Associates accepts written requests from telecommuters who are interested in employment.

Time Inc.
Address: 1271 Avenue of the Americas
         New York, NY 10020
Telephone: (212) 586-1212
Number of Telecommuters: See comments
Positions: Editor; writer
Telecommuter Status: Salaried employee
Comments: It's no wonder this prestigious newsweekly has telecommuters. All editors and writers receive computers for home use. "They give you a computer like they give you a pencil," says senior science correspondent Dick Thompson. *Time* writers and editors get "playbacks" of their stories each Friday afternoon to review. These typically include queries that they must respond to from editors or others at the magazine. The playbacks are uploaded on the company's electronic mail system. Most of its writers review their playbacks from home to keep from having to stay late in the office. *Time* also has stringers who telecommute.

Travelers Corporation
Address: One Tower Square
         Hartford, CT 06183
Telephone: (203) 277-0111
Number of Telecommuters: 50+
Positions: Programmer; programmer/analyst; senior analyst; manager; officer

Telecommuter Status: Salaried employee

Comments: Travelers initiated a pilot telecommuting program to test the waters. It's worked out so well that the company is now ready to dive right in.

A wide variety of Travelers employees now participate. With the exception of managers, they telecommute four and a half days a week, showing up at the office to pick up assignments and touch base with their supervisors. They work banker's hours—nine to three—finishing their day's work during off hours when computer response time is faster.

Telecommuters must have been with the company one year, be solid performers, have a good attendance record, have a job that's appropriate for telecommuting, and attend telecommuting training. Travelers has also set up telecommuter support groups that meet regularly.

Travelers plans to expand the program into more job groups and increase the number of telecommuters in the company.

*UMI/Data Courier

Address: 620 S. Third St.
             Louisville, KY 40202

Telephone: (800) 626-2823

Number of Telecommuters: 20–30

Positions: Abstracter; vice president

Telecommuter Status: Independent contractor

Comments: Abstracters work from home part time and are considered independent contractors. Also, UMI/Data Courier's vice president, who has a complete computer set-up at home, occasionally stays home when drafting speeches. Abstracters must live close enough to the company to pick up publications once a week. UMI/Data Courier provides IBM XT computers.

Very little training is required for this position, and the company does accept outside applicants. UMI/Data Courier has used telecommuters since 1976.

*United Press International (UPI)

Address: 1400 Eye Street, NW
             Washington, DC 20005

Telephone: (202) 898-8000

Number of Telecommuters: Unavailable

Positions: Correspondent; sales representative; radio anchor

Telecommuter Status: Salaried employee

Comments: Many of UPI's news bureaus are one- and two-person operations, located in small towns across the United States and in foreign cities. UPI allows these correspondents to work out of their homes. Also, UPI has several sales representatives who work from their homes, selling UPI's services to television and radio stations and newspapers. Finally, UPI created a radio mini-station in the home of one of its key radio announcers who was laid up following hip-replacement surgery.

*University Graphics, Inc.

Address: 11 West Lincoln Avenue

Atlantic Highlands, NJ 07716

Telephone: (201) 872-0800

Number of Telecommuters: 60

Positions: Data-entry clerk; graphic artist; proofreader

Telecommuter Status: Independent contractor

Comments: University Graphics does contract work for publishers, producing typeset pages from manuscript. Half its telecommuters are "on computers" and do entry work. The other half are proofreaders or page-layout specialists. The telecommuters are considered piece workers and work from twenty to forty hours per week.

University Graphics accepts outside applications for telecommuting jobs but prefers to hire people who live within commuting distance. Telecommuters must come into the office twice per week to drop off and pick up work. University Graphics plans to use more "cottage keyers," a type of worker it has now used for fifteen years.

University of Wisconsin, Center for Health Sciences

Address: 600 Highland Avenue

Madison, WI 53792

Telephone: (608) 263-6500

Number of Telecommuters: 6

Positions: Medical transcriptionist

Telecommuter Status: Salaried employee

Comments: This is an unusual program in that the telecommuters are union members (AFSME). Beginning as a pilot project in the early 1980s, the program is now formalized.

The program began in response to several problems at the center.

First, the center had trouble keeping its group of medical transcriptionists fully staffed. (The jobs are intense, with quotas.) It had tried contracting with workers outside the Madison area, but this made turnaround time too long. Also, the center had run out of office space. (These are the kinds of problems, incidentally, more and more businesses will face.)

In view of these problems, it created a unique telecommuting program—one that AFSME, the union that previously represented the transcriptionists, fully sanctioned. There's now a formal agreement between the employer and AFSME covering working conditions, down to the furniture the telecommuters use in their home offices.

The union meets regularly with telecommuters and their managers. It also runs a statewide electronic bulletin board for union members. "This is not your typical union," says spokesperson Alan Highman.

US West
Address: 3898 S. Teller, Room 208
          Lakewood, Colorado 80235
Telephone: (303) 978-6260
Number of Telecommuters: 300–500
Positions: Staff manager; assistant staff manager; systems analyst; programmer; records assistant
Telecommuter Status: Salaried employee
Comments: US West is one of the "Baby Bells" created when AT&T split up in 1984. Its revenues top the $8-billion level and it has more than 68,000 employees. US West also runs one of the oldest and largest of the formal telecommuting programs.

Telecommuting's success at US West owes much to the enthusiasm and drive of its sponsor, William Benham. Management originally initiated the program after formally investigating its potential. Specifically, it wanted to learn what it could gain through telecommuting. Approaching the issue strictly from a business viewpoint, US West found telecommuting made good economic sense. The program is well managed and executed and serves as a model to other companies. Prospective telecommuters and their supervisors attend training sessions together, both spending a day immersed in telecommuting. Telecommuting is presented in all its facets: everything gets spelled out. For example, US West makes it clear from the outset that it does not consider telecommuting a substitute for making other childcare arrangements. The company actively promotes its telecommuting program. It sells a videotape that describes telecommuting not only at US West but at other large employers as well (see Chapter 10).

Working Mother magazine named US West one of the nation's "50 Best Companies for Working Mothers." Actually, telecommuting is only one of the flexible work options this progressive company offers. Others include flextime, compressed work weeks; and "excused time," whereby a worker may take time off (without pay), schedule permitting. The company also offers job sharing, where two employees share the responsibilities associated with a single position. While accepting outside applicants for telecommuting jobs "has not been the pattern," Benham says, "that is not to say that we won't in the future." US West is well aware of telecommuting's power as a recruitment tool, which is one reason it sees its telecommuting program expanding.

Washington State Energy Office
Address: 809 Legion Way S.E., FA-11
       Olympia, WA 98504
Telephone: (206) 586-5000
Number of Telecommuters: Unavailable
Positions: Director; word processor; manager; engineer
Telecommuter Status: Salaried employee
Comments: The Washington State Energy Office is coordinating a telecommuting demonstration project in the Puget Sound region that it hopes will involve ten to fifteen employers and 200 to 300 telecommuters. Also, many of its own staff members telecommute to alleviate space problems and eliminate lengthy commutes (some live sixty to seventy miles away). For further information about the services the energy office offers prospective telecommuters, see its entry in Chapter 10.

Wendy's International, Inc.
Address: 4288 W. Dublin-Granville
       Dublin, OH 43017
Telephone: (614) 764-3100
Number of Telecommuters: 20–30 (varies)
Positions: "Jobs in accounting, finance, operations, marketing, and information systems"

Telecommuter Status: Salaried employee
Comments: Wendy's Bill Golden, when asked who started the program at Wendy's, writes: "I did, but employees 'drove' it." Wendy's provides laptop and portable PCs to those who either "wish to or must" do work at home. This usually takes place after hours or when someone is unable to be in the office.

Weyerhaeuser
Address: Forest Products Division
        Tacoma, WA 98477
Telephone: (206) 924-2345
Number of Telecommuters: Not available
Positions: Market researcher; program developer
Telecommuter Status: Salaried employee
Comments: Telecommuters here work for the marketing department. They work at home to research new markets, and develop new products (anything that's wood or wood-related).

Workstation Laboratories, Inc.
Address: 8111 LBJ Freeway, LB156
        Dallas, TX 75251
Telephone: (214) 644-1733
Number of Telecommuters: 2
Positions: CEO; president
Telecommuter Status: Salaried employee
Comments: Both the CEO and the president of this company telecommute from their homes, both of which are located on mountaintops! Workstation tests computers using a variety of industry standard and proprietary performance tests. President David Wilson literally has his work with him at all times: He has thirty-seven computers in his house. While the two head honchos at this hi-tech firm are its only telecommuters, other employees do "bring work home."

*Worldwide Church of God
Address: 300 West Green Street
        Pasadena, CA 91129
Telephone: (818) 304-6000
Number of Telecommuters: 5 (among regular staff); 5500 volunteer WATS workers
Positions: Computer programmer; television script writer; Span-

ish-language translator; newsstand coordinator; in-home WATS volunteer

Telecommuter Status: Both independent contractors and salaried employees

Comments: This Pasadena-based church has its own telephone program, "The World Tomorrow," which generates more than 30,000 calls per week.

Its use of telecommuters is interesting on many levels. Let's start with the jobs telecommuters hold. You have your basic computer programmer. After that, though, this church stands alone in employing a television script writer, Spanish-language translator, newsstand coordinator, and in-home WATS volunteer. The regular staff members initiated the telecommuting option themselves and usually work at home for family or health reasons. The 5500 volunteers, while not strictly telecommuters, are of great interest nonetheless. They volunteer fifteen minutes of their time one weekend day every three weeks to answer some of those 30,000 calls. Spread throughout the U.S., they save the church about $500,000 a year since they answer calls from their homes rather than from the Pasadena headquarters.

W. W. Norton & Company

Address: 500 Fifth Avenue
         New York, NY 10110
Telephone: (212) 354-5500
Number of Telecommuters: 30
Positions: Sales representative
Telecommuter Status: Salaried employee

Comments: A majority of this publishers' sales reps in its college division work from home when they are not on college campuses selling textbooks. The sales reps use an electronic bulletin board to post messages with one another and otherwise keep in touch. For example, if a professor asks a sales rep about a competitor's book that the rep does not know anything about he can post a message on the bulletin board and receive an answer within minutes.

While the reps can also use the company's voice mail system to keep in touch, they prefer the bulletin board because it allows them to get hard copies of their correspondence. The bulletin board also offers a psychological benefit: It provides human contact of a kind, which reps can sorely need when they are on the road.

7
Your Hi-Tech Home Office

Not long ago no one really thought that people who worked from home had "real" jobs like the rest of us. They didn't go to the office, so they weren't really working. It's hard to hold on to that kind of thinking these days. A look inside the hi-tech offices of programmers, writers, editors, illustrators, and other telecommuters shows how far working at home has come. Computers, modems, printers, fax machines, and telephone answering machines are now cheap enough for any office, whether it's in a glass-and-steel office building or a Main Street Cape Cod.

The difference is that at home you can make better use of these powerful tools. You've arranged to work not only when you want, but in a place where you can really produce. Gone is the boxy, depressing cubicle you had at the office. In its place, you've fashioned a comfortable work space that reflects *your* taste, not your employer's.

The Basics

In this era of so many hi-tech gadgets, anyone who works from home must soon break down equipment into two categories: must-have items and wish-list items. For telecommuters, especially the part-time telecommuter, the must-have list is small. If you regularly go to your office, you won't need to ensure that every piece of equipment you might possibly need is at home. A discussion of what your office should include, at a minimum, follows.

The Office Itself

At first you may create a make-do office—one that simply lets you get some work done as you ponder the business of setting up a more permanent work center. During this stage you may settle for the kitchen or dining-room table. Soon you'll hunger for a more permanent setup. There are drawbacks to using space that's meant for something else. In a kitchen, for example, you risk things spilling onto (and into) your equipment. Besides, the busiest room of the house is not where your office should be. You'll soon want a place mostly devoted to work so that you don't spend time tucking things away only to have to unearth them again later. Such tasks reduce your productive work time.

The Ideal. If you live alone, you can set up an office wherever you like to work. Most telecommuters have families, though, and fewer options. It's best to set up your home office in a room of its own with a door that closes. The door is both a sound barrier and a psychological barrier. Closing it behind you in the morning (or whenever you start your work day) signals that work has begun. Shutting it at night helps distance work from the rest of your life. If you have a spare room in your house, that's the obvious spot for a home office. Other options include large closets or areas carved out of a garage or basement.

In choosing a place for your home office, consider what your work day is like. If you spend a lot of time on the phone, seclusion is important. A basement or attic office may work out best, or a spare room with a door that you can close. If you expect visits from clients (for example, if you sell real estate) then you need a more spacious office with a grander entrance.

Remember, this will be a production place, so choose it on that basis, not just on the basis of convenience. One prospective telecommuter told the State of California's program manager he planned to set up an "ironing-board office," on his back porch. He reasoned that he could put his computer in a corner along with the family's washer and dryer, and use the ironing board for his work materials. To him, this was a satisfactory work setup. Before completing the training period, however, the consultant had helped him redesign and relocate his office.

If you live in an apartment, condo, or even a small house, you'll be accessible to the rest of the family when you are in your home office. You'll have to plan carefully to ensure enough privacy for work. Editor Dianne Breen's home office is in a room by itself and is therefore very private. However, "That's not always an advantage with a toddler in the house," says Dianne. "Sometimes I'd like to have my computer in the living room so I could work near her play area and keep an eye on her." (Dianne plans to buy a laptop so she can follow her around.)

The hideaway office. If you have the resources you can custom-design your office. Steve Hoge, a sales representative for W. W. Norton, planned his Williamsburg Colonial with working at home in mind. The desk, files, computer, and other gear comprising his home office are tucked into a specially designed three-foot-deep closet. The best feature is the closet's closing doors. Shutting those doors hides the clutter and transforms the office into a comfortable library that's "the meditative spot in the house," says Steve. "This would be hard to achieve if wires were staring at you." Steve also has a rolltop desk that lets him hide whatever work is on it. The design of the office means that Steve's 16-month-old son can use the room without disrupting anything. Claiming a tax deduction for a hideaway office, however, may be problematic (see the section on Home Office Tax Deductions).

Bad choices. There are a few places where, psychologically speaking, a home office does not belong. These boil down to two areas: your bedroom and your den.

If your office is in your bedroom you risk never being able to escape from your work. It's always right there just when you need to get away from it. With work that close by, it's tempting to follow through on ideas no matter what time of the night they strike. At times you'd want to act on these impulses, but doing so regularly works against you. Eventually it catches up with you, and productivity drops off. If a bedroom office is your only choice, consider getting a rolltop desk to hide your work at night.

The same goes for your den, family room, or other room where you go to relax. That pile of material acts as a reminder of something that's best left forgotten for a while.

No matter where your office is, however, one of the fascinating things any telecommuter can discover is that he's created a Shangri La, which may be great for the psyche but is poor for production. That beautiful grassy view that's always right there may do you more harm than good. One telecommuter has several windows in her office that present a splendid view of the Mississippi River. She eventually had to put up café curtains because she found it too easy to pass time away by enjoying the view.

Furniture

Desks. You'll need a desk or something that functions as a desk.

To start, even a hollow door that sits atop two two-drawer file cabinets will do. You can eventually buy a desk that's designed to accommodate a computer and keyboard, as you add that equipment. Such work stations are now widely available through department and furniture stores and computer retailers such as Radio Shack.

Chairs. While a lot of people occasionally "lie down on the job," most prefer chairs at least some of the time. Your chair is probably the most important piece of office furniture you'll buy. Invest in a quality desk chair that won't put additional strain on your body (sitting eight or more hours a day is strain enough). Home office consultant Paul Edwards says that too often people use extra dining room or kitchen chairs when setting up home offices. "People do terrible things to themselves using chairs that are uncomfortable and that don't give proper support to their spines," he says. This is especially important for telecommuters, since as information workers they spend a lot of time on the telephone or hunched over computers.

Most consultants recommend so-called ergonomic chairs. With executives spending more time in front of computers these days, ergonomic chairs have become a big business. New standards have reduced their design to a science. They specify recommended seat height (16.0 to 20.5 inches), seat depth (between 15 and 17 inches), seat width (at least 18 inches). They also call for footrests if your feet don't reach the floor.

The ultimate ergonomic chair, straight from the Jetsons, is in prototype. Before sitting down, you feed the chair relevant facts about your body type. These facts are embedded on a credit card-size piece of plastic that you insert into the chair's computer. Once programmed, the chair's cushions arrange themselves appropriately. You may never want to get up from such a contraption.

Many people buy ergonomic chairs for their home offices because these are what they may have had at work. But these chairs are so comfortable they encourage you to sit longer. This is just what you don't want. The longer you sit the more you risk backaches, according to furniture designer Nathan Edelson of Montana's Environments for Health. As descendants of hunters and gatherers, humans have to move around a lot to keep their joints lubricated and spry.

"Telecommuting," says Nathan, "is a chance to change not only where you work but how you work." His premise is that telecommuters are too uptight—not loose enough. "What's the point of doing it if you are just going to duplicate it?" Nathan notes that people have only recently sat while working. Shakespeare, for example, supposedly wrote all of his plays standing up. Computers only encourage us to sit more because they do so many things. Need to type something? Use your microcomputer. Have filing to do? Forget the file cabinet, your PC does that as well. The list continues. From your microcomputer you can fax something, do bookkeeping chores, and fire off mail. Never before have office workers had it so easy.

In response Nathan's company, Environments for Health, manufactures a work station that lets people exercise while they work. Basically, it's a treadmill complete with built-in pedestal support for a computer and telephone. The treadmill requires you to walk at a 1-to 2-mph clip. You type or talk on the phone as you walk. The $10,000 price tag keeps Nathan's desk out of reach, but the idea behind it is sound. Walking brings more oxygen to the brain, which makes for clearer thinking.

What to do then? The best solution is to go with an ergonomic chair but to keep Nathan's points about sitting too long in mind. Try to do as the experts counsel, and break for a five-minute stretch every hour or so. If you do find yourself working for longer periods, try some exercises at your desk to reduce strain. Edelson recommends shifting weight from leg to leg, bending and straightening knees, and periodically swaying back and forth.

Before you buy anything, ask your company for the furniture you need. Ergonomic chairs, which can cost $500, are an expense you can do without. Most companies have spare furniture.

File cabinets. We're still far from paperless offices. So, you'll need a file cabinet to keep paper out of sight and in some kind of order. Four-drawer file cabinets are expensive (your employer may be able to help out here—if not, buy a used one). With a paint job and some lubricant (to ensure smooth-working drawers) you'll never know the difference.

Telephones

You probably have one of these already. There are more telephones in the U.S. than there are people. A bit of advice: stick to AT&T phones or phones made by one of the Baby Bells (such as Northwestern Bell). There's a lot of junk out there. Also, an office telephone should have a hold button in case you get diverted during a business call. Many telephones now come with this feature, plus one-button redial and the capability to store ten or more often-dialed numbers.

You should also have a telephone answering machine. These are so cheap now there is no reason you should do without one. An answering machine ensures you can work uninterrupted if you need to, which is probably one of the reasons you decided to work from home in the first place.

Lighting

Lighting is something else you can control more at home than at your employer's office. Daylight is the best light source, but it's unlikely that you'll be able to rely on daylight alone. Full-spectrum fluorescent bulbs have many of daylight's properties. The problem is that all fluorescent lights give off a low-level hum that grates on your nerves even if it's not that noticeable. For that reason, home office expert Paul Edwards recommends incandescent bulbs. At any rate, to reduce eyestrain invest in a quality lamp that throws a lot of light on your desk space.

Glare. Many offices now include a new source of light—the computer monitor. There is no need to direct additional light at your monitor. That extra light makes it harder to read what's on your screen since it reduces needed contrast.

Lighting that's too bright creates glare. Glare, in turn, leads to eyestrain, dizziness, and blurred vision. Do what you can to reduce glare by directing light at your work surface rather than at your keyboard. But if glare is a recurring nuisance, it may pay to buy a glare screen, available either as a mesh screen or glass shield. In addition, make a conscious effort to blink every few seconds to lubricate your eyes. This is something that you might otherwise neglect to do as you sit transfixed before your screen.

Computers

Certainly not all telecommuters need computers to do their jobs. But few telecommuters could not benefit from having one, which is why they are in the must-have category. Few people know how telephones work, yet just about anybody can use one. The same thing goes for a microcomputer. Yet a basic knowledge of computers helps, because most people eventually expand their computers or have some minor problems with them.

A microcomputer system consists of hardware and software. The hardware is the machinery itself. The software is the set of instructions that directs the machinery.

Hardware: Inside the computer.

- *The Microprocessor.* This is the brains of the computer. Usually made by Intel or Motorola, this chip is so important to how computers function that some machines are identified solely by the type of processor they include. At present, for example, Intel's (the processor found in IBM machines and compatibles) 80386 processor is the fastest generally available. The 80486 only recently entered the market.
- *System Memory.* Just as humans have two types of memory, long-term and short-term, so do computers. Long-term memory in a computer is called ROM, for Read Only Memory. This contains the information your computer needs to check its own operation and perform basic tasks. The user cannot alter it. Short-term memory is called Random Access Memory, or RAM. This determines the size of the palette (or work space) you have to work with. The standard has become 640K (640,000 characters), although you can still get away with 512K for most applications. Unlike ROM, RAM can be manipulated.
- *Expansion Slots.* Many computers (especially IBM PCs and their clones) include the means for expanding the machine's capabilities via plug-in boards. These fit into empty expansion slots inside the computer itself. There are several types of board:

    —RAM expansion boards for boosting system
      memory.
    —Display adapter cards, to change from mono-
      chrome to color display.
    —Interface adapter cards for connecting external
      peripherals (add-on devices) such as printers or
      modems.
    —Modem cards (also known as internal modems)
      Like any othermodem, theselet you send andre-
      ceive data overphone lines.

- *Disk Drives.* Disk drives write and read information to and from the floppy disks (or diskettes) that store data. Computers have one or two disk drives.
- *Hard Disk Drives.* These store large amounts of data, such as

20 million bytes (20MB) or 40 million bytes (40MB). They offer the following advantages over diskette drives:

—The operating system (e.g., MS-DOS) does not have to be loaded separately, meaning you can get down to work faster.

—You don't have to play musical diskettes. Many word processors, for example, come on several diskettes. Loading the program may involve manually putting four or five disks into the disk drive as you need the data they contain. A spelling checker or thesaurus, for example, often comes on a disk of its own. And to store any documents you create you'd want to use another disk. With a hard disk, the entire program stands ready for use at your whim.

—Easier organization of your work. A hard disk makes organizing your information easier. Creating directories and multiple subdirectories is much simpler than it is with diskette-based systems.

—Hard disks have their disadvantages, too. They eventually "crash," which renders your precious data inaccessible. (This is why you must back up anything that resides on a hard disk.) Because they give you so much memory to play with it's also possible to send a file to your hard disk and have trouble subsequently finding it. Naming files carefully and using subdirectories helps locate them easily. So do software programs such as Gofer and MemoryMate, which let you search your hard drive by key word to find errant files.

Hardware: Peripherals. Peripherals are add-on devices that allow computers to interact by displaying, printing, or communicating information.

- *Monitors.* Monitors allow your computer to show you the work you are doing. Monochrome monitors are preferable to color monitors for word processing or database-management tasks. But if you'll be doing any graphics applications (for example, creating slides for presentations) you should probably get a color monitor.

- *Printers.* Printers allow you to create a paper copy of what's on your monitor. For a long time there were only two types of printers from which to choose: daisy wheel and dot matrix. These two choices have been joined by a third, the laser printer.

  Dot matrix printers form letters and numbers using small dots and cost the least. Those junk mail letters we all get that have a computer look to them display the quality of some dot matrix printers. Some dot matrix printers, however, have a letter-quality mode, and almost all print faster than daisy wheel printers.

  Daisy wheel printers, so named because their printer wheels are shaped like daisies, type slower but the result is better. They offer the same-quality type as a fine typewriter. You can also change type styles by replacing the wheel.

  Laser printers offer both speed and quality. They also cost a lot more than either dot matrix or daisy wheel printers.

  If you can afford it, the choice is clear: Go with a laser printer. But most telecommuters will find that a dot matrix printer with a letter-quality mode does just fine. The leading names here are Epson and Okidata. The new 24-pin models print closer to letter quality than do the 9-pin models. Finally, if you type out a lot of files and work at night, choose a quiet printer out of consideration for your family members—especially if your office is close to sleeping quarters.

- *Modems.* Modems allow you to send information over the telephone lines. People who use them to go on-line and communicate with others soon find them indispensible. The first thing to ensure is that any modem you buy is Hayes-compatible. That's the standard. The only question remaining, then, is whether you should buy an external modem, which sits alongside your computer, or an internal one, which fits in an expansion slot.

  External modems win this one hands down. Here's why:

  —You can use an external modem with any machine. Internal modems tend to be machine-specific.

—Internal modems add heat to the computer,
which may affect memory chips.
—Internal modems take up an expansion slot.
—External modems include lights so you can check
the status of your on-line session.
—If there is a problem with an external modem
you just pack it up and send it off. You don't
have to rip apart your machine to get to it.

The best argument in favor of internal modems is that they
don't take up any room in your work area. If space is tight,
that's an advantage worth considering. But you can place a
telephone on top of most modems. And, while external modems add some extra wires and plugs to your work space,
you'll have a lot of those to deal with anyway. What's a couple
more?

Hayes external modems are the safest choice, but they are
expensive. Good modems are now available from many repu-
table manufacturers, so there is no reason any more to go with
Hayes, if you shop carefully. On-line maven Alfred Glossbrenner says Avatex modems, sold by a company called Megatron-
ics, Inc. (Logan, UT) "do a fantastic job." These Hayes-compatible modems also received *Computer Shopper's* Best Buy
designation for three years running.

A 1200-bps Avatex external modem costs $70; the 2400-bps
model costs $150 (*bps* stands for bits per second and is a mea-
sure of how fast the modem transmits and receives data).

Software. There is a tremendous amount of software available,
especially for IBM and IBM-clone computers. But there are only a
few types of software packages that telecommuters really need right
off.

- *Word Processing.* The most important software application
for telecommuters is probably word processing. Most people
do at least some writing in the course of their jobs. An easy-to-
use and inexpensive word processor is PFS Professional
Write, from Software Publishing, Inc. Another is Sprint, from
Borland International. Sprint is fast (hence the name), having beaten out such major-league word processors as Word-

Perfect, WordStar, and Microsoft Word in speed tests. It also has a handy auto-save feature, which means you can never lose more than a few seconds' worth of work. It also accepts commands used by other word processors. So if you are already accustomed to using, say, WordPerfect, you can use Sprint to call up a WordPerfect file and edit it using WordPerfect commands.

In the high-end area, *Software Digest* recently judged Microsoft Word the top microcomputer-based word processor. It compared the program against "advanced word processors" on such criteria as ease of use, performance, error handling, and versatility. Microsoft Word includes such features as page preview and graphic display that are unavailable with lower-priced and shareware word processors. But its learning curve is longer. It also sells for $450 (retail), as compared to a price tag of under $200 for the packages mentioned earlier.

- *Communications.* A communications package controls your modem's operation. In the IBM world, the favorite of many users is Procomm+. Procomm earns high marks in three key areas: power, ease of use, and value. Power, because it does everything you need it to do: It can automate going on-line so you don't have to key in passwords every time you want to access an on-line service. It also has a mode that lets others call in and transmit files or other data even if your computer is unattended. Ease of use, because of the short learning curve. You can be up and running with it inside an hour. Value, because it's available through mail-order houses for under $50 ($89 from the manufacturer). A try-before-you-buy version, called the Procomm Plus Test Drive, is available through CompuServe and GEnie and many local bulletin boards and user groups.

  Apple Macintosh users have their own excellent telecommunications software packages to choose from. These include Red Ryder ($80 from a company called Freesoft), Microphone II ($295 from Software Ventures Corp.), and Smartcom II ($149 from Hayes). Of the three, the publication *MacUser* rates Smartcom II the highest.

  Once you've outfitted your computer with a modem and a communications software program you have all the equipment you need to "go on-line." This means not only that you can communicate with co-workers at your employer's office but that you can also do research or even network with other professionals, all from the comfort of your home. Freelance writer Tom Johnson says that going on-line has proved immensely valuable to him as a journalist: "I can go into DIALOG or VU/TEXT and pull down a bibliography in fifteen minutes that will give me 85 to 90 percent of the references I'll need. And many times I can now retrieve the full text of an article."

The ability to gather information on-line gives you an edge no matter what your field. Lawyers, for instance, have many resources available to them on-line, including court citations going back 200 years and case law from all fifty states. The technology is still expensive, but when used judiciously it saves time and can give you an edge over competitors. Telecommuting lawyer Fred Wilf says that, like many lawyers, he does his own research. ("Most lawyers do not wear $800 suits and drive $100,000 cars as may be seen on *LA Law*," says Fred, "and they don't have the money to pay paralegals and law clerks.")

Fred cites the following example of a time when on-line research gave him an edge: "In January 1988 my firm was called in to represent a client who had been sued on a trademark question in the federal court in Philadelphia. While the principal of the firm, Gerry Elman, conducted on-line research into the industry in question, I conducted on-line research and managed to get the registration information on the trademarks at issue. Within hours we knew more about certain aspects of the case than the larger law firms representing the other side, and at a lower cost."

Using an on-line service's electronic mail feature also eliminates telephone tag. You simply send a message (or letter or report) to someone's electronic mailbox. The next time your correspondent logs on, the system tells him there's a message waiting. However, with rare exceptions, both people must subscribe to the same on-line service.

Writer Tom Johnson recently used electronic mail to collaborate on a writing assignment: "An editor at the *New York Daily News* called me to say he was buying a travel piece I

had written. I left a message on GEnie (an on-line communications service) telling my photographer (based in Blooming-
ton, Indiana) that I needed the pictures he had shot to go
along with the particular story. I also gave him the editor's
name. A day later I checked on-line to see he had read my message and gotten in touch with the editor."

- *Integrated Software Packages.* These are good bargains because they include multiple applications all in one software
package. The most highly regarded integrated software package is Microsoft Works, which includes word processing,
spreadsheet, chartmaker, database manager, report genera-
tor, and communications.

- *Free Software.* One of the most humbling things about buying
a microcomputer is that you soon learn your expenses are only
starting. One telecommuter refers to hers as "the other member of the family, always outgrowing things and needing
something new." Chief among these expenses is software. But
it doesn't have to be that way. For many applications (word
processing, communications, database management) perfectly good software is available for little more than the cost of
the diskette. Tracking the software down, though, remains a
mystery to many people who buy only through retailers.

Some of this software is considered shareware or tryware—
satisfied users are asked to send in a small registration fee
(about $30) if they find the software useful. Some software is
in the public domain—and thus free.

Chapter 10 lists Alfred Glossbrenner's hand-picked recommendations of free software packages especially suited for
telecommuters.

Protecting Yourself and Your Equipment

Radiation. There's been a lot of controversy over the years as to
whether or not the radiation video display terminals (VDTs) emit is
harmful. The issue still isn't settled. It does appear, though, that
there may be a link between long exposure to VDTs and miscarriages. The most damning evidence came from a 1988 study at the
Kaiser Permanente Medical Care Program in California, which
found that women who use VDTs more than twenty hours per week
during the first trimester of pregnancy have more miscarriages than
women who do not. It's still not certain, though, whether other fac-

tors enter into this correlation, such as the stress that goes along with the VDT operator's job. In the meantime, pregnant women who use VDTs should take some precautions.

Several options are available:

- Laptops or transportables. Unlike VDTs, laptops and portables (laptops that require an AC adapter) use Liquid Crystal Display (LCD) screens, which do not pose a radiation threat.
- Radiation-free desktop monitors. These are just now entering the market. Because they are not widely available they are expensive—in the $1000 range as compared to under $200 for a typical monochrome monitor.

  Buying a quality monitor in the first place will help as well. A crisp image not only reduces eyestrain, it lessens exposure to radiation. Because radiation dissipates with distance, the closer you sit to a monitor the higher the level of radiation you'll be exposed to. With a crisp image you can move the monitor back a bit (even just a few inches can make a difference).
- Glare screens. The better ones reduce radiation as well as glare.

Static electricity. Many parts of the country have serious static electricity problems. This is not only uncomfortable for the computer user, it can harm the computer. At under $50, antistatic mats, which fit under the computer keyboard, are cheap protection against static electricity. There are also sprays you can buy that reduce static charge.

Power spikes. Surge protectors are a must for smoothing out power to your computer. They cost from $20 to $150. Buy a six-outlet model with an on-off switch and circuit-reset button. It's also a good idea not to put the computer on the same line with other energy hogs such as the air conditioner, heater, or refrigerator.

Maintenance agreements. It's a good idea for telecommuters to take out extended warranties that cover maintenance for their equipment. In a "regular" office, if a computer circuit gets fried you simply call in a technician. In the meantime, you can probably switch to another machine. It's not a big deal. In a home office, though, the problems are yours to deal with. Calling in a technician is an option but that costs a small fortune. You can send it out, but that leaves you without equipment for a week or more.

Unfortunately, you are often told about these agreements when you are already shelling out a lot of money, so you may be tempted to save the expense. But if you are buying the equipment yourself and regularly using it for work-related tasks, it seems the least your employer could do is pick up the cost of the extended warranty. After all, your uninterrupted productivity benefits your company too.

Homeowners insurance. Most homeowners policies don't adequately cover home office equipment. For a small increase in your monthly premium you can boost your liability coverage so your equipment and furnishings are insured.

Home Office Tax Deductions

Salaried employees who work from home may be able to deduct a percentage of their overall household expenses. These include real estate taxes, mortgage interest, casualty losses, rent, utilities, insurance, depreciation, and office-related costs not covered by your employer.

The amount you can deduct depends on what your home office represents as a percentage of your overall living area. For example, if your home is 1200 square feet and your office is 240 square feet, it's 20 percent of the total. That means you can deduct 20 percent of the expenses mentioned earlier. To qualify, that part of your home (or apartment, condo, or even boat, for that matter) must be used *regularly and exclusively* for business. Many telecommuters pass that test if they have separate home offices. But the IRS also says that salaried employees must work at home for the "convenience" of their employers, not just because it's "appropriate and helpful" in their jobs. That's the test that many telecommuters fail.

Basically that means that you must telecommute because you have no choice. For example, your work requires a lot of overtime and your office doors close at five. Or your employer is based in another state. Full-time telecommuters who can prove there is no space for them at the office or that the equipment and other facilities they need to do their jobs are not available at the office have the best chance of qualifying.

For further information, get publication 587 (*Business Use of Your Home*) from the IRS.

The Telecommuter's Wish List

There is a lot of pressure on people who work from home to buy every available gadget for their offices. This pressure will only increase now that well-heeled manufacturers such as Sharp and Sony are targeting this market. Whether or not you need a fax machine, for example, depends largely on whether the work you do could be enhanced by having one. The descriptions that follow should help.

But also consider convenience. You don't really need a dishwasher, for example, but if you have one you know what a timesaver it is. The same goes for office equipment. If you'll have childcare responsibilities for part of your working day, two pieces of equipment may prove useful for that reason alone: a cordless telephone and a laptop computer. Both extend mobility. Also, facsimile machines and copiers can save trips to the post office and copying center (or your employer's office).

Second Phone Lines

These are a good idea if you'll be doing a lot of on-line work, including sending and receiving facsimile messages. A less obvious advantage of having a separate business line is that it makes it easier to keep business calls (including associated charges) separate from personal calls. Business lines cost just under $100. This covers the cost of installation and the line itself. Then there's a monthly fee of about $15.

Fax Machines

Heading every telecommuter's wish list today is a fax machine. Many people, once they finally buy a fax machine, say they don't know how they'd get along without it.

Fax (short for facsimile) machines are important if your work requires you to transmit documents, drawings, or designs or if you do any work internationally. Telecommuters find they are the handiest way to get memos and other documents back and forth to their employer's office. Fax messages can be sent for the price of a phone call, so they often work out to be cheaper than overnight delivery services. For Dan Swanson, freelance illustrator/telecommuter, a fax machine was an early purchase which he says has been uniquely valuable. "On a dedicated phone line it's always available to receive work requests, sketches, proofs, etc.—unattended. My current machine, a Canon FAX-450, can also be switched to voice mode by the sound of the caller's voice."

Operating a fax machine couldn't be simpler. You put the docu-

ment in the feeder tray, dial the fax number of the person you're sending the fax to, wait for the tone, then push a button to start the
transmission.

Features. Many fax machines include built-in telephones. Some
also make copies. Other conveniences include an auto-dialer and document feeder. A feeder is especially useful because fax machines
work slowly. Without one, you have to manually feed each page of a
multipage document.

Prices. Standalone fax machines now average about $950. During
1990, the average price may drop to about $750. Right now, you can
buy a Murata 900 fax machine, a no-frills machine that performs
well, for $899 retail. Through discount sources such as 47th Street
Photo in New York, it's available for hundreds of dollars less.

Some telecommuters will prefer to use fax machines rather than
modems when transmitting information, despite the poorer readabili-
ty of fax messages. Reporters at the *Los Angeles Times* when out in
the field prefer to fax their stories into the office rather than "modem" them in, even though via modem the text could be sent right
into the text-processing system. Why? With a modem, one wrong
beep over the phone line (line noise) can change a figure of 10,000
into 10 million.

Fax line managers. Heavy telephone users will want a second
phone for business purposes, which is why they are included in the
must-have category. But there is a lot of demand for business lines
these days with telephone calls, fax transmissions, and connections to
on-line services all using the same portal. If you'll be on-line a lot or
doing much faxing, you may want to consider a fax line manager
(available for $199 from Technology Concepts Inc. of Belmont,
Calif.). This connects directly to a telephone line, intercepting all
calls, then routing them to the right device. Data calls go to the modem or fax machine—whatever is appropriate. Phone calls go to the
telephone.

If you will just be using your phone line for fax messages and telephone calls, consider buying a fax machine that includes an automatic fax/tel switch. These are now becoming standard in the low-end
machines.

Fax boards. With a fax board you can use your microcomputer to
transmit and receive facsimile messages. A fax board fits in an expansion slot and offers the convenience of sending a fax directly from
your PC. Fax boards transmit documents at a higher resolution than

stand-alone fax devices. This is a real advantage because poor legibility can cause serious mistakes where documents such as purchase orders or contracts are involved.

While stand-alone fax machines are as easy to use as copiers, fax boards are another matter. These require some training. In addition, messages intercepted by fax boards come in as graphics files. These not only eat up a lot of disk space, they must be changed to text files before you can do much with them. Finally, while expensive ones operate in a background mode, some fax boards tie up your computer when receiving fax messages. And to use one round the clock you must leave your computer on.

Fax boards can cost as much as or even more than a stand-alone model, running from $300 to $1000 and up.

Because of these drawbacks, fax boards don't sell as well as the more conventional fax machines. Perhaps they work best when used to complement a stand-alone fax machine rather than take the place of it.

Two leading vendors of fax boards are:

The Complete PC, Inc.
521 Cottonwood Drive
Milpitas, CA 95035

Intel PCEO
Mailstop CO3-07 5200 NE Elam Young Parkway
Hillsboro, OR 97124

Fax via an on-line service. If you subscribe to an on-line service such as CompuServe, MCI Mail, or Delphi you can send fax messages without a fax board or your own fax machine.

You simply type in an electronic letter as you normally would. Then, instead of giving an electronic mail address, you type in the fax number where you want the electronic letter sent. Because the message does not have to be scanned (as it would with a fax machine), there's no loss of resolution on the receiving end. Another advantage of going this route is that once you've uploaded the letter earmarked for fax delivery you are done with it. If the line is busy the on-line service will keep trying it until it gets through. Sending faxes this way may even be cheaper than using a fax machine. If most of what you have to fax is ASCII text created on your PC and you subscribe to an on-line service, there may be no reason to buy a fax board or fax machine.

Laptop Computers

In the early 1980s telecommuters, specifically journalists, eagerly latched onto laptop computers such as the Tandy TRS-100 and TRS-200 models. They loved their portability. But few others used them. The screens on these early laptops were hard to read. Like the moon, they counted on reflected light to be seen. A lack of storage options, expansion slots, and decent graphics also worked against them.

Today, laptops are as different from these early models as electronic typewriters are from the old manual models. They often have their own light source behind the screen (and thus are backlit), and include hard disks so storage is never a problem. As a result, sales of laptops are growing faster than sales of any other type of microcomputer.

These are not office machines, so it's fair to say that telecommuters are fueling this growth. "Every reporter I know who's away from the office uses this stuff constantly," says writer Tom Johnson.

For telecommuters, already freed from the nine-to-five office routine, a laptop extends that freedom even further. It lets them work not only when they want but where they want—in the home office, backyard, or at the park.

Features. Laptops are generally more expensive than desktop computers, because their components are miniaturized and they require special features that keep power needs low. They cost from about $1800 (for a Tandy Model 1400) to $12,000 (for the GRiD-Case 1535, a high-end machine for business, scientific, and engineering use).

Complete with battery, laptops weigh ten to eighteen pounds. Smaller, sleeker, and therefore more portable laptops that may only weigh one pound are coming soon. The Ultra-Lite, a $3000 model weighing in at four pounds, is already available from NEC Corporation.

There's also a whole range of laptop peripherals you can buy, including portable printers, and modems small enough to fit in your shirt pocket. The Auto-Pro, available for $98.50 from distributors of computer equipment, attaches to a car seat and lets you position a laptop four ways. It also protects the en route laptop from sudden stops.

Some laptops now come with cellular modems, giving new meaning to the term *portability*. With these laptops, you can not only work from anywhere, you can communicate from anywhere—you don't even need a phone jack.

Zenith and Toshiba are the market leaders. Other manufacturers include GRiD, Sharp, and Data General. Apple also recently introduced a Macintosh laptop.

Other Office Equipment

Copiers. Along with personal microcassette recorders, transcribers, and calculators, we now have personal copiers. Home office models are rudimentary compared to office models, but they do make copies—and when you need one you need one. About the cheapest copier now available is the Canon PC-3. These make just one copy at a time, however, and like most low-end copiers, cannot reduce or enlarge. It sells for about $500 from mail-order suppliers. Ricoh sells a hand-held copier for about $540 that weighs less than three pounds. It includes attachments that enable it to double as a fax machine or scanner.

Scanners. Scanners turn graphics and hard-copy text into a bit stream that you can feed directly into your computer. They can save a lot of keystroking. Illustrators and other artists find them indispensable, as do desktop publishers. Right now they are too expensive to place very high on the telecommuter's wish list.

Shredders. Even further down the telecommuter's wish list is a paper shredder. You may need one of these if you bring confidential documents home. The cheapest model available from mail-order giant Quill is a "personal paper shredder" that sells for $169.99 and is manufactured by a company called Boston.

Buying Equipment

Office products are available from many sources, offering a broad range of prices and support packages. Sometimes, getting the best deal on an item may require more research than a consumer usually does before making a purchase. With such a variety of shopping options, and with so many vendors selling essentially the same equipment in different cases, careful shopping is a must.

For help in evaluating microcomputers, copiers, fax machines, and other office equipment see publications such as *PC Magazine* and *Home. Office Computing,* which review office products with each issue. To pinpoint reviews when you need them, use a service called *Computer Library,* available through the CompuServe on-line service. It lets you search electronically for the issues containing the product reviews you want. You can summon to your screen the complete text of the article for only $1.50 plus connect time rates of $24 per hour.

Microcomputers: Two Choices

In the microcomputer world, there are only two names you really need to know: IBM (or IBM-compatible) and Apple.

Here's the difference. The Apple, specifically the Macintosh, uses a different microprocessor than do the IBM and its clones, Motorola's instead of Intel's. Apple computers also work on a system of icons and menus to retrieve information. They provide a warmer and less threatening introduction to computers than the IBM PC's "A:/ " prompt that awaits your command.

Still, the IBM and compatibles such as Tandy's computers make the most sense for the great majority of telecommuters. Freelance journalist Tom Johnson, former editor of the trade journal *Mac-WEEK,* thinks the choice between Apple and IBM is actually no choice at all. Here's why:

—The smaller Macintosh screen is harder to see; this also makes editing more difficult.

—IBM machines (specifically clones) cost less.

—You can't upgrade a Macintosh that easily. The low-end model can't be expanded at all, except through add-on devices attached through ports on the unit's back. Also, many people like to use RAM-resident programs (the kind that pop up at the push of a key or two). These are not as easy to use on a Macintosh.

—Apple only offers a ninety-day warranty on its hardware. Most other vendors offer a year. You can, however, buy a service agreement that extends that warranty to three years.

—There is a lot more software available (especially business software) for IBM machines.

However, for a select group of telecommuters, those who can appreciate and make use of its superior graphics capabilities, a Macintosh is the better choice. This includes illustrators, architects, and designers. Others would be better off with IBM or IBM-compatible machines. The top suppliers are IBM, Tandy Corporation, and Compaq.

That makes it a choice between microprocessors. That's where the rubber meets the road. There's always pressure on microcomputer users to upgrade to the fastest machines available. Buyers for large businesses have forsaken the XT-class (with 8088 processors) machines and are buying the 80286 and 80386 machines in about equal numbers. That won't continue for much longer. The 80386 will supplant the 80286.

Actually, there's no reason you can't use an IBM XT. If you are doing computer-intensive things that swallow a lot of processing power (spreadsheets, computer-aided design, or manufacturing applications), then you need a computer with a fast microprocessor. But for garden-variety applications, word processing and communications, you can get by with a slower and cheaper computer.

Still, buying an 80286 (AT-class) machine currently makes the most sense. They are faster than the XT-class machines. But they don't cost as much as the 80386 computers. Through a mail-order company such as CompuAdd or Dell you can get an excellent machine for under $1,500.

Mail-Order Sources

Buying equipment by mail order is no longer the risky business it once was. Dell and CompuAdd, both described in Chapter 10, are excellent sources for computers and other office equipment. For instance, Dell's 386SX system comes with self-diagnostic software, toll-free technical support, and a thirty-day money-back guarantee.

Ann Kelly, a technical editor and freelance writer, recently bought a computer through CompuAdd. Ann was new to computers when she went about choosing the right model and dealer for her needs. The process she went through in selecting a computer and dealing with a mail-order house is recounted here.

> Prior to purchasing my microcomputer I did extensive research on the various types of systems out on the market. First, I determined what I would use it for. I listed all of the tasks I thought I could use a PC for and realized the majority of the work to be done was word processing. The second runner-up was database management—primarily for merging mailing addresses. The third choice was budgeting personal income and expenses.

Now that I had narrowed down software choices I could determine roughly how much hard disk and memory I would need. Next I read back and current issues of *Personal Computing, PC Week, Computerworld,* and several other computer publications. Then I asked users what they would recommend and listened to their suggestions.

The next step in evaluating the choices was to go to three retail stores and test equipment. Unfortunately, the sales staff was not much help—often I felt I knew more about their systems then they did!

After going the retail route, the next step was to test out mail-order houses and their seemingly incredible low prices. But how do you test them? If they said call for prices I called their toll-free number to make sure their prices were legitimate. To test their technical support force I called the 800 number and noted how many times the phone rang before they picked up. After doing this to a number of mail-order companies I found the company with the best phone record (CompuAdd) also had among the lowest prices on the market.

After placing a charge card order (which I used so if I had a problem with delivery it was my option not to pay the bill) I received the order, which included an 80286-based machine, 20MB hard drive, monitor, keyboard, diskettes, manual, word processing software, printer, paper, and all the necessary cables in six working days—four days less than the company's promise. I received all merchandise intact and complete.

Buying the microcomputer as part of a configured package from the mail-order house saved me about $500, as opposed to buying separate pieces, on sale. Plus, I had all the necessary cables, diskettes, paper, software, and documentation to begin using the computer from day one.

Included in the purchase price was a thirty-day money-back guarantee and one year of free technical phone-in service, a benefit seldom offered by retail outlets.

System installation was easy, except for the printer. After several attempts to send a file to the printer I gave up and called the company. They suggested trying another cable. I called them again and they gave more technical suggestions; however, after a closer inspection of the cable opening I realized I hadn't plugged the printer in all the way!

Give It Time

Set up your office the way you think you want it, then live with it for a while. Is the keyboard at a comfortable height? Is your monitor too close? Is glare a problem? Are your files handy enough? How about the noise level? You can then change things based on what you've learned. But right from the start, plan to get as comfortable a chair and work surface as you can afford. Otherwise you may get more tired working at home than you did working in the office.

One of the pleasant things about working from home is that it gives you more options. Who's to say you have to work from your home office all the time? Link Resources' Carol D'Agostino, for example, has her office in her bedroom. She reads and makes telephone calls in her living room, however, which gets more sunlight. In this more relaxing environment she can put her feet up. She also gets a change of scenery. Other telecommuters take their laptops to the park or backyard.

Working from home is a growth opportunity and a learning experience. Your home office will be shaped by this growth and learning. As your situation changes your office will change too. A new job, the need for more or different equipment, more money at your disposal— all can lead to changes in your office. Software writer Diane Yaeger-McIntosh, who has worked at home exclusively for more than four years (and at least part time since 1974), began with a "desk" that was a board on top of two side-by-side stacks of large books. Over the years, however, Diane bought matching desks with hutches and pull-out keyboard shelves for her computers, chairs (although she still prefers the floor sometimes), a pair of four-drawer file cabinets, a tall bookcase, plus a couple of brick-and-board arrangements.

You probably won't set up the perfect office overnight. Even now, Diane has her wish-list items: laser printer, copier, fax, high-quality portable laptop, and a second hard disk. You'll have yours too.

8
Telecommuting and the Disabled

Telecommuting has brought freedom to a lot of people, but one group it has failed, some would say, is the disabled. Telecommuting was once heralded as a godsend for the nation's 36 million disabled people. At first glance, there does seem to be a good fit between the two.

Some Striking Demographics

Unemployment Among the Disabled

Of all demographic groups, the disabled has the smallest percentage of people working. A striking two-thirds of disabled people between the ages of sixteen and sixty-four don't work. Although the disabled comprise 8 percent of the U.S. population, they make up only 1 percent of our work force. Yet a Louis Harris Poll found that a majority of disabled people not working would like to. What's more, the same poll found that an overwhelming number of employers who have disabled workers rate their performance good or excellent.

Would Telecommuting Help?

Telecommuting would spare a disabled person the ordeal of a twice-daily commute. And in these days of labor shortages, businesses can't afford to turn down whole groups of candidates. Yet experts in that field disagree with this approach. Most disabled people can get around and are certainly mobile enough to come into a nearby office one or more times a week. True, blind people can't drive cars. But by using a seeing eye dog, taking advantage of special services such as van pools, or otherwise arranging to have someone drive them in, they can still get to an office.

By setting up disabled (or "physically challenged") people as full-time homeworkers we risk creating a ghetto of sorts. It may appear that we are doing them a service by setting them up to work at home, but it's not to their benefit if it also continues to cut them off from society. They then never really become a part of it.

Few employers, of course, would purposely set out to do this. Unfortunately, it can still happen. "Some employers may use telecommuting programs as a way to hire disabled workers without coming to terms with their effects on the work place," says Susan Herman, general manager of the City of Los Angeles' Telecommunications Department. The fact that disabled people make many able-bodied people uncomfortable is one reason employers don't go out of their way to hire them. By the same token, some disabled people themselves find the corporate environment difficult and prefer to work from home.

Other barriers have been removed. Buildings, for example, are now accessible to disabled people thanks to the Architectural Barriers Act of 1968, which says that ramps, entrances, and parking facilities must accommodate people with impaired mobility. The tools the rest of the work force now uses, such as personal computers, are also accessible. A recently passed law, Public Law 99-506, ensures that, in places employing federal employees, the electronic office equipment is outfitted in a way that permits disabled people to make use of it. Any new equipment federal contractors and agencies buy must be purchased with access by the disabled in mind.

There are already more than 1600 devices available that help disabled people use computers. These include Braille computer printers, attachments that enlarge information on computer screens up to sixteen times normal size, talking terminals, and voice-activated keyboards. The Kurzweil Personal Reader, for example, which its manufacturer bills as the device that lets Stevie Wonder "read" his mail, is an excellent example of what today's technology can do for disabled people. The reader includes a special scanner that, when moved across a printed page, groups letters into words. The attached computer (about the size of a laptop model) recognizes the pairings of letters and words and reads them aloud. The reader recognizes most kinds of type, and even numbers and punctuation, according to its manufacturer, Xerox.

Mainstreaming

Many experts in both fields—telecommuting and serving the disabled—now advocate mainstreaming. Lift, Inc., for example, works with programmers who have severe disabilities such as polio and cerebral palsy. Most cannot go to an office every day. Yet Lift requires its programmers to go into the office at least once a week. A small percentage do report to the office every day.

In some cases, even the few trend-setting employers who saw telecommuting as a way to hire disabled workers favor mainstreaming wherever possible. United Airlines, for example, at one time had several disabled people working for it at home. Now the company tries to bring disabled workers into its workplace. Other companies that aggressively recruit disabled workers are McDonald's and Wendy's.

When Telecommuting Makes Sense

Even with this kind of technology moving into the workplace, under some circumstances working from home *is* the best option for a disabled person.

Temporary Disabilities

In the case of a temporary disability (say, a severely broken leg) it may not pay for you to make special arrangements to get in to work when you know you'll only be laid up briefly. In that case, working at home for a while, even full time, may make the most sense.

Unpredictable Disabilities

For people with disabilities that are unpredictable, such as arthritis, part-time telecommuting may be the perfect solution. That way, if someone had a day when the pain was especially bad, he could gradually ease into his work day. On such days the worker could still feel productive.

The Truly Immobile

The third category of disabled people for whom telecommuting may make sense is those who are truly immobile. This group, however, represents the smallest segment of the disabled population.

While telecommuting offers benefits for some disabled people, it's not the automatic answer. In most cases, whether or not a disabled person should telecommute should depend on the same things anyone thinking about it must consider: the suitability of the job, the person, and the employer.

Recommended Resources

The following organizations assist disabled individuals who are interested in using technology to work.

National Council on Disability
800 Independence Ave., S.W., Suite 814
Washington, D.C. 20591
(202) 267-3846
An independent federal agency created to inform the public and the disability community. As part of its work, it holds forums in many states and sponsors conferences. The National Council on Disability also publishes a useful newsletter, *Focus.* It is distributed quarterly without charge.

National Rehabilitation Information Center (NARIC)
8455 Colesville Road, Suite 935
Silver Spring, MD 20910
(800) 346-2742
NARIC, funded by the U.S. Department of Education, says it "provides information for an independent life." When you call its 800 number a staff member takes your name, address, and daytime telephone number and asks "the nature of your disability." A trained counselor then returns your call, usually within a couple of days.

NARIC's services include referral, "quick" and general reference, document delivery, and database training all for a nominal fee. The organization publishes a useful, information-packed newsletter, *NARIC Quarterly.* Subscriptions are free.

Apple Computer, Inc.
Office of Special Education
20525 Mairiani Avenue
Cupertino, CA 95014
(408) 996-1010
Apple created this special office to bring together teachers, therapists, and rehabilitation engineers to discuss and work on ways of making Apple computers more accessible to people with disabilities. The center produces a database that describes thousands of adaptive devices, software programs, and disability-related organizations, publications, and networks. Some of this same information is available in hard-copy form through a resource guide Apple publishes called *Connections.*

IBM National Suppport Center for Persons with Disabilities
P.O. Box 2150
Atlanta, GA 30055
(800) IBM-2133

IBM hired its first disabled worker in 1914. Since then, the company has remained committed to finding opportunities for disabled people within its work force. This clearinghouse provides information about computers and computer-aided devices for people with disabilities. It provides information about products available from both IBM and other vendors. The center also sponsors Executive Awareness Programs in which staff members travel to various cities to discuss the types of jobs people with disabilities can do with the aid of computers.

Job Accommodation Network
809 Allen Hall
P.O. Box 6122
West Virginia University
Morgantown, WV 26506
(800) 526-7234

A clearinghouse and referral service providing information to employers who may need to make special accommodations for disabled workers. The network was established by the President's Committee on the Employment of People with Disabilities.

CompuServe Information Service
5000 Arlington Center Boulevard
Columbus, Ohio 43220
(800) 848-8199

The CompuServe electronic information service includes several forums that deal with disablilites. Because the forums are available through an on-line service, they include a lot of information on how technology can assist the disabled.

For information on telecommuting opportunities, network with forum members by posting messages on forum message boards. There is no charge for access beyond CompuServe's normal on-line fees. In addition to the forums included here, the Working From Home Forum, discussed in Chapter 10, can also furnish contacts and leads.

Each of the following forums has its own strengths:

Disabilities Forum. An electronic meeting place for people interested in sharing information about disabilities and the potential of disabled people. The message board here is active and is broken down into the following categories:

General Interest
Developmental Disorders
Emotional Disturbances
Hearing Impairments
Learning Disabilities
Mobility Impairment
Rights/Legislation
Education/Employment
Family Life/Leisure

Separate libraries of files that can be downloaded are also available under these same categories. Access by typing GO DISABILITIES.

Rehabilitation Database. An on-line service provided by the Veterans Administration Office of Technology Transfer. This is not updated as frequently as some of the other services available on CompuServe. There is no message board, either. Its best features are a separate section on information about wheelchairs, provided by the National Rehabilitation Information Clearinghouse, and back issues of the *Journal of Rehabilitation Research and Development*. Access by typing GO REHAB.

Handicapped Users Database. The best resource of its kind. If you are disabled or just have a strong interest in the subject, the presence of this Special Interest Group is reason enough to subscribe to CompuServe. It offers an on-line listing of resources for the disabled that would take you days to compile any other way. The repository breaks down as follows:

Nonprofit Organizations
Commercial Companies
Organizations
Self-help Group Clearinghouses
Organizations for the Deaf
Blind-related Sports Organizations
Wheel Chair Sports Associations
Microcomputer Support Organizations

The reference library area includes areas on Computers in Education, Physically Handicapped, Helplines, and Making Technology Happen. Access by typing GO HUD.

IBM Special Needs Database. For IBM owners with special needs or problems. This is more of a general-interest service than the other Special Interest Groups profiled. The way its message board is broken down reflects this:

> General Information
> Software
> Hardware
> Special Needs
> Developers
> Beginner's Corner
> IBM Bits and Bytes

Access by typing GO IBMSPEC.

Lift, Inc.
350 Pfingsten   Suite 103
Northbrook, IL 60062
(312) 564-9005

Lift hires, trains, and places computer programmers with severe physical disabilities. Typical disabilities are spinal-cord injury, muscular dystrophy, and blindness. Almost all of its programmers work from home at least part time. The company recruits candidates that meet the specific requirements of its corporate clients.

Over the past fourteen years Lift has hired 132 computer programmers. Ninety-two were subsequently placed with corporate clients such as Allstate Insurance Company, Dun and Bradstreet Corporation, and Union Oil Company of California.

9
Working with Consultants

Like most fields, telecommuting has its own consultants. These are independent experts who make their living advising companies that want to set up telecommuting programs or even just explore the idea. Whatever your role—would-be telecommuter or manager—you can benefit from knowing how consultants operate. The employee who wants to telecommute assumes the role of consultant as he makes his case to management. He therefore needs to know what consultants do. And, as explained below, there are several reasons a manager who's looking into telecommuting may very well want to hire a consultant.

Consultants—Two Types

The Telecommuter as Consultant

Telecommuting is uncommon; it still goes against the norm. On that basis alone some managers will hesitate when an employee suggests it. So, in order to effectively pitch their cases, many would-be telecommuters assume the consultant's role, explaining what telecommuting is and how it might benefit the company. While they don't necessarily go through all the steps a consultant would (especially if only speaking for themselves), they go through at least some of them. These steps are recounted here.

Outside Consultants

Companies with only one or two telecommuters don't need outside consultants. But as soon as a manager starts thinking of going beyond this to how it may work out for larger groups of employees (such as entire departments) consultants make sense. When a company wants to implement telecommuting on a large scale it must be custom-fit to the organization; it's not a plug-in solution. In those cases, it's comforting to know that there are consultants who can take over the whole process.

Granted, some companies with large human resources departments may consider setting up programs on their own since anything a consultant is going to do the company could do itself. The problem is that most companies in this lean and-mean era are short-staffed. They can't spare internal people to do the research and other work involved in creating a pilot program from scratch.

What Consultants Do

Help Companies Avoid the Pitfalls

The main reason to use a consultant is to avoid repeating the same mistakes others have made. Consultants can help companies design programs geared to their organizations instead of going the trial-and-error route. They can also recommend shortcuts and proven procedures that have worked before.

Hand-hold the Company Through the Process

Telecommuting doesn't work the same for everybody. Not all jobs are suitable for telecommuting or even the same form of it. Consultants can help companies consider the content of people's jobs to see how suitable they are for moving from the traditional office. Some can be done from anywhere. Others depend on a certain location. If your job requires you to be at a counter greeting people, you have to be where the public is. On the other hand, a software engineer who interacts with computers more than people can work anywhere. Between these extremes, there are all sorts of shades in the middle.

But unanticipated problems can crop up beyond the expected concerns. If you plan to let only a few people telecommute, for example, how do you explain to the others who would like to that they can't? And in unionized companies, the unions may object to their members working from home, out of their reach.

Implement Programs Quickly

By forsaking the trial-and-error route, companies that use consultants can move more quickly and effectively when starting telecommuting. Sometimes, getting a telecommuting program under way quickly is more important than anything. For example, at Ortho Pharmaceutical, a Johnson & Johnson division, overcrowding was so bad that double-decker cubicles seemed the only solution. By bringing in a consultant they were able to alleviate this problem much sooner than they would have otherwise.

Getting Ready for the Consultant

Understanding What Telecommuting Is

"You have to do your homework before you can work from home" is the motto of one expert in the field. This also applies to companies when they work with consultants. Preparation allows for more productive and cost-effective use of the consultant's time. This is one reason consultants prefer to work with companies that have a basic working knowledge of telecommuting.

Deciding on a Reason for Telecommuting

Companies should also know what business problem they want telecommuting to address. While consultants can offer advice there as well, the point is to be sure that telecommuting is an appropriate solution for the problem. Telecommuting should not be instituted merely for its own sake, for experimentation. The idea is to be problem-focused and look at telecommuting as a tool to manage your business.

Four Steps to Telecommuting

All telecommuting consultants go through the same four steps once a company hires them, although their approach and emphasis vary with what the company wants and the consultant's way of doing things.

The Briefing

This is where the consultant brings managers up-to-date on what telecommuting is: its history, where it stands, and what its prospects are. There's a reason that consultants take a top-down approach and brief managers first. They've found they don't have any trouble convincing prospective telecommuters that it's a good deal, but the real issue is to get management support from the top of the organization.

Consultants generally handle briefings in the same way. Gil Gordon, for example, spends a day or so in a seminar format, giving its history and explaining what telecommuting is and is not. His objective is to ensure that everyone is on the "same sheet of music." This may include debunking myths that have developed so everyone is thinking and visualizing the same thing. During the briefing, the consultant may also address whether it might be appropriate for the company, and how the company might get started in it.

Screening / Discussion Stage

If after the briefing management thinks it's worth continuing, the consultant talks at length with the managers about who would participate. This is also when the telecommuters themselves get involved, as the consultant works with managers to choose the best candidates for telecommuting. Selecting the right candidates is crucial to telecommuting's success.

The approach a consultant takes reflects his background. Jack Nilles, for example, a former rocket scientist, takes a very scientific approach. He's developed some tests for both prospective telecommuters and their supervisors. He then analyzes these and uses them as the basis of recommendations to the company as to who should telecommute and in what form and how often. The tests look at two areas: the nature of the job and the work-related sociopsychological characteristics of both the telecommuter and his supervisor. They concentrate on the match between those two, not just one or the other. The idea is to be certain both are suited for it—one for telecommuting the other for managing a telecommuter.

For example, here are some traits that make a manager a good candidate for managing telecommuters:

1. Measures performance objectively
2. Is willing to try something new
3. Has a reasonably flexible managing style

Managers who always do things by the book, without exception, and who are very highly process-oriented won't be good telemanagers unless all of their employees are the same way. This is rarely the case.

By the same token, it's important to choose the right telecommuters. If people self-selected based only on their perceptions, many will jump into telecommuting to get out of the traffic. They don't consider all that's involved—what it's going to be like to be their own boss, how they are going to handle the work vs. family issues, and so on.

While some consultants use commercially available tests or personality profiles to measure dimensions that would seem relevant (e.g., need for socialization), other consultants hesitate to use such tests. They reason that clients who ask for them are insecure or uneasy about the whole process.

During this second step the consultant links telecommuting to what's going on in the business, conducting a feasibility analysis to select the best departments for programs. He may consider several departments that appear to be good prospects and ask key questions: Do they have space problems or staffing problems? Do they have the kind of operation that might benefit from the extended hours telecommuting provides? Once participants are selected they get briefed on, as Gil Gordon puts it, "the good, the bad, and the ugly about telecommuting."

Plan and Implementation

After the candidates are selected and everyone is briefed, the consultant writes a formal plan for how telecommuting should proceed. This is where all the details are hammered out, from the equipment the telecommuters will need to what other departments in the company should be involved to how it gets rolled out. They try to cover everything, to think of as many downside possibilities as possible.

Training. This is also when formal training begins. This often includes manuals for the supervisors, for the telecommuters, and for the trainers (assuming that medium-to-large companies will have their own trainers). It may also include further in-depth sessions for the telecommuters, their managers, and for both together. While that's going on, there are background issues being considered—technical issues, logistics such as getting materials back and forth, planning about meeting schedules, and all the little details should not be left to chance.

"A prescription for failure, says consultant Gil Gordon, "is to say 'OK Charlie, take your PC home, plug it in, and start working from home next week.' You don't have to go to the other extreme of making it a five-year project. But we know enough now about what things have to be planned for that people are really programed to succeed."

(Some companies did switch on telecommuting that abruptly. Invariably, they ran into problems.)

Consultant Joanne Pratt believes training is the most important part of the process since it builds trust. "Without the trust you may not want an employee leaving your office at all." The key to establishing this trust is good communications. Pratt feels that in most offices, supervisors and employees rarely sit down and level with each other, because they lack the time and they hesitate to really let each other know what they are feeling.

"As a facilitator coming in I can help make that happen. I sit the telecommuter and supervisor together, away from the daily pressure of phone calls and other obligations, and get them to ask questions and answer questions face to face. Although it's just a matter of opening communications, it takes an outside person to do that."

Often people assume they communicate effectively when really they may not. To make this clear, Joanne Pratt conducts exercises that exaggerate normal day-to-day situations. For example, she'll have the employee and his boss sit back-to-back while the supervisor gives a set of instructions. The employee then tries to get the supervisor to clarify what's been said by asking "You mean you want me to. . . ?" This continues until the task is fully defined.

This exercise shows that ordinarily when you give someone instructions, you count on the other person watching your face, hand movements, and gestures to fill in the blanks. Joanne says she could spend an hour trying to make this point, but sitting them down and having them do the exercise gets it across in ten minutes. As a result of this, "One of the benefits of telecommuting for supervisors is that they learn to give clearer instructions."

Following the training, people start telecommuting on a limited basis, perhaps one or two days a week. The consultant moves into the background during this stage.

Follow-up and Evaluation

Once telecommuting begins, the consultant's role becomes that of monitor and evaluator. He tracks the progress over the first few months. He may meet with the telecommuters during this time to find out how it's going. He'll ask about work output, effect on home life, and anything else that may reflect the new work arrangement. Fine-tuning follows. Some sort of final evaluation caps their service.

What Consultants Charge

Expertise does not come cheap. There is generally a flat fee for the briefing part of the process. After that, the charge varies with the amount of time the consultant puts into the project.

Jack Nilles says that for him there is a fixed amount of time it takes to get the project planned. This is relatively independent of the project's size. He usually quotes a fixed price rather than an hourly rate. "It tends to be $10,000 or more to get the plan together. The plan for the State of California project, because of its size, was $30,000 [in 1985 dollars]."

Gil Gordon charges between $3500 and $5000 for an introductory two-day program. The first day is a telecommuting seminar, the second a feasibility analysis. The company does not have to commit to any further services beyond that. Costs from there are harder to estimate, but Gordon gives a ballpark range of $10,000 to $50,000. The low end is where a company supplied a lot of its own resources and the pilot was limited. "The other extreme," says Gordon, "is where I am going to carry the whole ball; it's a larger pilot, there are more technical planning issues, all of which means more time on my part."

For some suggestions on tracking down telecommuting consultants, see Chapter 10.

10
Resources for Telecommuters

Whether you want to track down companies with telecommuters or just stay abreast of the field, you'll need to tap the most up-to-date sources. Telecommuting is not new, but it's a fast-changing field that's constantly growing.

The idea is to get the information while it's fresh, when it will do you the most good. For example, in mid-1989 the Washington State Energy Office, as part of a demonstration program it was planning, asked to hear from people who wanted to become telecommuters. Obviously, the sooner you acted on such information, the better your chances of participating in the program.

The best way to make sure developments in a technology you are tracking don't escape you is through computer databases, which is why this book (and this chapter, especially) stresses them. Beyond that, the resources below will help you learn more about the technology that feeds telecommuting, create a home office, or just work or get work as a telecommuter.

Books

Very few books discuss telecommuting from the telecommuter's viewpoint. There are, however, many books available that cover working at home, and the technology that plays into that. Naturally much of what they cover applies to telecommuters as well.

Careers Tomorrow: The Outlook for Work in a Changing World. Edited by Edward Cornish. Bethesda, MD: World Future Society. 1988. $7.95. Selected articles reprinted from *The Futurist* magazine, the journal of the World Future Society. Most are at least two years old. Still, the book gets you thinking about career options.

The Complete Computer Career Guide. Judith Norback. Blue Ridge Summit, PA: TAB Books. 1987. $12.95. Computer scientist, systems analyst, programmer, technical writer—just about any computer-related job you can think of is suitable for telecommuting. This book fully describes twenty-five computer jobs, giving benefits, drawbacks, and career-opportunity details. Its listing ofemployment agencies specializing in computer jobs is a greatresource for would-be telecommuters. Counselors at these agencies know a lot about local employers and can possibly suggest a few who already allow some employees to work from home. Telecommuters may also find the section on home study useful.

The Computer Industry Almanac 1990. Egil Juliussen and Karen Juliussen. New York: Brady Books. 1989. $29.95. Anyone who is at all interested in computers will find this reference work fascinating. The biggest, best, fastest, they are all detailed here—as long as it relates to computers. Features include profiles of industry companies, forecasts for the computer marketplace, salaries of top executives, and product trends and product award winners. Written by two telecommuters and updated yearly.

Computing Across America: The Bicycle Odyssey of a High-Tech Nomad. Steve Roberts. Medford, NJ: Learned Information, Inc. 1988. $9.95. Author and "technofreak" Steve Roberts outfitted his one-of-a-kind bike with five computers, a cellular phone with modem, speech synthesis, five solar panels, a TV set, a fax machine, and much more to create a mobile electronic "cottage." He then set off to explore America, occasionally sending stories in to various computer publications to cover costs. A most unusual first-person account of telecommuting.

The Electronic Home Advisor. Howard J. Blumenthal. New York: Andrews and McMeel. 1988. $9.95. Excellent advice on buying any kind of electronic equipment. Written in a simple, straightforward manner. Telecommuters will find the chapter on The Electronic Office especially useful.

Growing a Business/Raising a Family. Edited by Jan and Charlie Fletcher. Seattle: NextStep Publications, 1988. $8.50. A collection of essays based on the experiences of parents who have integrated working at home with parenting. Recommended for anyone who wants to explore this option.

Home Offices and Workspaces. Menlo Park, CA: Lane Publishing Co. 1986. $6.95. A picture book of ideas for setting up a home office. You can't look at this book without coming away with several new ideas for crafting a new workspace or improving the one you have. Includes many full-color photos of sample home offices, plus suggestions on how to set a home office. There's even a section on home office furniture you can build. A worthwhile investment for anyone who plans to work at home for any length of time.

How to Get Free Software. Alfred Glossbrenner. New York: St. Martin's Press. 1989. $18.95. For owners of IBMs and compatible computers. Why pay hundreds of dollars for software when programs costing virtually nothing are sometimes just as good? This book shows how to locate the most useful free programs from on-line services such as CompuServe. The best thing about this book is that the author names what he considers the best free software programs for given applications.

How to Look It up On-line. Alfred Glossbrenner. New York: St. Martin's Press. 1987, $14.95. How to use on-line databases to get any kind of information you want from books and articles. There is simply no more readable introduction to this subject than Glossbrenner's book. It also covers how to navigate databases and make the best use of the services database vendors provide.

The Jobs Rated Almanac. Les Krantz. New York: Pharos Books. 1988. $14.95. A career reference book that's actually fun to browse through. Rates 250 jobs on such categories as environment, salary, benefits, travel, and physical demands. Most valuable to people thinking of changing careers. Out of the top ten jobs (considering all criteria combined), seven are suitable for telecommuting: Actuary, computer programmer, computer systems analyst, mathematician, statistician, industrial engineer, and paralegal. (Rounding out the top ten are hospital administrator, physicist, and astrologer.)

New Emerging Careers: Today, Tomorrow, and in the 21st Century. S. Norman Feingold and Maxine H. Atwater. Garrett Park, MD: Garrett Park Press. 1988. $15.00. Describes the most promising occupations for the coming years and how to prepare for them. The authors are experts in the field of emerging careers.

The New Era of Home-Based Work: Directions and Policies. Edited by Kathleen Christenson. Boulder, CO: Westview Press. 1988. $49.95. Draws on research from a national gathering of experts in the field.

Overcoming Writer's Blocks. Karin Mack and Eric Skjei. Los Angeles: J. P. Tarcher. 1979. $6.95. Many telecommuters write for a living, which makes this an extremely useful book. The writer who's in the throes of a block may find this unique book a lifesaver. It offers tricks for both getting started and keeping the writing process going. There are also chapters on business, technical, and academic writing.

Signal: Communication Tools for the Information Age. Edited by Kevin Kelly. New York: Harmony Books. 1988. $16.95. From the people who brought you the *Whole Earth Catalog,* this book reviews more than 900 "communications tools," including software packages, books, newsletters, databases, and computers. There's much here of interest to telecommuters, including a section (too short, unfortunately) on recommended tools for working at home. Written in the characteristically casual yet knowledgeable manner of its predecessor. Fun to page through.

Sitting on the Job. Scott W. Donkin. Boston: Houghton Mifflin. 1989. $7.95. Written by a chiropractor, this is a survival guide for the millions of us who sit while working.

The Telecommuter's Toolkit. Joanne H. Pratt. Dallas: Reverchon Press. 1989. $5.95. Notes and worksheets based on the author's training of State of California telecommuters and her ongoing workshops.

The Telecommuters. Francis Kinsman. New York: John Wiley & Sons. 1987. $44.95. The F.I. Group, a British firm that has employed telecommuters for more than twenty-five years, sponsored freelance journalist Francis Kinsman in the writing of this book. It provides extensive background information on the technological, social, and economic forces behind telecommuting. Included are case histories and useful checklists for managers who are thinking of adopting telecommuting for their organizations. Throughout, the accent is on British companies and "teleworkers"; a chapter called "Telecommuting in the World at Large" mentions U.S. companies.

Telecommuting:The Future Technology of Work. Thomas B. Cross and Marjorie Raizman. Homewood, IL: Dow Jones Irwin. 1986. $25.00. Much more academic (read: dry) than the Gordon/Kelly book that follows, this book considers telecommuting from the manager's view. The authors cover the technologies associated with telecommuting in great detail. The best chapters are the first (Telecommuting Overview) and the last (Telecommuting Resource Guide).

Telecommuting: How to Make It Work for You and Your Company. Gil E. Gordon and Marcia Kelly. Englewood Cliffs, NJ: Prentice-Hall. 1986. Available for $15.95 from Gil Gordon Associates, Monmouth Junction, NJ. Written by two of the top names in the telecommuting field, this book covers telecommuting from the employer's viewpoint. You might want to browse through this book before discussing telecommuting with your employer. Topics include handling technical details, training managers of telecommuters, and implementing telecommuting programs.

The Third Wave. Alvin Toffler. New York: Bantam. 1984. $4.95. Way ahead of its time (the hardbound edition was published in 1980), this book popularized the idea of electronic cottages.

What Color Is Your Parachute? Richard Nelson Bolles. Berkeley, CA: Ten Speed Press. 1989. $9.95. The book that sets the pace for all job-hunting manuals. The best thing about *Parachute* is that it stresses introspection, the prelude to finding the right job that all too often other books treat lightly. This is especially important for telecommuters, since they *must* really enjoy their work to succeed at telecommuting.

The Woman's Work-At-Home Handbook. Patricia McConnel. New York: Bantam. 1986. $9.95. Although the subtitle, "Income and Independence with a Computer," suggests another get-rich-with-your-computer book, this one offers much more. Geared to entrepreneurs, it also includes a lengthy chapter on telecommuting and important information on how several disabled people work at home with computers.

Working from Home. Paul and Sarah Edwards. Los Angeles: Jeremy P. Tarcher. 1987. $12.95. Covers everything you'd need to know about working from home, from deciding whether working from home is right for you to designing a work space to marketing a home business. There's also a chapter on telecommuting. Perfect for home-based entrepreneurs, there is enough information that also applies to telecommuters to justify buying a copy.

The Work-at-Home Sourcebook. Lynie Arden. Boulder, CO: Live Oak Publications. 1988. $12.95. A names-and-addresses book of companies that use homeworkers. While it includes a few telecommuting opportunities, it also lists offbeat things like drapery-sewing positions and field surveying jobs. Of particular value to people who see working at home as a way to supplement their families' income rather than provide the bulk of it.

Free Software

There is no reason to pay hundreds of dollars for software when perfectly fine packages are available for little more than the cost of the floppy disk. But, as with so many "bargains," separating the values from the ripoffs requires an insider's expertise.

Fortunately for readers of this book, Alfred Glossbrenner, author of *Alfred Glossbrenner's Master Guide to Free Software for IBMs and Other Compatible Computers* took the risk out of the process.

Telecommuters will find the following programs useful. They are available through on-line bulletin boards, services such as CompuServe, or directly from Mr. Glossbrenner. Buying these packages, instead of going the retail route, "will save a telecommuter $1000, guaranteed," he says.

To order any of the programs listed below from Alfred Glossbrenner, send $5 for each disk ($6 for 3.5-inch), plus $2 per order for shipping and handling. Include your mailing address and zip code and the name of the disk(s).

Send your check or money order, payable to FireCrystal Communications, to:

Glossbrenner's Choice
699 River Road
Yardley, PA 19067
(215) 736-1213

Word Processing
- PC-WRITE 1—Program Disk (Some say PC-WRITE is the finest word processor available at any price.)

- PC-WRITE 2—Utilities Disk
- PC-WRITE 3—Reference Disk
- PC-FASTYPE (A typing tutor.)

Spreadsheets
- As-Easy-As (A Lotus 1-2-3 [Version 1A] clone.)

Filing
- FILE EXPRESS 1—Program Disk
- FILE EXPRESS 2—User's Guide and Supplemental Programs (a Filing program for inventories or mailing lists.)

Communications
- ProComm 2.4.3—Program Disk (Everyone's favorite communications package for IBM and IBM-compatible machines.)
- ProComm Utilities
- The Communicator's Toolchest (A collection of programs of value to all on-line communicators.)
- Minihost BBS Package (A program for those who need remote access to their own systems.)

Magazines

There are many magazines for home-based entrepreneurs but only one that includes a significant amount of information for telecommuters—*Home Office Computing.* This and other useful magazines are listed here.

Computer Shopper. 5211 S. Washington Ave., Titusville, FL 32780. $29.97/year. Features many ads from mail-order houses specializing in computers.

Consumer Reports. 256 Washington Street, Mount Vernon, NY 10553. $18/year. The best source for objective ratings of home office equipment.

Home Office Computing. Scholastic, Inc., 730 Broadway, New York, NY 10003. $19.97/year. Bills itself as "the only magazine for people who enjoy the freedom of working from home." While it has the entrepreneur (as opposed to telecommuter) market in its sights, many of its features also apply to telecommuters. For example, here you'll find articles about choosing among 286- or 386-based computers, using a fax board to turn your computer into a fax machine, and dialing into on-line databases.

PC/Computing. 80 Blanchard Road, Burlington, MA 01803. $24.97. The best of the many PC magazines. It's accessible and intelligent, yet it doesn't take itself too seriously. In other words, it assumes that while computers are important to you, they are not your only interest.

Mail-Order Sources

As a telecommuter, you may be able to get all the office supplies you'll need from your employer. Sometimes, however, that can't be arranged. Or perhaps you want to first create a productive home office and then convince your employer to let you telecommute. In that case, your best source of supplies is often mail-order houses.

Mail order offers so many advantages (lower prices, convenience) that most people will chance it even though it means ordering merchandise they've never seen. This is especially true for buyers of computer equipment, who can literally pay hundreds of dollars less for software packages when bought through the mail and thousands of dollars less for computers bought this way. A survey by FUJI found that 26 percent of people with home offices used mail order. The only "purchase outlet" (a market-research term, no doubt) with a higher percentage was computer specialty stores at 28 percent.

The following are recommended mail-order outlets/sources for home office supplies.

Boston Computer Exchange Corporation. Box 1177, Boston, MA 02103. Dubbed the world's "first and largest computer brokerage," the Boston Computer Exchange brings together sellers of used computers with buyers and eliminates the risk to both. The exchange's electronic trading system is modeled on the idea of the New York Stock Exchange.

To get started, you call the Exchange's toll-free number (800-262-6399) and tell a BoCoEx broker what you want to buy or sell. (To get a feel for prices you can check recent BoCoEx prices on several on-line services: CompuServe [GO BCE]; MCI [BO-COEX]; or Delphi: [BOCOEXCO]. Or a BoCoEx broker can assist you.)

Buyers and sellers agree on a price. The buyer sends the funds to the Exchange. Once received and verified, the seller ships the equipment to the buyer. The buyer then has forty-eight hours to make sure the equipment is in good working order. If everything checks out, the funds are released. (Sellers pay the exchange a 10 percent commission fee on the final price.) Companies such as General Electric, Sun Oil, Kodak, and Lotus use the Exchange to sell their used equipment. For those seeking to buy or sell used computers, the only other options are newspaper ads or word of mouth—hardly as safe.

CompuAdd. 12303 Technology Boulevard, Austin, TX 78727. A mail-order house specializing in computers and computer accessories sold direct to customers. Many people swear by this company's low prices and customer service. An excellent bargain is the CompuAdd Professional Starter Kit which, at the time of this writing, included an 80286 computer with 512KB RAM, a monitor, a Panasonic 1180 printer, all the cables you'd need, and CompuAdd's own Productivity software package for $1,495.

Curtis Manufacturing Company, Inc. 30 Fitzgerald Drive, Jaffrey, NH 03452. Offers a variety of high-quality (and sometimes expensive) computer accessories: from surge protectors to cleaning kits to printer stands. Recommended: The Curtis Clip ($6.95), an ingenious fastener for positioning copy that mounts to the side of your computer terminal with Velcro strips. The nice thing about the Curtis Clip (aside from the reasonable price) is that it doesn't take up any desk space. It also folds flat against your terminal when not in use.

Dell Computer Corporation. 9505 Arboretum Blvd., Austin, TX 78759. Dell sells its own line of computer systems and laser and dot matrix printers direct to buyers. If you are going the mail-order route for a new computer, this company and CompuAdd are about your safest bets. Reviewers at trade journals rate Dell's equipment highly. For example, *PC Magazine* gave Dell's Dell System 325 its Editor's Choice award.

Environments for Health. 526 Hickory Street, Missoula, MO 59801. Developers of unique furniture for home offices, including the Edelson wedge and the Edelson Computer Desk. The furniture strives to eliminate the "postural fixity" that comes with sitting in one place for too long.

47th Street Photo, Inc. 36 East 19th Street, New York, NY 10003. If you expect hand-holding from your electronics retailer, you'd better look elsewhere, but if it's low prices you want send for 47th Street's free catalog. It's packed with a wide variety of consumer electronics items (going way beyond camera equipment), including many for the home office.

Frank Eastern Company. 599 Broadway, New York, NY 10012. An office- and computer-furniture retailer, in business since 1946. Among the company's specialties are its Ergo-Flex chairs, designed with advanced orthopedic features that can make "eight hours of work feel like four."

Quill. P.O. Box 4700, Lincolnshire, IL 60197. Quill's semiannual catalog (free) is a 375-page bonanza of fax machines, desk organizers, binders, print wheels, adding machines, diskette holders—everything you'd possibly need for your home office. This is where stationery freaks (you know who you are) go for a fix. What's more, everything is discounted. The best thing about Quill, however, is its service. The company knows that people worry about ordering products through the mail; therefore it lets you return merchandise that doesn't live up to expectations, no questions asked. Quill recently added a new wrinkle to its service: a software package that lets you order by modem. The program is so appealing that it actually makes ordering office supplies fun. It lets you both order when you want and keep your phone charges low since your phone tab (by modem) is less than it would be if you telephoned in your order.

The Reliable Corporation. 1001 West Van Buren Street, Chicago, IL 60607. A Quill competitor that some people prefer because, according to the *Whole Earth Catalog,* its prices "are a tad cheaper." Send for their free catalog and judge for yourself.

Wilson Jones Office Products. 6150 Touchy Avenue, Chicago, IL 60648. Sells an impressive array of products for safeguarding your data—from surge protectors to antistatic mats to antitheft locks for computers.

Newsletters

Electronic Cottage Report. Lis Fleming, P.O. Box 1738, Davis, CA 95617. An electronic newsletter, available at no charge (except for the on-line time spent downloading it) to members of Compu-Serve's Working From Home Forum. Monthly. Focuses on home businesses, also devotes extensive coverage to telecommuting. Articles frequently include contacts and resource lists for obtaining additional information. A nice benefit of a CompuServe subscription if you are joining anyway.

Home Business Advisor. NextStep Publications, 6340 34th Avenue, SW, Seattle, WA 98126. $24/year. Subtitled "Helping Parents Work at Home," provides advice on how to merge working at home with childrearing. This thoughtful, well-written newsletter has an authoritative feel. Its focus is working at home with children, but it also covers issues of interest to entrepreneurs such as direct marketing, post-startup problems, and measuring success. (Telecommuting coverage is planned.) One of the newsletter's most interesting features is its "Home Business Ads" section, which carries ads from businesses that blend New Age ideas with parenting. Here you'll find ads from "Baby Clouds," special cushions that "surround baby in a cloud of comfort"; vegetarian cookbooks for cooks on the run, and resources for parents who want to educate their children at home.

Independent Contractor Report. James R. Urquhart, Editor, 2021 Business Center Drive, Suite 112, Irvine, CA 92715. $95/12 issues. Written by a lawyer who specializes in the independent contractor-versus-employee issue. Articles cover relevant IRS rulings pertaining to independent contractors and their "employers." Heavy reading, but recommended for people who feel they need to be on top of this issue, or for employers.

Telecommuting Review. TeleSpan Publishing Corporation, 50 West Palm Street, Altadena, CA 91001. $157/12 issues. Geared to managers who want to stay on top of telecommuting. Gil Gordon, one of the top authorities in the field, writes this is in a friendly, comfortable style. Because it looks at the broad view, it sometimes covers issues only marginally related to telecommuting. For example, a regular feature called "The Changing Workplace" recently looked at a temporary-help firm that's offering its workers some benefits.

On-line Services

Many telecommuters use on-line services to connect with other telecommuters, send and receive messages from their employers, add to their software collections, or perform research.

CompuServe. 5000 Arlington Centre Boulevard, P.O. Box 20212, Columbus, OH 43220. With more than 500,000 members, the CompuServe Information Service is the leading service of its kind. Recommended services for telecommuters include the EasyPlex electronic mail service, and CompuServe's many forums—including the Working From Home Forum—and those covering laptops, translation, journalism, the law, consulting, public relations, and specific types of computers. Subscribe by purchasing a CompuServe Subscription Kit from computer retailers for $39.95 (including $25 of free connect time) or less from mail-order sources. Also, if you buy a modem, there's a good chance it will come "bundled" with a CompuServe password, a forty-five-page descriptive brochure, and $15 of free connect time. If you go this route you can always purchase a CompuServe User's Guide from the company for $12.95. All subscribers also pay a $1.50-per-month service charge.

CompuServe has its roots in the hacker community, but to describe it as a hacker's haven is no longer accurate. CompuServe can benefit just about anyone who wants to connect with other people, whether to advance in their careers or just acquire knowledge.

CompuServe's best feature is its forums. Devoted to every conceivable topic, from types of computers to operating systems to the disabled to journalism—there are more than 100 operating. Each forum, akin to an electronic meeting place, includes a message board for posting messages for other forum members. This is where the real action is and where you will derive the real benefit from your CompuServe subscription.

DIALOG Information Services, Inc. 3640 Hillview Avenue, Palo Alto, CA 94304. DIALOG is the leading vendor of on-line databases. Readers of this book should consider subscribing to DIALOG's after-hours on-line service, Knowledge Index ($35 start-up fee, including a User's Workbook and two free hours of use to get to know the system). "Power users" who don't mind navigating on-line services via commands may prefer a regular DIALOG password, which lets you search anytime (not just during off-peak hours) and provides access to all of DIALOG's 300 databases. In that case, buy the DIALOG Starter Kit ($150), which includes $100 of free on-line connect time, complete system documentation, and training.

Knowledge Index gives you access to seventy or so of DIALOG's databases at a much-reduced rate of just $24 per hour. This includes all telecommunications charges, print charges, etc. The only drawback is that few of the databases are full-text. That is, they'll provide pointers to the articles (title, author, source) and in some cases an abstract, but not the actual text. So you've still got some work ahead of you. DIALOG plans to add more full-text sources shortly.

Knowledge Index is still one of the on-line world's best bargains. Databases available through the service that are of special interest to telecommuters are:

—*ABI/INFORM.* Contains lengthy article abstracts culled from more than 500 business journals. In many cases, the abstracts are all you need. A very valuable research tool.

—*Books in Print.* The best way to track down books now in print or those about to be published (as far as six months in advance). According to DIALOG, the database "represents virtually the entire content of the U.S. book publishing inventory."

—*Computer Database.* Of all the databases covering the computer field (and naturally there are scores of them), this one covers the most ground. If a significant article has been published, it's likely to be indexed here. Recommended highly for telecommuters or would-be telecommuters.

—*Consumer Reports.* Contains the full text from the eleven regular monthly issues of the magazine of the same name. You may want to see what their product testers said about telephone answering machines, printers, or other office machines before buying anything yourself. Going on-line is the fastest way to do it. The database contains every monthly issue from 1982 on.

—*Magazine Index. Magazine Index* is very similar to the *Reader's Guide to Periodical Literature,* only it covers even more periodicals. Again, no full text, only references.

—*Newsearch.* Updated daily, contains references to articles found in more than 370 U.S. magazines and newspapers, including *People, Business Week, The Wall Street Journal,* and *The New York Times.* This is kind of a holding area for new references en route to their permanent homes in more static databases such as *Magazine Index*. Using this database is one of the best ways to keep on top of developments in the telecommuting field. The only problem (and it's a big one) is that Newsearch does not include the full text of the articles, only the references.

—*Standard & Poor's Corporate Descriptions*. Provides key business and financial information for more than 8000 publicly owned companies. Use this database to check the solvency and market position of potential employers.

—*Trade and Industry Index*. Similar to *Magazine Index*, it focuses more on business publications than on general-interest publications.

Dow Jones News/Retrieval. P.O. Box 300, Princeton, NJ 08543. The only on-line source for the full text of *The Wall Street Journal.* It also offers access to full-text articles from national and regional business publications *(Business Week, Barron's)* and company and industry news. Standard membership is $29.95, which includes five free hours of connect time, a User's Guide, and a subscription to the company's *Dowline* magazine.

GEnie. GEnie, short for the General Electric Network for Information Exchange, is CompuServe on a smaller scale. GEnie contains many of the same types of features, including forums. Because its universe of users is much smaller than CompuServe's (160,000 vs. 550,000), its forums have that many fewer people participating and fewer files for downloading. Telecommuters should check into The Home Office Roundtable, an electronic gathering place for people who work from home, including telecommuters. Recent discussion topics included an ongoing bibliography for people who work from home, women in business, the types of modems round-table participants use, and small business association information. As with CompuServe's Working From Home Forum, the accent is on entrepreneurs, but telecommuters would still find some information (and contacts) of interest.

MCI Mail. 1150 17th St., N.W., Suite 800, Washington, DC 20036. An electronic mail service that's a favorite among writers, editors, and journalists. It offers a variety of delivery options (including PC to fax). Annual subscriptions are $25; electronic mail messages cost $.45 for up to 500 characters (about 100 words), with prices increasing incrementally beyond that. A handy option lets you send up to forty messages per month for $10. Heavy electronic mail users should probably subscribe both to CompuServe and MCI Mail.

Mead Data Central (Nexis). 9393 Springboro Pike, P.O. Box 933, Dayton, OH 45401. Mead Data Central, a subsidiary of the paper-company giant Mead, offers the most desirable, but unfortunately one of the most expensive database services around—Nexis. Nexis contains the full text of articles from hundreds of newspapers, magazines, and newsletters. There is no simpler and faster way to gather a large amount of background information from many sources. Nexis is so expensive that it's more appropriate for businesses than for individuals.

Organizations

Association of Part-Time Professionals. Flow General Building, 7655 Old Springhouse Rd., McLean, VA 22102. $45/1-year membership. A nonprofit organization that offers a wealth of information and access to other resources for people thinking about the part-time route, an increasingly popular work option. Membership includes a subscription to its monthly newsletter, *The Part-Time Professional,* which has ads from employers looking to fill part-time positions. Members can also purchase any of the association's publications (e.g., its *Employer Directory*) at a discount.

Electronic Bar Association. Paul Bernstein, c/o LAW MUG, 505 N. Lasalle Street-575, Chicago, IL 60610. $250/yearly membership fee. Lawyers are lucky in that they have their own organization to turn to for information on using computers to do research, automate their offices, or telecommute. The membership fee includes an annual subscription to the Lexis on-line service for lawyers; a subscription to the *LAW MUG* newsletter (MUG stands for Microcomputer User's Group), an excellent, lengthy publication that for lawyers may by itself justify the cost of the membership fee; membership in the Chicago Computer Society; and discounts on selected software.

National Association for the Cottage Industry. P.O. Box 14850, Chicago, IL 60614. $45/yearly individual membership fee. Coralee Kern, who started Maid to Order, a Chicago-area cleaning and party service, also founded this association. Although it's mostly for people with their own home-based businesses, it also provides useful information for telecommuters. Members receive a bimonthly newsletter, *Cottage Connection,* which like many of the publications in this field has a friendly yet informative tone. Members also receive special group health and life insurance rates, car rental discounts, and discount subscriptions to certain business magazines.

New Ways to Work. 149 Ninth Street, San Francisco, CA 94103. $25/yearly membership. Founded in 1972, this is one of the oldest organizations in the alternative work options field. Its specialty is job sharing, where two people share the responsibilities associated with one job. The association also provides information on other work options such as part-time employment, sabbaticals, leaves, flextime, and compressed work weeks. It publishes a quarterly newsletter, *Work Times,* available separately for $30 per year; members receive a discount. NWW also provides counseling and workshops. San Francisco-area readers will want to check out NWW's library on work issues, open to the public by appointment.

The Telecommuting Advisory Council. c/o Pat Mokhtarian, Schimpeler-Corradino Associates, 433 S. Spring Street, Suite 1004 North, Los Angeles, CA 90013. A group of telecommuting experts that meets once every three months to share information on telecommuting in the region. The chair, Pat Mokhtarian, was formerly with the Southern California Association of Governments and was the driving force behind that organization's push for telecommuting (both for itself and other organizations). The council meets both via audioconferences (telephone meetings) and face-to-face meetings.

Washington State Energy Office. 809 Legion Way S.E., FA-11, Olympia, WA 98504. Contacting the Washington State Energy Office (WSEO) should be among the first things you do if you are looking for up-to-date information about telecommuting. This holds not just for people in the Washington State area but also nationwide. WSEO is coordinating a large telecommuting demonstration project in the region. It hopes to involve hundreds of people as telecommuters and ten to fifteen area employers. The energy office has also invited people in the region interested in working as telecommuters to contact them for help. If WSEO feels your job lends itself to being done from home, it will talk to your employer about it on your behalf. Others should contact the office for its bibliography on the subject and other materials it may have available to aid prospective telecommuters.

Women's Computer Literacy Center. Box 68, Jenner, CA 95450. This organization, founded by Deborah Brecher, who has more than twenty years' experience in the computer field, was set up to offer courses to women who want to learn more about computers: how to use them on the job and feel comfortable with them. Contact the center for details on classes in your area. If you can't get to one of its classes, consider buying its excellent manual for computer beginners of both sexes: *The Women's Computer Literacy Handbook.*

World Future Society. 4916 St. Elmo Avenue, Bethesda, MD 20814. $25/yearly membership. An organization dedicated to keeping its members on top of the social and technological developments shaping our future. The reasonable membership fee includes a subscription to *The Futurist,* a bimonthly magazine covering everything from artificial intelligence to robotics that's excellent for browsing. Regular departments include Tomorrow in Brief, Future Scope, and World Trends and Forecasts. It often covers work-related topics, including telecommuting. Members also get a discount on the scores of fascinating books sold through The Futurist Bookstore in Washington, D.C. In addition, members receive special rates for all assemblies and conferences sponsored by the society and a subscription to the society's newsletter, *Newsline.* Finally, members receive discounts on their U.S. Sprint phone bills; if you make a lot of long distance calls the money you save in just a few months can easily cover the cost of your membership.

Consultants

As mentioned in Chapter 9, companies that are setting up formal telecommuting programs may want to hire outside consultants. You can count on one hand the number of consultants that specialize in telecommuting.

Aside from the consultants listed here, however, some help is available from public agencies (state and local governments such as the Southern California Association of Governments) that have used tax dollars to set up telecommuting programs. In developing their programs, these agencies prepared a lot of training materials, such as questionnaires. They sometimes furnish these to other agencies looking to start programs of their own. Companies thinking of using materials developed by another company or government agency should keep in mind that often the materials were created for pilot programs that had unique objectives or for an organization with a different culture.

Three leading telecommuting consultants are:

Jack Nilles
JALA Associates
971 Stonehill Lane
Los Angeles, CA 90049
213-476-3703

Gil Gordon
Gil Gordon Associates
10 Donner Court
Monmouth Junction, NJ 08852
(201) 329-2266

Joanne Pratt
Joanne H. Pratt Associates
3520 Routh Street
Dallas, TX 75219
(214) 528-6540

Miscellaneous Resources

Office Chatter/Computer Chatter. (Audiotapes) When you work from a home office, business callers are more likely to hear home sounds in the background (squalling kids, doorbells) than office chatter (typewriters, file cabinets). With many people working from offices these days, home sounds may strike the still-wary, office-bound types as unprofessional. Single mom of four Laura

Newman solved the problem for herself and thousands of others by creating a cassette tape full of office sounds: Office Chatter. It includes ringing phones, sliding file drawers, and the tap-tapping of typewriters' keys.

Office Chatter and its spin-off, Computer Chatter, are available for $15 apiece from:

Zable's Business Services
156 Wall Street
Kingston, NY 12401

Taking Work Home. (Videotape) This ten-minute film from U.S. West Communications packs a lot of information into its time frame, and does it in an entertaining way. It concentrates on the formal telecommuting programs at Mountain Bell (a U.S. West company) and the city of Fort Collins, Colorado. It includes interviews with both managers of telecommuters and telecommuters. It's expensive, but it certainly gives you more of a sense of what telecommuting is all about than you would otherwise get from just reading about it.

Available for $100 from:

U.S. West Communications
1005 17th Street
Denver, CO 80202

The Whole Work Catalog. The New Careers Center, 1515 23rd Street, P.O. Box 297, Boulder, CO 80306. One-stop shopping for the best job books available today. Regularly updated, this 32-page catalog (price: $1.00) describes scores of books for job hunters. No discounts; but orders of $40 or more qualify you for free bonus books. A section covers books on working from home.

Appendix

Getting Telecommuting Under Way: Sample Memo

There may be several people in your department for whom telecommuting would be appropriate. In that case, a good way to get telecommuting started is to suggest that several people (rather than just yourself) give it a try. In other cases (such as small companies), you may be the only likely candidate, so you'll only represent yourself when making a case.

Either way, after first presenting the idea to your boss, you may need to present your plan more formally, through a memo. This should briefly cover what telecommuting is, stressing its benefits to your company.

Reprinted here is an actual memo (with the names changed) a prospective telecommuter submitted to his employer. The would-be telecommuter was recommending that telecommuting be offered as an option for an entire editorial department. Feel free to use this as a template for your own memo.

Be sure to include a list of companies in the same field that have telecommuters (referred to in the memo as Attachment A). Use Chapter 6 for this.

MEMORANDUM

TO: Bill Sharp
FROM: Jack Rogers
SUBJECT: Telecommuting at Acme Publishing

What Is Telecommuting?

Telecommuting refers to working for a company from home or another remote location (e.g., a satellite office), for one or more days a week. In practice, many telecommuters use computers and modems both to do their jobs and stay in touch with their offices. Hundreds of companies now have telecommuters, including many in the publishing field (see Attachment A).

What Jobs Are Suitable for Telecommuting?

- Jobs that do not require a lot of face-to-face interaction.
- Jobs with clearly defined and measurable tasks.
- Jobs that are portable. That is, do not require a lot of resources available only at a centralized location.

What's in It for Acme Publishing?

Handled right, telecommuting is a win-win situation. Both the company and the employee stand to gain. These are some of the benefits to the company:

- Increased productivity. Telecommuters are an average of 20 percent more productive than their office-based counterparts, according to Professor Jack Nilles, the ''father of telecommuting'' and a telecommuting consultant to Fortune 500 companies. Freed from lengthy commutes and the distractions of an office, telecommuters

work for longer stretches. They can also work
when they are at their best: morning people early in the morning, night owls, later in the day.

- Money savings. An employee who works from home is
  not using company resources such as parking
  spaces, bathrooms and lunchrooms, computer
  equipment, desks, chairs, etc.

Fleming LTD, telecommuting advisors to the
State of California and other employers, have
compiled the following figures to show how telecommuting's savings can add up for an employer:

Telecommuter at home 2 to 3 days per week

Personnel Factors	Benefit-Savings
Productivity (quantity)	$3,000
Productivity (quality)	$1,000
Recruiting-training-retention	$1,000
Absenteeism	$1,000
Facilities	
Office Space	$1,800
Parking	$200
Annual total per employee	$8,000
$8,000 X 100 telecommuters	$800,000

(Figures based on annual salary of $20,000, pro-
ductivity increase of 20 percent, reduced personnel costs of 10 percent, parking @$500 per year re-
duced by 40 percent and use of central office
facilities of 150 square feet @ $30 per square foot
rent per year reduced by 40 percent.)

- Fewer sick days taken. People who work from home
  will often still work with colds or other minor
  ailments. Office workers with these ailments,
  on the other hand, may just stay home and call it a

''sick day.'' The State of California, which has one of the country's largest formal telecommuting programs, found that the dollar impact of reduced sick days taken by its telecommuters was almost as high as money saved due to increased production.

- Improved recruiting. Companies like Hewlett-Packard have found that telecommuting is an excellent recruiting tool. With the unemployment rate at a 15-year low it's getting harder to fill many positions.

  If we could tell prospective employees that telecommuting is an option here, we could better compete for scarce talent. (Although you may not want a new hire working from home, he could be allowed to do so after six months to a year.) This is especially important when recruiting ''technical'' people who could easily be lured away by bigger salaries elsewhere.

- Reduced turnover. Companies like JCPenney have found that telecommuting programs reduce turnover markedly.

- Better morale. Telecommuters are happier. They appreciate the improved flexibility telecommuting brings to their lives. They also like working in synch with their body clocks.

How It Might Proceed at Acme Publishing

We should start small. Employees may, for instance, telecommute only one day a week to start. Those with clearly defined and measurable tasks (say an editor copy editing a manuscript) would be a good test case.

Telecommuting could be rolled out according to the following schedule:

1) Managers are briefed on telecommuting. They learn what it is, what its benefits

are, and for whom it's suitable. They are also given some hints about managing employees from afar. Possible candidates are discussed.

2) Telecommuters are selected. This should be entirely voluntary, of course. Some factors that managers may want to consider, though, are:

- Whether the employee has a home office set up, including a computer (although we may be able to help here by providing loaner laptops).

- The level and ''trustworthiness'' of the editor. This may be more appropriate for mid- to senior-level editors, employees who do not need close supervision, and employees who are not new to the company.

- The manager's willingness to give it a try. Both the manager and the telecommuter should be comfortable with the idea.

3) Telecommuters are briefed on what telecommuting is, what will be expected of them, and how they can retain ties to the office while working at home. Some suggestions for avoiding pitfalls such as distractions at home are also covered.

4) Telecommuting begins. Again, it starts gradually. A core of people get it under way.

5) Program evaluation. Telecommuters and their managers are called in after a month or so to discuss how it's working. Possible problems are brought out and discussed and the program is amended accordingly.

Index

ABI/INFORM, 222
Abstracter, 68-69, 140, 166
Accountant, 69
Actuary, 69-70
Advertising copy writer, 70
Advertising representative, 70-71
Allergan, Inc., 118
Allstate Insurance Company, 96, 118-19
American Express Company, 119
Appalachian Computer Services, 81, 119-20
Apple Computer, Inc., 114
    Apple *vs* IBM computer, 192-93
    and disabled, 199
    software, 182
    telecommuting jobs at, 120
Architect, 71
Arden, Lynie, 215
Association of Part-Time Professionals, 224
AT&T, 24, 90, 97, 102, 120-22
Atwater, Maxine H., 212
Auditor, 71-72
Author, 72-73
Avatex modems, 181

Baltimore *Evening Sun,* 76, 78, 83, 92, 105, 122
Bank officer, 72
Beneficial Corporation, 122
Benefits, employee, 34
Berlitz Translation Services, 109, 122-23

Bernstein, Paul, 89-90, 224
Best Western International, Inc., 102, 123-24
Blue Cross/Blue Shield of Maryland, 124
Blue Cross/Blue Shield of South Carolina, 5, 81, 100, 124-25
Blumenthal, Howard J., 211
Bolles, Richard Nelson, 214
Book author, 72-73
Booking agent, 66, 73
Bookkeeper, 74
Books, on telecommuting, 210-15
Books in Print, 222
Boredom, 30, 43
Boston Computer Exchange Corporation, 217-18
Brecher, Deborah, 226
Budget analyst, 74-75
Business Week, 16, 75

California State Department of General Services, 71, 81, 89, 90, 96, 103, 104, 125-26
California State Employees' Association, 34
California Western States Life Insurance, 32-33, 81
Careers Tomorrow: The Outlook for Work in a Changing World (Cornish), 210
Chairs, ergonomic, 175-76, 219
Chief executive officer (CEO), 75, 170

Child care, 17-20, 62
Christensen, Kathleen, 19, 29, 213
Citibank, 126
City manager, 76
Columnist, 76, 131
Communications software, 182
Commuting time, 6, 13-14
Companies with telecommuters, 5
  hi-tech, 51, 114
  information intensive, 115
  large *vs* small, 51, 112-13
  profiles of, 112-71
  publishing, 114
  See also specific names
Companion HealthCare, 100,
  127-28
*Complete Computer Career Guide,
  The* (Norback), 211
CompuAdd, 193, 218
Compucare Company, The, 128
Compuserve Information Service, 23,
  91, 133, 189, 192, 200, 220-21
  disabilities forums, 200-202
  Working From Home Forum, 50,
  52, 219
Computer(s), 177
  for disabled, 197, 199, 200-201
  hardware, 178-81
  laptop, 185, 190-91
  mail order sources for, 217-18
  maintenance of, 184-85
  and safety precautions, 184-85
  selecting, 192-94
  software, 180-84, 215-16
  See also Database services
Computer Chatter, 227-28
Computer Database, 222
Computer Industry Almanac, The, 75,
  211
Computer Library, 192
Computer Service Technician, 77
Computer Shopper, 181, 216
Computer systems analyst, 77-78
*Computing Across America: The Bicy-
  cle Odyssey of a High-Tech Nomad*
  (Roberts), 211
Consultant
  as telecommuting job, 78, 83-84

on telecommuting programs, 203-
  9, 226-27
Consumer Reports, 216
  on-line service, 222
Continental Communications Agen-
  cy, Inc. (CCA), 82, 128-29
Control, sense of, 5, 13
Control Data Corporation, 96, 129
Copiers, 191
Copy editor, 78
Copy writer, advertising, 70
Cornish, Edward, 210
Correspondent, 79, 131, 167
Cost estimator, 79-80
Cottage Connection, 225
Critic, 80, 122
Cross, Thomas B., 214
Curtis Manufacturing Company, Inc.,
  218
Custom Data Solutions, 52
Customer service representative, 80-
  91, 142, 158

Database administrator, 81-82
Database services
  and disabled, 200-202
  Knowledge Index, 220-23
  Nexis, 224
  telecommuting jobs at, 84
Data-entry clerk, 81, 167
Data General Corporation, 96, 104,
  130-31
Dell Computer Corporation, 193,
  218
Desk, 174-75
Desktop publisher, 82, 147
Detroit *Free Press,* 76, 92, 105, 131
DIALOG Information Services,
  Inc., 221-23
Digital Equipment Corporation, 78,
  97, 102, 104, 131-32
Digital News, 92, 106, 132
Direct Data, 82, 132-33
Disabled workers
  organizations assisting, 199-202
  telecommuting programs for, 129,
  135, 145, 151, 161

telecommuting *vs* mainstreaming, 196-98
unemployment among, 196
Disk drives, 178-79
Donkin, Scott W., 213
Dow Jones News/Retrieval, 223
Dress, freedom to, 14, 27-28
Du Pont (E.I.) de Nemours & Co., 101, 133

EasyCom, Inc., 97, 101, 133
Economist, 82-83
Editor, 138, 148, 156, 165
copy, 78
electronic news, 84-85
Educational consultant, 83-84
Educational software writer, 84
Edwards, Paul, 175, 214-15
Edwards, Sarah, 214-15
Eldercare, 20, 132
Electronic Bar Association, 124
Electronic Cottage Report, 219
Electronic Home Advisor, The (Blumenthal), 211
Electronic Services Unlimited, 69
Entrepreneurships
vs telecommuting, 7-8
telecommuting jobs with, 52, 113
Environments for Health, 175, 176, 218
Equipment. *See* Computer(s); Home office, equipment and supplies
Equitable Life Assurance, 133-34
Expansion slots, 178

Family, and telecommuting, 17-20, 29-31, 132
Family Circle, 19, 29
Farallon Computing, Inc., 102, 104, 134
Fax boards, 188-89
Fax line managers, 188
Fax machines, 4, 86, 164, 187-90
Federal government, telecommuting jobs with, 72, 134-35
Federal Reserve Bank of Atlanta, 25
Feedback, 25
Feingold, Norman, 212

FI Group, 25
File Cabinets, 176
Financial manager (bank officer), 72
First Chicago Corporation, 72, 135
First National Bank of Chicago, 72
Fleming, Lis, 59, 219
Fleming LTD, 55, 231
Fletcher, Charlie, 211
Fletcher, Jan, 19-20, 211
Flexible schedule, 3, 11-12, 21, 56
Fort Collins (Colorado), City of, 96, 126-27, 228
Fortune, 22, 138
47th Street Photo, Inc., 218-19
Frank Eastern Company, 219
Fundraiser, 85-86
Futurist, The, 226

Gallup Polls, 93
Gannett, 92, 136
General Electric Network for Information Exchange (GEnie), 182, 184, 223
General Services Administration, 134, 135
General Telephone of California, 78, 96, 136
GEnie, 182, 184, 223
GE Plastics, 102, 136-37
Globalink Language Services, 108, 109, 137
Glossbrenner, Alfred, 181, 184, 212, 215-16
Gordon, Gil, 37, 53, 54, 59, 126, 205, 207, 209, 214, 220, 227
Growing a Business/Raising a Family (Fletcher), 211

Hard disk drive, 178-79
Hardware, 178-81
Heart specialist, 86
Hewlett-Packard Company, 104, 137-38
Hi-Tech Public Relations, 97, 138
Home Business Advisor, 220

Home office
  control of environment, 15-16,
    194-95
  designing, 174, 212
  equipment and supplies in, 41, 57,
    61, 63, 172, 186-87, 191; evaluat-
    ing, 190-91, 193-94; fax ma-
    chines, 4, 86, 164, 187-90; mail or-
    der services for, 192-93, 217-19;
    telephone, 176-77, 187, 188; *See
    also* computer(s)
  furnishing, 174-76, 218, 219
  inspection by employer, 58, 61, 62
  insurance of, 186
  lighting, 177
  location of, 19-20, 172-73
  reimbursement for expenses of, 41,
    62, 63
  tax deduction for, 62, 174, 186
  worker's compensation in, 58, 61, 62
Home Office Computing, 138, 191,
  216
Home Offices and Workspaces, 212
Honeywell, Inc., 138-39
How to Get Free Software (Glossbrenner), 212
How to Look It Up On-line (Glossbrenner), 212
Hughes Aircraft, 104, 139

IBM. *See* International Business Ma-
  chines Corporation (IBM)
IBM National Support Center for
  Persons with Disabilities, 200
ICL, 34
Illustrator, 86-87
Independent contractors, 33-35, 52-
  53
Independent Contractor Report, 220
Indexer, 87-88, 138-39, 151-52
Industrial indemnity, 51
Information Access Company (IAC),
  69, 140
Information broker, 88
Insurance claims representative, 88-89

Interactive Systems Corporation, 78,
  140-41
International Business Machines
  Corporation (IBM)
  and disabled, 200, 201
  IBM *vs* Apple computers, 192-93
  software, 182
  telecommuting jobs at, 141
Isolation, 6, 22-26

Janal Communications, 52, 141-42
Jet Propulsion Laboratory, 142-43
Job Accommodation Network, 200
Jobs, telecommuting, 4
  assessing feasibility, 38-40, 45-49
  clerical, 40-41
  in entrepreneurships, 52
  geographical areas for, 50-51
  opportunities for, 38-40, 49-51,
    113-14
  professional, 41
  profiles of, 68-111
  rating, 67
  salary range of, 66-67
  top fifteen, 68
  See also specific job
Job Rated Almanac, The (Krantz), 69,
  212
John Hancock Mutual Life Insurance Company, 78, 143
Journal Graphics, 107, 143-44
Judge, 89
Juliussen, Egil and Karen, 75, 211

Kelly, Kevin, 213
Kelly, Marcia, 214
Kern, Coralee, 224-25
Keyers/coders, 124, 125, 167
Kinsman, Francis, 213
Knowledge Index, 221-23
Krantz, Les, 212
Kurzweil Personal Reader, 197

Lanier Business Products, 78, 83, 144

LAW MUG newsletter, 224
Lawyer, 89-90, 121, 146, 164
Legal assistant, 90, 130, 147
Letter Perfect, 145
Librarians, freelance, 88
Lift Inc., 96, 119, 145, 198, 202
Lighting, home office, 177
LINK Resources Corporation, 22, 26, 91, 146
Los Angeles, City of, 94, 127
Los Angeles, County of, 44, 72, 94, 129-30

McConnel, Patricia, 214
McGuire, Woods, Battle & Boothe, 90, 147
Mack, Karin, 213
MacWeek, 53, 85, 87, 106, 147
Magazine Index, 222
Magazines, on telecommuting, 216-17
Manufacturers Hanover, 51
Market research analyst, 90-91, 146, 164, 170
Mayo Clinic, 93
MCI Mail, 189, 223-24
Mead Data Central, 224
Meckler Publishing Corporation, 81, 147-48
Medical records technician, 91
Medical transcriptionist, 167-68
Medical reviewer, 100, 125
Merrill Corporation, 8, 39, 148
Microphone II, 182
Microprocessor, 178
Microsoft Word, 182
Microsoft Works, 184
Modem, 17, 52, 57, 180-81
Mokhtarian, Pat, 225
Monitors, 179-80, 185
MultiLink, 23, 39, 83, 97, 115, 148-49

National Association for the Cottage Industry, 224-25

National Council on Disability, 199
National Opinion Research Center, 93, 149-50
National Rehabilitation Information Center (NARIC), 199
NCNB Corporation, 72, 97, 150-51
New Emerging Careers: Today, Tomorrow and in the 21st Century (Feingold and Atwater), 212
New England Telephone and Telegraph, 151
New Era of Home-Based Work, The (Christenson), 213
NewsBank, Inc., 88, 151-52
Newsbytes, 84
Newsbytes News Service, 152-53
Newsearch, 222-23
Newsletters, on telecommuting, 219-20
New Ways to Work, 225
New York Life, 153
Nexis, 224
Nilles, Jack, 2, 11, 13, 19, 44, 125, 206, 209, 227, 230
Norback, Judith, 211
Norton (W.W.) & Company, 102, 171
Nurse, registered, 100, 125

Office. *See* Home office
Office Chatter, 227-28
Olsten Corporation, The, 153-54
On-line services, 90-91, 183, 189-90, 220-24
Operations research analyst, 92-9
Orange County *Register*, 92, 154
Ortho Pharmaceutical Corporation, 154-55, 204-5
Overcoming Writer's Blocks (Mack and Skjei), 213
Overeating, 27

Pacific Bell Telephone Company, 11, 31, 59, 91, 155-56
Pathologist, 93

PC/Computing, 217

PC Magazine, 191

PC Week, 155-56

PDN Software Newsletter, 156

Penney (JC) Company, 5, 43, 80, 107, 142

Personal Computer Support Group (PCSG), Inc., 75, 104, 156-57

PHH Homequity, 157

Philips Publishing Inc., 85, 106, 157-58

Pollster, 93

Pratt, Joanne, 8, 41, 126, 207-8, 213, 227

Presentation stage, 66

President's Council on Management Improvement (PCMI), 135

Prime Computer, Inc., 77, 81, 158

Printers, 180

Probation officer, 94

Procomm +, 182

Production stage, 66

Productivity, 6, 10-11, 54

Professor, 94-95

Programmer, 66, 95-96, 118, 119, 145, 157, 164

Proofreader, 151, 167

Psychological Services, Inc., 39-40, 78, 96-97, 158-59

Psychologist, 96-97

Public relations professional, 97, 121, 142

Publishing, 72-73, 114

Purchasing agent, 97-98

Quill, 219

Radio announcer, 98, 167

Radiologist, 98-99

Raizman, Marjorie, 214

RAND Corporation, The, 101, 159

Random Access Memory (RAM), 178

Read Only Memory (ROM), 178

Real estate agent, 99

Records manager, 100

Red Ryder, 182

Rehabilitation Research and Training Center (RRTC), 135

Reliable Corporation, The, 219

Remote Control, 107, 159-60

Reporter, 91-92, 122, 131, 136, 152, 154, 161

Researcher, 88, 100-101, 159

Research stage, 65

Reservations agent, 101-2, 123,24

Reviewer, 156

Roberts, Steve, 211

Rockwell International, 160

Rosenbluth Travel, 81, 101

Sales representative, 102, 121, 137, 167, 171

Scanners, 191

Sears, Roebuck & Co., 98, 160-61

Seattle *Times,* The, 92, 161

Secretary, 103

Shredders, 191

Signal: Communication Tools for the Information Age (Kelly), 213

Sitting on the Job (Donkin), 213

Skjei, Eric, 213

Social worker, 103

Software, 180-84, 215-16

Software engineer, 104

Software writer, educational, 84

South Coast Air Quality Management District (SCAQMD), 97, 110, 161-62

Southern California Association of Governments, 45, 60, 69, 110, 164

Speechwriter, 104-5, 134

Sportswriter, 105, 122

Sprint, 181-82

Standard & Poor's Corporate Descriptions, 223

State of California Franchise Tax Board, 75, 90, 163-64

Stockbroker, 105

Taking Work Home, 228

Taxation, 34, 62, 186

Technical writer, 106

Techprose, 52, 82, 91, 164

Telecommuters/telecommuting
  advantages of, 5-6, 10-21, 56; for
    communications, 16; commuting
    time eliminated, 6, 13-14; dis-
    tractions eliminated, 14-15; emo-
    tional, 5, 12-13; for employer,
    53-56, 232; for family, 17-20; flexi-
    bility, 3, 11-12; freedom of dress,
    14; monetary, 15; productivity, 10-
    11, 54; technological skills, 16-
    17; work space, 15-16
  arrangements: conditions of, 60-
    63; on experimental basis, 64; for-
    mal/informal, 5, 43-45; indepen-
    dent contractors, 33-34, 52-53;
    negotiating, 53-60, 63, 229-34
  consultants, 203-9, 226,27
  and disabled. See Disabled worker
  disadvantages of, 6, 22-37; bore-
    dom, 30, 43; for career growth, 34;
    co-worker relations, 36-37; dis-
    tractions, 28-29, 43; exploitation,
    32-35, 40-41; for family, 30-31;
    family demands, 29-30; invasion of
    personal time, 35; isolation, 6,
    22-26; loss of office services, 31;
    overeating, 27; slovenliness, 27-
    28; workaholic tendencies, 26-
    27; zoning regulations, 32
  vs entrepreneurship, 7-8
  information/resources on, 210-28
  job stages and, 65-66
  numbers of, 2
  personal evaluation for, 42-43, 46,
    49
  trends favoring, 2-4, 51
  and unions, 34, 44
  See also Companies with telecom-
    muters; Home office; Jobs,
    telecommuting
Telecommuters, The (Kinsman), 213
Telecommuter's Toolkit, The
  (Pratt), 213
Telecommuting Advisory Council, The,
  225
Telecommuting: How to Make It
  Work for You and Your Company
  (Gordon and Kelly), 214
Telecommuting Review, 220
Telecommuting: The Future Technol-
  ogy of Work (Cross and Raizman),
  214
Teleconferencing, 149
TeleMagic, 106-7
Telemarketer, 106-7, 160
Telephones, 176-77, 187, 188
Third Wave, The (Toffler), 214
Thyng Associates, Inc., 99, 164-65
Time Inc., 165
Toffler, Alvin, 214
Trade and Industry Index, 223
Transcriber, 107-8, 144
Translator, 108-9, 123, 129, 137
Travel agent, 109
Travelers Corporation, 5, 43, 96,
  115, 165-66
Typesetter, 110

UMI/Data Courier, 69, 166
Unemployment rate, 2, 51, 196
Unions, 34, 44
United Airlines, 198
United Press International (UPI),
  98, 102, 166-67
University Graphics, Inc., 81, 87,
  167
University of Wisconsin Center for
  Health Sciences, 91, 108, 167-68
Urban Planner, 110-11
US West, 3, 24, 43, 78, 168-69

Washington State Energy Office,
  104, 169, 210, 225-26
Wendy's International, Inc., 69, 93, 169-
  70
Weyerhaeuser, 91, 170
What Color Is Your Parachute?
  (Bolles), 214
Whole Work Catalog, The, 228
Wilson (H.W.) Company, The, 88, 139-
  40
Wilson Jones Office Products, 219
Woman's Work-At-Home Handbook,
  The (McConnel), 214

Women's Computer Literacy Center, 226
WordPerfect, 182
Word processing software, 180-81
Word processor, 111
Work-at-Home Sourcebook, The (Arden), 215
Worker's compensation, 34, 58, 60-61, 62
Working from Home (Edwards), 214-15
Workstation Laboratories, 75, 170
World Future Society, 226
Worldwide Church of God, 96, 170-71

Writer, 131, 132, 147, 165, 213
    book author, 72-73
    editorial, 83
    freelance, 85
    software, 84
    speech, 104-5, 134
    sports, 105, 122
    technical, 106
    See also Reporter
Writer's Market, 73
Writing Edge, The, 78-79

Zoning laws, 32